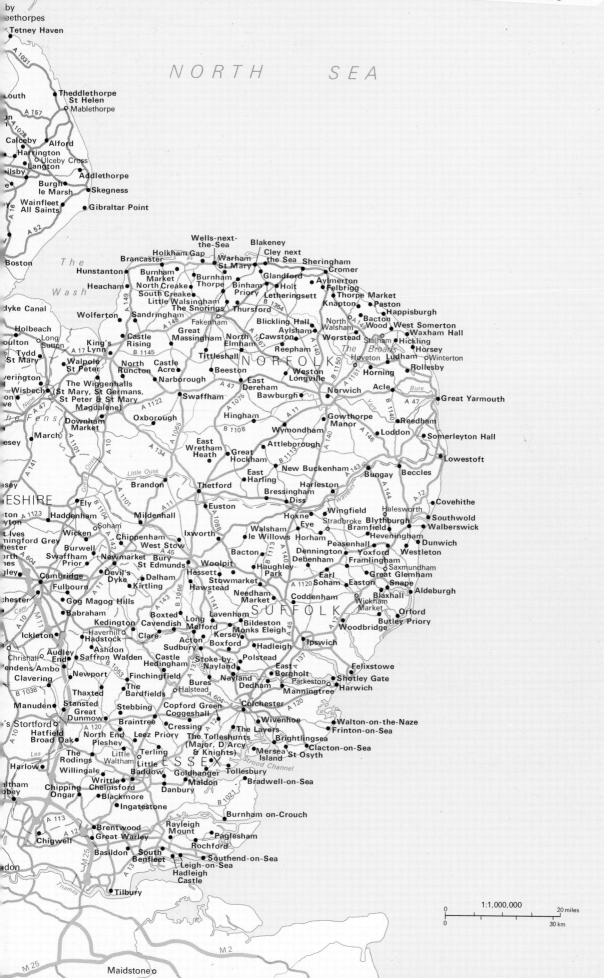

NORTH SEA

by
eethorpes
Tetney Haven

outh
Theddlethorpe
St Helen
Mablethorpe

Calceby
Alford
Hartington
Ulceby Cross
ilsby
Langton
Burgh
le Marsh
Addlethorpe
Skegness
Wainfleet
All Saints
Gibraltar Point

Boston
The
Wash

Wells-next-
the-Sea
Blakeney
Holkham Gap
Cley next
the Sea
Sheringham
Brancaster
Warham
St Mary
Hunstanton
Burnham
Market
Burnham
Thorpe
Glandford
Cromer
Aylmerton
Felbrigg
Heacham
North Creake
Binham
Priory
Holt
Letheringsett
Thorpe Market
Paston
South Creake
Little Walsingham
The Snorings
Thursford
Knapton
Happisburgh
Wolferton
Sandringham
Fakenham
Blickling Hall
North
Walsham
Bacton
Wood
West Somerton
Waxham Hall
dyke Canal
Great
Massingham
North
Elmham
Aylsham
Worstead
Hickling
Horsey
Holbeach
King's
Lynn
Castle
Rising
Cawston
The Broads
Stalham
Winterton
oulton
Long
Sutton
Tittleshall
Reepham
Hoveton
Ludham
Rollesby
Tydd
St Mary
Walpole
St Peter
North
Runcton
Castle
Acre
Beeston
East
Dereham
Weston
Longville
Horning
erington
Narborough
Acle
Wisbech
The Wiggenhalls
(St Mary, St Germans,
St Peter & St Mary
Magdalene)
Swaffham
Bawburgh
Norwich
Bure
Great Yarmouth
on
ve
Downham
Market
Oxborough
Hingham
Gowthorpe
Manor
Reedham
he Fens
esey
March
Wymondham
Loddon
Somerleyton Hall
East
Wretham
Heath
Attleborough
esy
Brandon
Great
Hockham
Lowestoft
Thetford
East
Harling
New Buckenham
Bungay
Beccles
Ely
Haddenham
Mildenhall
Euston
Harleston
Covehithe
Wicken
Soham
Bressingham
Diss
A 1123
t Ives
nningford Grey
hester
Ixworth
Hoxne
Wingfield
Halesworth
Southwold
orth
nes
Burwell
Swaffham
Prior
Chippenham
West Stow
Walsham
le Willows
Horham
Eye
Stradbroke
Bramfield
Blythburgh
Walberswick
Newmarket
Bury
St Edmunds
Bacton
Dennington
Peasenhall
Heveningham
Dunwich
gley
Cambridge
Fulbourn
Devil's
Dyke
Dalham
Kirtling
Woolpit
Haughley
Park
Debenham
Yoxford
Westleton
Hessett
Earl
Soham
Framlingham
Saxmundham
Great Glemham
Gog Magog Hills
Stowmarket
Hawstead
Needham
Market
Easton
Snape
Babraham
Coddenham
Blaxhall
Aldeburgh
Boxted
Lavenham
Bildeston
Wickham
Market
Ickleton
Kedington
Hadstock
Long
Melford
Cavendish
Monks Eleigh
Kersey
Orford
Butley Priory
Haverhill
Ashdon
Clare
Acton
Boxford
Woodbridge
Audley
End
Saffron Walden
Sudbury
Hadleigh
Chrishall
endens Ambo
Castle
Hedingham
Polstead
Ipswich
Clavering
Newport
Finchingfield
Stoke-by-
Nayland
East
Bergholt
Felixstowe
B 1038
Thaxted
The
Bardfields
Bures
Nayland
Parkeston
Shotley Gate
Manuden
Stansted
Great
Dunmow
Stebbing
Copford Green
Coggeshall
Halstead
Dedham
Manningtree
Harwich
s Stortford
Braintree
Colchester
Hatfield
Broad Oak
North End
Pleshey
Leez Priory
Cressing
The Layers
Wivenhoe
Walton-on-the-Naze
Frinton-on-Sea
Harlow
The
Rodings
Little
Waltham
Terling
The Tolleshunts
(Major, D'Arcy
& Knights)
Brightlingsea
Clacton-on-Sea
Willingale
Little
Baddow
ESSEX
Mersea
Island
St Osyth
altham
bbey
Writtle
Chelmsford
Goldhanger
Tollesbury
Chipping
Ongar
Blackmore
Danbury
Maldon
Bradwell-on-Sea
Ingatestone
Burnham on-Crouch
Brentwood
Rayleigh
Mount
Paglesham
Chigwell
Great Warley
Rochford
Basildon
South
Benfleet
Southend-on-Sea
Leigh-on-Sea
Hadleigh
Castle
ndon
Tilbury

Maidstone

1:1,000,000
0   20 miles
0   30 km

BEAUTIFUL BRITAIN

EAST ANGLIA

Published by the Reader's Digest Association Limited, London for the Automobile Association,
Fanum House, Basingstoke, Hampshire RG21 2EA

EAST ANGLIA
was edited and designed by
The Reader's Digest Association Limited
for the Automobile Association,
Fanum House, Basingstoke, Hampshire RG21 2EA

This book contains material from
the following titles originally
published by Drive Publications Limited:
*Treasures of Britain, Discovering Britain,
Book of British Towns, Illustrated Guide to
Britain, Book of British Villages, AA Illustrated
Guide to Country Towns and Villages of Britain;*
and from *Folklore, Myths and Legends of Britain*
and *The Past All Around Us,* both published by
the Reader's Digest Association Limited.

ISBN 0-86145-519-3

Filmset by MS Filmsetting Ltd, Frome
Separations by Litra Ltd, Edenbridge
Printed by Blantyre Printing and Binding Co Ltd, Glasgow
Bound by Hazell Watson & Viney Ltd, Aylesbury

Printed in Great Britain

The map on the endpapers was produced by
Thames Cartographic Services, Maidenhead,
and is based upon Ordnance Survey material
with the permission of the Controller of
Her Majesty's Stationery Office, Crown
copyright reserved. A name printed on the
map in bold type indicates that the place
is featured in this book.

Cover photographs: Salhouse Broad, Wroxham
by Tim Woodcock (*top*);
Ufford by Neville Fox-Davies (*bottom left*).
Windmill at Cley by Penny Tweedie (*bottom right*).
Introduction (*pages 6–7*): Dunwich Common by
Michael Freeman.

CONTENTS

Introduction | 6–7

Gazetteer | 8–155

Index | 156–159

Acknowledgments | 160

This land of shadows, pierced by a crystalline winter sun, has inspired artists for centuries. The former kingdom of East Anglia was made up of the North Folk (Norfolk) and the South Folk (Suffolk). Its boundaries were defined by the sea, the treacherous Fens and the forests of the south. But with the draining of the Fens, the disappearance of the forests and the breeching of the defensive earthworks by main thoroughfares to London and the west, the boundaries became blurred. Today the urban countryside of Essex, the Fens and uplands of Cambridgeshire, and Lincolnshire's massive acres of wheat, potatoes and barley, have all been welcomed into the loose confederation of East Anglia. The Angles gave their name to the region, and the Vikings too left their mark in the form of name and word-endings of towns, villages, streams and hamlets. The Saxons left innumerable burial grounds, and the Romans a bulwark of fortifications and roads. Hundreds of years later the Flemish brought their weaving and brewing skills, and the Dutch converted the inhospitable marshlands into rich farms.

These counties can boast a roll-call of the great: here Boudicca ruled, Mary Tudor lived and Catherine of Aragon died. Nelson, Wolsey and Cromwell were all East Anglian men. Not forgetting the countless scholars, scientists, writers and statesmen who owe their place in history to the great university town on the quiet River Cam.

A

ACLE
Norfolk
8 miles west of Great Yarmouth

The Church of St Edmund in Acle has an 11th-century round tower, but the octagonal upper stage and battlements are of a later date. Both north and south porches are two storeys high. The font dates from 1410, with carvings of lions, wild men, and the Trinity.

Two miles outside the village is a brick-built water pump of 1883, known as the Stacey Arms Windpump. It was used to draw off surplus water from flat marshland sunk below sea-level. A turbine pump lifted water 7 ft to the River Bure.

About 2 miles south is Tunstall, whose pool is said locally to lead directly to Hell. The church bells were once stolen by the devil, who escaped to his realm through the pool. To this day, muffled peals are sometimes heard.

ACTON
Suffolk
3 miles northeast of Sudbury

Acton village is most notable for its Church of All Saints which was originally constructed c. 1300. Its tower, however, is early 20th century. There is a very good brass of Sir Robert de Bures c. 1302, shown as a cross-legged knight wearing chain-mail and holding a shield; also a monument of c. 1722, which might be by Thomas Green of Camberwell, with a reclining man against an architectural background, with his wife sitting at his feet.

ADDLETHORPE
Lincolnshire
4 miles north of Skegness

Addlethorpe's 15th-century Church of St Nicholas lost its chancel in 1706. Some of the medieval glass still remains, and much of the woodwork is original in the screens, pew ends, and angels in the roof. The church has recently been extensively restored.

At Ingoldmells about 1 mile west, the Church of St Peter and St Paul is a large and impressive church with a 15th-century porch. The chancel was demolished in the early 18th century. An interesting brass of the 16th century depicts a man called William Palmer, with his 'stylt' or crutch at his side. The church also has a fine Perpendicular font.

ALDEBURGH
Suffolk
6 miles southeast of Saxmundham

The flourishing town of Aldeburgh, with good hotels and mixed architectural styles, grew up after the prosperous medieval fishing and ship-building centre of Slaughden was destroyed by the sea. Slaughden was still prosperous when the Rev. George Crabbe lived and worked there at the beginning of the 19th century before writing *The Borough*, a collection of tales which was the inspiration for Benjamin Britten's opera *Peter Grimes*, which is set in the village. Aldeburgh's world-famous music festival is held every June. Founded in 1948 by the two composers Benjamin Britten and Eric Crozier and the singer Peter Pears, it takes place in the Snape Maltings, the 15th-century Church of St Peter and St Paul and the Jubilee Hall, and is always a popular event.

The River Alde, its banks bright with small craft, cuts in close behind the yacht club and divides the mainland from a long, marshy spit. The river passes Orford Ness, with its unapproachable radar installations, and Havergate Island, nesting-place of the avocet, before joining the River Ore.

Two miles to the north, Thorpeness is a gay mock-Tudor extravaganza with a water tower disguised as a house and known as 'The House in the Clouds'.

ALFORD
Lincolnshire
11 miles southeast of Louth

The 14th-century Church of St Wilfrid in the pleasant small town of Alford was extensively restored and enlarged by Sir Gilbert Scott in 1869. The five-sail windmill, built in 1813, is in full working order, and a lively craft market takes place on summer Fridays in Alford. West of the town, sheep graze on the gentle slopes of the Wolds, and there are pleasant lanes for walking between Ulceby, Skendleby and Claxby. Ulceby is a pretty village set in woodland, and has an 18th-century manor house and a brick church dating from 1826.

ALVINGHAM
Lincolnshire
3 miles northeast of Louth

One thing in particular sets Alvingham apart from other villages: it has two churches in a single churchyard. One church, St Mary's, belongs to the neighbouring parish of North Cockerington. The other, Alvingham's parish church, St Adelwold's, lay abandoned for most of the 19th century, but was restored in 1933. Both churches can only be approached through a farmyard.

St Mary's Church was once the chapel of a Gilbertine priory, which was founded in Alvingham in the 12th century. The parishioners of North Cockerington were allowed to use it as their church when forced to abandon their first church as a ruin. It still retains some original Norman features, including the font base. There is part of a Saxon window in the chancel.

TURNING SAILS *Alford has two windmills, one of which, Myer's mill, built in 1837, is still working.*

ASHDON *Next door to the church is the 16th-century timber-framed Guildhall, today a private house.*

Across the yew-shaded churchyard stands the largely 14th-century Church of St Adelwold, the only church in Britain dedicated to this Saxon saint. Adelwold became Bishop of Winchester in the late 10th century, and was a man renowned as a severe disciplinarian but an outstanding teacher.

Bordering the southern side of the churchyard is the old Louth Navigation Canal which links Louth, 3 miles southwest, to the sea. On the north side, Church Lane leads to a watermill near the two churches. A mill has stood on the site for at least 900 years. The present mill, housed in a three-storey building, has been partially restored and is open to visitors on Bank Holidays and on certain days each week in summer. There are two other craft workshops: the smithy in Yarburgh Road, which sells wrought-iron work; and a nearby pottery, housed in the old wheelwright's workshop.

ANCASTER
Lincolnshire
5 miles west of Sleaford

A village set in pleasant wooded country, Ancaster is best known for its stone, quarried in medieval times to give Lincolnshire many of its churches. The quarries are 2 miles south of the village. Ancaster was important in Roman times, and traces of a 9 acre camp, Causennae, on Ermine Street can be seen. Causennae was the last posting-station along this main road from London to Lincoln. Finds of coins, pottery and mosaics from the site are in Grantham Museum.

ASHDON
Essex
4 miles northeast of Saffron Walden

One of the ground-floor rooms in the 17th-century Rose and Crown in Ashdon village still has its original wall decorations – painted panels with geometric patterns and texts in Gothic lettering.

The Church of All Saints crowns the hill above the village and dates from the 14th century, though the lower sections of the columns are thought to be Saxon. Next to the church is the early 16th-century timber-framed Guildhall, now a private house. Waltons, originally an Elizabethan house 1 mile northeast of Ashdon, was destroyed by fire in 1954, but was rebuilt by its owner and given a Georgian front. He also restored the derelict 18th-century post-mill in a field opposite the house.

The Bartlow Hills, 3 miles north, are the site of the best Romano-British burial mounds in the country. There were seven at one time, four of which remain in good order. In the 1830s, these graves were opened up and yielded bronze, enamel and glassware which obviously once belonged to men of high rank. The best examples were taken to Easton Lodge, near Great Dunmow, but were destroyed in a fire there in 1847.

ATTLEBOROUGH
Norfolk
14 miles southwest of Norwich

The Church of St Mary at Attleborough was formerly cruciform, but the church's chancel and apse have disappeared, while the central tower remains. Some Norman work exists and the remainder is mainly

AYLMERTON
Norfolk
3 miles southwest of Cromer

The Shrieking Pits is the name given to a number of circular depressions in the area surrounding Aylmerton. Though they are probably the remains of prehistoric houses or flint mines, they have gained notoriety through matters ectoplasmic rather than archaeological. The tall white figure of a woman has sometimes been seen peering into the pits, wringing her hands and uttering piercing shrieks. Some say it is the ghost of a Stone Age woman, others of someone murdered nearby; but her shrieks have terrified local residents on many occasions.

The Church of St John the Baptist has the round tower often found in East Anglican churches; the rest is a marriage of Decorated and Perpendicular styles.

AYLSHAM
Norfolk
12 miles north of Norwich

Red brick and flint are the building materials in Aylsham, and a flint facing protects the 14th-century parish church of St Michael, just north of the Market Place. Inside are some good memorial brasses, including two depicting the grinning skeletons of its 15th-century benefactors, Richard and Cecilie Howard. Humphry Repton, the landscape gardener who designed many of the great English parks of the late 18th century, was buried in the churchyard in 1818. One of his favourite flowers was the rose, and rose bushes still cover his grave. The inscription on his memorial reads:

Not like Egyptian tyrants consecrate,
Unmixed with others shall my dust remain,
But mold'ring, blending, melting into Earth,
Mine shall give form and colour to the Rose,
And while its vivid blossoms cheer Mankind,
Its perfumed odours shall ascend to Heaven.

The ample, four-square, red-brick buildings of the Market Place make an apt centrepiece for this solidly prosperous market town. For 500 years, until the Industrial Revolution, it was an important centre for the manufacture first of linen and then of worsted. The Black Boys Hotel, in the square's southwest corner, might not be quite as it was in the 17th century, but its bow front and curious frieze of little black boys still convey a sense of elegant comfort.

On Blickling Road are Aylsham Old Hall, a fine late 17th-century mansion, and the Queen Anne Knoll House. On Norwich Road, Old Bank House is 18th century and the Manor House is early 17th century.

By the River Bure, and forming a distinct community within Aylsham, is Millgate, once busy with flat-bottomed sailing wherries plying the waterways to Norwich and Yarmouth. But the railways and a disastrous flood in 1912 finished Millgate as a trading centre. It is now a peaceful residential area of imposing 18th-century houses, such as Bure House and the former wherry inn, Bridge House, both with fine doorways. A large mill that was built in the 18th century remained in use until 1969.

Decorated, with a good west window and a two-storey porch. The late 15th-century rood screen has painted decoration and together with its loft is considered one of the finest in England – one of the few that survived the Reformation intact. There is a cast-iron lectern of 1816, some original stained glass, and fragments of medieval wall painting depicting, among other subjects, Moses and David.

AUDLEY END
Essex
1 mile west of Saffron Walden

Audley End House is approached by a stately Adam bridge over the River Cam. Built in 1603 for Thomas Howard, 1st Earl of Suffolk, who became Lord High Treasurer, it was originally far larger, about twice its present size, and prompted James I to remark that it was 'too big for a king, but might do for the Lord Treasurer!' What is left is nonetheless immense, and includes a magnificent entrance hall and staircase. The front facing is of stone, with splendid porches into the Great Hall. The latter is two storeys high, with a magnificent panelled ceiling and a Jacobean screen. There is much fine Adam work, lovely 18th-century furniture, and a notable collection of stuffed birds.

Red-brick Tudor/Jacobean stables – which today house a garden centre open to the public – flank the house, and in the grounds there are landscapes by 'Capability' Brown, a round temple, a Palladian bridge carrying a summer house, the Temple of Concord (1781), several decorative lodges, the Lion Gateway (1786) and the tall Springwood column (1774). The village is a well-planned estate, mainly Georgian, with Jacobean almshouses.

AUDLEY END *The Tudor brick stables may incorporate some of the remains of the early priory which once stood here* (overleaf).

B

BABRAHAM
Cambridgeshire
7 miles southeast of Cambridge

Babraham's Church of St Peter was begun in the 12th century, and its oldest surviving section is the tower. The new east window was designed by John Piper. A 17th-century sculpture by John Bushnell is of two figures with carved drapery.

Nearby at Sawston, to the southwest, is Sawston Hall. The present building was erected by Mary Tudor as a reward for the loyalty of the Huddleston family, who sheltered her from the followers of Lady Jane Grey in 1553. The Huddlestons, who lived at the Hall until 1970, have always been Catholic. There is a priest's hole beneath the staircase of the tower, cunningly built by Nicholas Owen, a Jesuit carpenter who built similar hiding places all over England during the reign of Elizabeth I. He died under torture rather than betray his friends, and was canonised in 1970. The ghost of Mary, who counted the Huddlestons among her truest friends, is said to have been seen walking in the Long Gallery.

BACTON
Suffolk
5 miles north of Stowmarket

The Church of St Mary at Bacton is a fine example of a Decorated and Perpendicular church with a west tower. There is decorative stone and flint work in the clerestory, and a double hammerbeam roof in the nave. Inside is a contemporary font with angels: also benches, a screen, and medieval doom-wall painting.

About 3 miles to the east is the village of Mendlesham, where the 13th-century Church of St Mary stands. The west tower and two porches have much flushwork decoration in flint and stone. There is a good font cover and pulpit of 1630. The north porch contains an unusual feature – a parish armoury (viewable by appointment), with pieces of armour from the 15th to 17th centuries.

BACTON WOOD
Norfolk
2½ miles east of North Walsham

A short way south of the coastal village of Bacton stand the ruins of the 12th-century priory of Broomholm. Today deserted and fogotten, in medieval times it was a popular place of pilgrimage, for one of its relics was believed to be a piece of the true cross. In Chaucer's *Canterbury Tales*, the Reeve tells how the startled miller's wife screamed 'Holy cross of Bromeholme keep Us!'

The ruins stand within sight of the sea beside the B1150 road. Southwest along the same road, barely 3 miles inland, lies Bacton Wood, tucked away in a pocket of land that dips into a shallow valley. Part of the Forestry Commission's scattered Wensum Forest,

it is also known locally as Witton Wood. Some 30 kinds of tree grow here – old-established species such as sweet chestnut and birch, and others from Japan, northern Europe, Corsica and the northwest coast of America. The imported trees have replaced those felled during the Second World War, so that Bacton Wood is a relatively young forest, although the area was probably wooded in Saxon times.

THE BARDFIELDS
Essex
Between 2 and 6 miles south and southwest of Finchingfield

The picturesque villages of Great Bardfield, Little Bardfield and Bardfield Saling are flanked by the little River Pant. The Hall at Little Bardfield dates from the 16th century. St Katherine's Church has a Saxon tower and an 18th-century organ. Great Bardfield, once a market town, has many medieval and Georgian houses, a restored windmill, and a mainly 14th-century church, St Mary the Virgin, notable for its fine stone screen across the chancel arch. The High Street, where a fair used to be held, is wide and was probably once a green. Tucked away here is a 16th-century museum. It features displays of rural history and village crafts. It has books and poetry and a wide range of corn dollies – medieval symbols of the Harvest Spirit, now sold as decorations and good luck charms.

BARNACK
Cambridgeshire
3 miles southeast of Stamford

Everything in and around Barnack is stone-built: drystone walls; grey and buff-coloured farm buildings looking like miniature castles; an 18th-century windmill; two old inns; the church – and England's largest and grandest Elizabethan mansion, Burghley House, which stands in parkland 2 miles northeast of the village. South of the village are the grass-covered hummocks of the long-abandoned quarries from which much of this limestone came. Workings there ceased in the 16th century, and the area is now the Hills and Holes National Nature Reserve.

The tower windmill was preserved in 1961, when a new cap was fitted, and although not in working order, the machinery is intact. The windmill is open to the public at weekends by appointment. The Saxons built the Church of St John the Baptist. Its tower dates from the early 11th century, and within the north aisle is a fine 11th-century sculpture of Christ in Majesty. The spire dates from the 13th century, but the pinnacles and a rood screen bearing the de Barnack arms were added in the 20th century.

During the Middle Ages the quarries provided material for the cathedrals at Ely and Peterborough, and for Corpus Christi and other Cambridge colleges. In Bishop's Walk, in the village, the old rectory is now named Kingsley House after its association with the

novelist Charles Kingsley, author of *The Water Babies*, who came here at the age of five with his clergyman father. Kingsley House is now divided into two private houses, but still retains the exterior that Kingsley knew.

BASILDON
Essex
26 miles east of London

Until the railway arrived in the 19th century, Basildon was a village of fewer than 200 people, whose cottages clustered around the 14th-century Holy Cross Church, said to be haunted by a red-robed figure of unknown identity. As a new town, today it has a population of just under 100,000.

Pitsea Hall, Pitsea, was built in the late 16th century, and the gabled Great Chalvedon Hall, in the same suburb, is several years older.

On the western edge of Basildon is Laindon, whose small Church of St Nicholas is of the 14th and 15th centuries, with carved wood decoration in the south porch. Attached to the west end is a two-storeyed priest's house of the 17th century. The font is 13th century. The church may be visited by appointment.

BAWBURGH
Norfolk
5 miles west of Norwich

A farmhand named Walstan made Bawburgh a place of pilgrimage. He died on May 30, 1016, and a spring is said to have gushed forth where his body was laid to rest in the village. He was canonised, and the village's little church, with its rocket-shaped round tower, is dedicated to him and to St Mary. The Bawburgh spring became St Walstan's Well: a place of international pilgrimage in the Middle Ages. So many pilgrims came

SUN DAPPLED WOOD *Just outside Norfolk's seaside village of Bacton, bracken and over 30 kinds of tree create a quiet haven.*

to the miraculous spring, and the shrine that was built over it, that a vicar and six priests were employed full-time to look after them.

The cult came to an abrupt end with the Reformation in the 16th century. Visitors today will find that the church is usually locked. The key is available from the nearby Church Farm.

A row of cottages – mostly brick built – lines one side of the village green beside the river. On the other side is a large water mill, once the site of another owned by a miller named Jeremiah Colman, who began his career here in 1802. He moved to Stoke Holy Cross to found in 1823 the mustard company that still bears his name. The present mill, built in 1876, last turned in 1967; it is now a private house.

BECCLES
Suffolk
8 miles west of Lowestoft

The mellow old town of Beccles is best seen from the north bank of the River Waveney. Gardens run down to the water, fringed with boat-houses and landings.

The stone-faced bell tower of the 14th-century parish church of St Michael stands apart from the building. It is 97 ft high and has a peal of ten bells.

Fires destroyed most of the old town in the 16th and 17th centuries and Beccles re-emerged as a handsome place of red-brick Georgian houses. Many of the surviving older buildings show Dutch influence, however, particularly the gabled Roos Hall dating from 1583. It was once the home of Sir John Suckling, an ancestor of Lord Nelson.

The Church of the Holy Trinity at Barsham, 2 miles

west of Beccles, is Norman with later enlargement. Holy Trinity has a round west tower, and a highly decorated east wall with a stone and flint flushwork trellis which incorporates the window as part of the scheme. The church has two fonts, one Norman, the other Perpendicular, and a pulpit with Jacobean woodwork. The 19th-century east window is by C. E. Kempe. There is a brass, and a 16th-century monument.

Two miles east is Worlingham Hall. A notable feature is its 1799–1800 octagonal hall with double staircase. Worlingham can be visited by appointment.

BEESTON
Norfolk
5 miles west of East Dereham

The lovely Church of St Mary in Beeston is mainly Decorated, with a Perpendicular clerestory added in 1410. The hammerbeam roof, the painted rood screen and two parclose screens are particularly fine. The churchyard has a memorial to Jem Mace, world champion bare-fisted boxer born in the village.

About 2 miles to the northwest is Letcham, whose Church of All Saints has a fine rood screen of 1436, with panel paintings of 22 saints. They include the child William of Norwich, who was supposedly murdered by the Jews in the 12th century.

BELTON
Lincolnshire
3 miles northeast of Grantham

Belton House – built in the village of Belton by an unknown architect in the style of Christopher Wren – is regarded as 'the finest surviving example of its class'. It was the ancestral home of the Brownlow family for 300 years before its acquisition by the National Trust.

Built in 1685–88, it is H-plan in shape, and has a hipped roof with dormer windows and, above, an elegant cupola. A broad flight of steps leads up to the main doorway, over which is the Brownlow coat of arms. About 1776 James Wyatt altered the house and in 1811, his nephew, Sir Jeffry Wyatville, built the orangery. In the house are good examples of furniture, tapestries and European old masters. The Chinese Bedroom, with its simulated bamboo panels, handpainted wallpaper and porcelain elephants, is particularly fine.

There is an exhibition of mementos devoted to the Duke of Windsor, and in the Stable Block a restaurant and shop. The house also has a rose garden and an extensive adventure playground for children. Belton's Church of St Peter and St Paul was altered from its original Norman style in the 18th century, and in 1816 Sir Jeffry Wyatville designed a chapel which contains monuments to the Brownlows.

BILDESTON
Suffolk
5 miles north of Hadleigh

A doctor's generosity probably saved Bildeston from a lethal epidemic in the late 19th century. In 1877 diphtheria – often fatal in those days – struck the villagers. The local physician, Dr Grouse, spotted an open drain running from the butcher's slaughterhouse, and realising that it was probably polluted and the source of the disease, he paid for a new covered drain to be built.

The doctor's diagnosis proved to be correct: once the drain was covered, the threat of an epidemic faded away. But it faded too late for Dr Grouse's own family. Two of his children had already died.

In the 13th and 14th centuries Bildeston was a wealthy wool town, especially noted for making blankets and blue cloth. Although competition from the Cotswolds later killed the industry, the village retains traces of its former greatness. Fine old half-timbered houses, plastered in many colours and built as homes for wealthy merchants, line the streets that radiate from the market place. A row of 15th-century cottages still lines Chapel Street. At one time all the attics formed a long, single common room, used for manufacturing coconut fibre and matting by workers who moved in after the wool industry moved out. Not far away stands what was once a wool merchant's fine timbered home, built in 1495. When the trade died it became a pub – The Crown.

On a steep hillside just outside the village, the unusually large 15th-century Church of St Mary Magdalene stands with its original carved door intact. The church had until recently a tower at its west end, but on May 31, 1975 – Ascension Day – a corner of the tower collapsed, and most of the rest was pulled down to make the other parts of the building safe. Inside the church is a memorial to Edward Rotherham, captain of Collingwood's flagship *Royal Sovereign*, which led the British fleet into action at Trafalgar in 1805.

BINBROOK

Lincolnshire
7 miles northeast of Market Rasen

In the 19th century Binbrook was a centre for the recruitment of agricultural labourers, both men and women, who were employed to work in the fields under intolerable conditions. Their long hours and miserable pay aroused public reactions that played a part in the formation of the National Union of Agricultural and Allied Workers in 1872.

Binbrook once had two churches, St Gabriel's and St Mary's, but St Gabriel's fell into ruin and was pulled down in 1820. Set back from the wide square behind trees, St Mary's ironstone tower and broach spire soar above a church surprisingly large for so small a village. Most of its interior is Victorian, but there are a few relics from the earlier building, including an 18th-century hatchment (a memorial panel bearing his coat of arms) to Richard Bewley Caton of Binbrook, an army major who later took holy orders. In Georgian times the Caton family were substantial local landowners.

During the Second World War, units of the Royal Australian Air Force were stationed at the airfield near Binbrook, and it was from here that squadrons of No 1 Bomber Group flew their Lancasters on night raids over Germany. On the night of March 30, 1944, 24 aircraft from Binbrook took part in a raid on Nuremburg; three failed to return.

BINHAM PRIORY

Norfolk
5 miles southeast of Wells

Binham was founded as a Benedictine Priory in 1091. It owes its fame to Richard de Pasco, who was prior from 1226 to 1244. He built the magnificent west front of the monastic church – a rare example of Early English architecture in East Anglia.

The priory was never very prosperous and Pasco's successor, William de Somerton, sold its few treasures to raise money for his research work as an alchemist. Having impoverished the priory he fled to Rome, leaving a deficit of £600. The priory as such came to an end when it was dissolved in 1540.

The monastic church is now used as a parish church. The large window with its geometric tracery may have been added at a slightly later date to the rest of the arcaded and dog-tooth ornamented front. Inside, the join between the 12th- and 13th-century work is clearly visible. There is a Perpendicular seven-sacramental font and the stalls have misericords. Ruins of the old priory surround the church.

BLACKMORE

Essex
8 miles southwest of Chelmsford

Blackmore's Priory Church of St Laurence possesses one of the finest of the few wooden belfry towers left in Essex.

Linked to the nave of the 12th-century church – all that remains of a former priory – the 15th-century tower rises in a series of pagoda-like steps, terminated by a shingled-broach spire. Strutted, braced and jointed together, a complex framework of timbers forms a rigid structure, capable of resisting the erratic strains imposed by the swing of the bell or gale-force winds – clearly owing much to the combined skills of continental invaders and medieval shipwrights.

There is a rare cresset stone in the tower. Used as nightlights in monasteries, cresset stones had cup-like hollows in them, filled with oil and a floating wick.

BLAKENEY

Norfolk
5 miles northwest of Holt

The picturesque port of Blakeney, built mainly of flint, is well known to yachtsmen, wildfowlers and naturalists. Because of its extreme northern position on the Norfolk coast, Blakeney makes a good landfall for migrating birds, particularly in autumn.

Beside the main coastal road between Sheringham and Wells-next-the-Sea stands Blakeney's Church of St Nicholas. Its tower, over 100 ft high, is a landmark for miles around, and at the eastern end of the church is a smaller tower built as a beacon to guide ships into Blakeney harbour.

High Street runs from the main road down to the Quay between cottages of brick and flint and a few houses of red brick. On the Quay is the Georgian Red House. The old Guildhall, in High Street, which is now a hotel, has a 14th-century brick vaulted undercroft. The waterfront was a commercial port until the beginning of this century. Now the estuary has silted up, and only small pleasure craft can sail up the narrow channel.

The broad Quay faces the wide, flat marshes stretching into the distance towards Blakeney Point. Blakeney Point's 'spire' is a ridge of shingle running along its entire length on the seaward side. On the

BLAKENEY *A long stretch of dunes, owned by the National Trust, acts as a welcoming sanctuary for shore birds* (overleaf).

landward side there are sand-dunes, and there is also plenty of vegetation and other wildlife. This long arm of sand and shingle has a nature reserve, owned by the National Trust, which can be visited by boat from Blakeney Quay, if the tide permits, or by a 5 mile walk from the neighbouring village of Cley.

BLAXHALL
Suffolk
4 miles south of Saxmundham

Local people say that the Blaxhall Stone at Stone Farm in Blaxhall is constantly increasing in size. The stone is supposed to have been the size of a small loaf when it was first noticed a century ago, and has since grown to its present weight of about 5 tons. The belief that pebbles actually grow in the soil and develop into large stones was once common in East Anglia.

BLICKLING HALL
Norfolk
1½ miles northwest of Aylsham

Blickling Hall — with its red-brick Jacobean facade, cupolas, turrets, chimneys and shaped gables framed between two yew hedges — is beside a church and an inn on the road between Aylsham and Saxthorpe. It was designed by Robert Lyminge — architect of Hatfield House — between 1616–24, for Sir Henry Hobart, Lord Chief Justice. The estate was at one time owned by the Boleyn family; it is said that Anne Boleyn, Henry VIII's second wife and mother of Elizabeth I, was born and spent her childhood in an earlier house on the site. The house had been bought by her great-grandfather from Sir John Fastolf, one of the models for Shakespeare's Falstaff. Anne Boleyn was beheaded on May 19, 1536, having fallen from the king's favour for failing to produce a male heir. Legend has it that on this day every year her ghost returns to Blickling, severed head in lap, in a ghostly carriage pulled by four headless horses and driven by a headless coachman.

Blickling Hall is now owned by the National Trust. Bedrooms portray different periods up to Edwardian times. There are formal gardens and a workshop for the conservation and repair of tapestries and fabrics throughout East Anglia.

BLYBOROUGH
Lincolnshire
3 miles south of Kirton in Lindsey

The Early English Chuch of St Alkmund in Blyborough has a 13th-century chancel arch and part of a 15th-century Flemish rood. Later work includes the 18th-century tower. There is a reclining effigy of a priest who died in 1434.

About 2½ miles south is Harpswell, whose Church of St Chad has a Saxon tower with an inscription which records that the clock that once stood there was given to commemorate the Battle of Culloden. There is a Norman font and a 17th-century south aisle. In 1891 the effigy of a priest was discovered in the floor and there are two others, of the 14th and 17th centuries. In the north wall of the chancel is the Whichcote brass, depicting a knight and his lady.

BLYTHBURGH
Suffolk
4 miles west of Southwold

In the 15th century Blythburgh was a thriving port, but it declined as medieval shipwrights launched vessels too big to navigate the river, which silted up until even the fishermen went.

The beautiful Church of the Holy Trinity is Blythburgh's glory. Visible for miles across the marshes, locals call it the 'Cathedral of the Marshes'. It is huge for a village — but then Blythburgh was big, too, when work began on the church in 1412. Its tie-beam roof, jointed without a single nail, covers a nave 127 ft long. The tower, a century older, belonged to an earlier church and once had a steeple. Holy Trinity has a 15th-century font, a Jacobean pulpit and benches carved with the Seven Deadly Sins, instead of the usual poppy-head common to Suffolk churches.

In 1577, lightning struck the church during a service, and toppled the steeple into the nave, killing a man and a boy. Scorch marks on the church door were believed by frightened villagers to have been made by the Devil's claws. The marks can still be seen.

In 1644 Cromwell's reformer William Dowsing and his followers smashed ornaments, windows and statues, and blasted shot into the carved, wooden angels soaring along the roof beams. Haltermarks and hoofmarks in the nave still show where the Puritans tethered horses.

As in Southwold, services are still started by a 17th-century Jack-o'-the-clock. Above the south porch an ancient private room for the priest has been restored, with an altar made of wood from Nelson's flagship *Victory*.

The Dutch-styled gables of the old White Hart Inn show East Anglia's long links with the continental lowlands. Inside, panelling and moulded ceilings survive from its days as a courthouse for Quarter Sessions. A path along the riverbank below the inn winds to Walberswick, skirting a nature reserve.

Wenhaston, about 3½ miles northeast, has a Norman church, St Peter's, with several later additions; the west tower has flushwork decoration. Inside is a large painting on wood, dating from about 1500, of the Last Judgement, *The Doom*.

BOOTHBY PAGNELL
Lincolnshire
5 miles southeast of Grantham

In Boothby Pagnell stands a small Norman manor house built in 1178 in the grounds of Boothby Hall; it had a moat for defence and substantial construction — in places the walls are as much as 4 ft thick — disguised by ashlar stone dressings. Inside is a vaulted ground floor with hall and solar. It is among the most important examples of its type and period in England.

The Church of St Andrew was built in the 12th century and has fine Norman arches and Saxon motifs on the bell openings. The pews, roof, oak screen and much of the stained glass were completely renewed in 1897 as a gift from Mrs Cecil Thorold, who lived at the Hall.

CATHEDRAL OF THE MARSHES *Blythburgh's Church of the Holy Trinity dominates the coastal marshes beyond Southwold.*

THE BOSTON STUMP *Once a beacon for sailors on The Wash, the steeple of St Botolph's is visible across miles of reclaimed Fens.*

BOSTON

Lincolnshire
28 miles southeast of Lincoln

The 272 ft lantern tower of the 14th-century St Botolph's Church, on the bank of the River Witham, is known as the Boston Stump. It was once a beacon for Fenland travellers and navigators on The Wash. From the top on a clear day you can see Lincoln.

Boston is the port from which a band of Puritans set sail for America in 1630 – ten years after the Pilgrim Fathers made their voyage to the New World. The Puritans founded the settlement of Boston in what is now Massachusetts, and St Botolph's contains a memorial to John Cotton, the 'rebel' minister who led a number of his congregation across the Atlantic. There are also memorials to the five Lincolnshire men who were afterwards appointed Governors of Massachusetts. The elaborately carved misericords (brackets on the choir seats) date from the end of the 14th century, and the chancel has a fine medieval painted ceiling.

To the south of the church is Queen Anne-style Fydell House, built in 1726 for a former Lord Mayor of Boston, William Fydell. Inside is an American Room for the use of visitors from the town's namesake, and the house itself is open to the public by arrangement. Next door is another building with an American connection – the 15th-century Guildhall, now a museum. It includes the cells occupied by the Pilgrim Fathers in 1607 after their first – and unsuccessful – attempt to escape to the Netherlands in search of religious freedom. They were betrayed to the authorities by the ship's captain and arrested, but afterwards they were allowed to go to Holland. Later they returned and in 1620 sailed to America from Southampton on board the *Mayflower.*

Boston's heyday as a port was in the 13th century, when it rivalled London. By the 16th century its fortunes had declined, mainly because of floods and silting of the Witham. But with the drainage of the fens and improvements to the channel such as the opening of the Grand Sluice in the 18th century, trade revived. By the 19th century its docks had once again come into their own – and still do a busy international trade in grain, timber, steel and fertiliser.

Freiston Shore, 5 miles southeast of Boston, is a village lying close to the sea amid rich agricultural land, intensively farmed for market produce. The marshes are dangerous, although there are well-worn hard paths through the safe parts of the Saltings. The marshes are excellent for bird-watching.

BOURNE
Lincolnshire
10 miles west of Spalding

The market town of Bourne was once the refuge of Hereward the Wake, last of the Saxon nobles to resist William the Conqueror. His Saxon manor house stood on the site of Bourne Castle, now marked by mounds and part of a moat. Bourne is also known for the BRM racing cars which were once manufactured here. Today, the town services the agricultural community around it. Bourne's water is said to be among the purest in the country, and there are extensive watercress beds.

Sir William Cecil (1520–98), Lord High Treasurer to Elizabeth I, and created Baron Burghley in 1571, was born in a house which is now the Burghley Arms Hotel. The town was also the birthplace of Frederick Worth (1825–95), founder of the House of Worth in Paris, which became a centre of the fashion world. Bourne has a number of good Georgian houses, including the

RED HALL *The 17th-century mansion later became the station master's house. Now it is a preserved landmark in Bourne.*

Maltings and the Manor House. The Tudor cottages in South Street, dated 1636, are single-storey structures in brick with stone gable-ends and modern mullioned windows. Only the 13th-century church remains of the Augustinian abbey founded in 1138.

BOXFORD
Suffolk
14 miles west of Ipswich

The wooden porch, on the north side of the 14th-century Church of St Mary at Boxford, is probably the oldest one in the country. The Perpendicular south porch, built a century later, is of Caen stone from Normandy. Inside is a 17th-century font cover, an 18th-century pulpit and medieval paintings.

There are two interesting monuments: a brass depicting a child who died in 1606; and another to four-times widowed Elizabeth Hyams, hastened to her end apparently 'by a fall, that brought on mortification … in her 113th year'.

BOXTED
Suffolk
10 miles south of Bury St Edmunds

A flint-and-stone church with a hammerbeam roof in the chancel, Boxted's Church of the Holy Trinity is thought to have been built by an outlaw, Gilbert de Bek, as a penance exacted by the Abbot of Edmundsbury between 1199 and 1216.

The church has the private pew of the Poleys – a family associated with Boxted for over 600 years. Such pews were raised above the general floor level of the church for the practical purpose of keeping out draughts and dogs, as well as to emphasise the social superiority of their occupants. Pews were partitioned

to separate the family from its low-born retainers.

Holy Trinity is in Boxted Hall park and has a 17th-century effigy of Sir John Poley, who may have been immortalised in the celebrated nursery rhyme: 'Frog who would a wooing go, with a roly poly, gammon and spinach.' Rowley, Poley, Bacon and Greene are all families still living in Suffolk. There is also an interesting monument with wooden effigies, c. 1587.

BRADWELL-ON-SEA
Essex
7 miles northeast of Burnham-on-Crouch

A nuclear power station 1 mile north of Bradwell-on-Sea dominates the broad estuary of the Blackwater, but 2½ miles east stands the tiny chapel of St Peter-on-the-Wall, which St Cedd built in AD 654 from the stones of the great Roman fort of Othona. The fort's walls can be traced in the grass, and the chapel, one of the earliest shrines of Christianity on the English mainland, stands astride the entrance. For centuries it was a smuggler's hide-out, then it became a beacon tower, a barn and a cattle shed; in recent years the surviving Saxon nave has been reconsecrated, though no services are held there.

Bradwell Lodge, in the village, is a Tudor and 18th-century building. There are good inns, and a tiny lock-up set in the churchyard wall. From the chapel it is possible to walk 12 miles or more along the lonely sea-wall southwards to Burnham-on-Crouch and scarcely see a house or human being.

BRAINTREE
Essex
11 miles northeast of Chelmsford

Textiles have meant prosperity to Braintree for more than 400 years. At first the trade was in woollen cloth, and when this declined at the start of the 19th century the Courtauld family introduced silk-weaving – an industry that still flourishes in the town. The Heritage Centre in the town hall describes Braintree's former international importance in wool, silk and engineering.

Braintree stands on the old Roman road from St Albans to Colchester, and the parish church of St Michael includes some Roman bricks. Braintree Market, first chartered in 1199, is still held.

Six miles to the northeast, Gosfield Hall is a Tudor courtyard house, much altered in the 18th century and added to and restored in the 19th by the Courtauld family. It has a Tudor panelled long gallery, ballroom and hidden room. It is now owned by Mutual Households Association.

BRAMFIELD
Suffolk
3 miles south of Halesworth

An acorn fell to the ground in Bramfield at about the time that Alfred the Great was burning the cakes. It grew into a sapling as the Vikings were driven out of eastern England, and was a sturdy oak when the Normans conquered the Saxons in 1066. Soon afterwards, Bramfield and its oak became part of the feudal estates of the Earl of Richmond, son-in-law of William the Conqueror.

In the 13th century a massive round tower – with walls 5 ft thick in places – was built as a defensive sanctuary in Bramfield. It is now the tower of St Andrew's Church. Unusually, tower and church are set apart, and the 14th-century church building is thatched. Inside is a magnificent rood screen, elaborately carved and with painted panels, which was made in the 15th century.

Sir Edward Coke (1552–1634), who owned the neighbouring manor of Huntingfield, became Lord Chief Justice and champion of the rule of law against the whim of the current monarchs. His son and daughter-in-law, Arthur and Elizabeth, who both died in the 1620s, can be seen in effigy in St Andrew's, with Arthur kneeling in full armour and Elizabeth holding a baby in her arms.

Twenty years later, while the Civil War raged, the Puritan William Dowsing descended on the church and destroyed '24 superstitious pictures: one crucifix and picture of Christ: and twelve angels on the roof'.

During the 16th century a family named Rabett moved into Bramfield Hall and became custodians of the oak. The Rabetts stayed for more than 300 years, and four of their coats of arms still hang in the church. The rabbits on their painted shields are a pun on the family name.

In 1843 the last two branches of the oak fell. Now only the stump remains as a monument to more than a thousand years of village history.

BRAMPTON
Cambridgeshire
2 miles west of Huntingdon

Among its dusky red and yellow cottages, Brampton includes Pepys's House, the home of Samuel Pepys's family. The celebrated diarist lived in this picturesque, twin-gabled farmhouse or small manor house when attending Huntingdon Grammar School in 1644. He owned the house from 1664 to 1680, fleeing here from the plague in 1665. Brampton's 13th-century church has a fine font, an oak screen, and three finely carved choir stalls of the 14th century.

The road to Huntingdon passes Hinchingbrooke House. The finely sculpted gatehouse is believed to have been brought here from Ramsey Abbey in the 16th century, but the mansion was built by Oliver Cromwell's prosperous great-grandfather, Sir Richard Cromwell, around the remains of a nunnery. After the Restoration the Ist Earl of Sandwich added to the west side of the court. A serious fire in 1830 did extensive damage, but the house was meticulously restored and it is now a school that is open to the public view at certain times during the spring and summer.

BRANCASTER
Norfolk
4 miles west of Burnham Market

The red-roofed village of Brancaster has a 14th-century church, from which a mile-long lane leads to the beach through thickets of tall reeds and across the saltings. Although the sandy beach is large and attractive, tides make swimming dangerous. From Brancaster Staithe, 1½ miles east, there is a boat service to Scolt Head Island, a bird sanctuary and nature-study area 1 mile to the north. The island stretches for 3½ miles from Brancaster Harbour to Burnham Harbour, its sand-dunes, shingle banks, marshes and salt-marshes forming an isolated segment typical of the whole North Norfolk coastline.

BRANDON
Suffolk
6 miles northwest of Thetford

The town of Brandon stands on flint, is largely built of flint, and was for long the home of England's oldest industry, flint knapping. Arrowheads and prehistoric tools were hammered out of mined slabs. Gun flints were supplied from Brandon to the British Army during the Napoleonic wars. Demand for gun flints from Africa and from muzzle-loading enthusiasts in America has been so great that knapping has been moved from behind The Flintknapper's Arms to a bigger yard on the Bury St Edmunds road.

Near Brandon, 3 miles to the northeast, is Grime's Graves, the largest prehistoric flint mine in Europe, with 350 known shafts. The vertical shafts, 20–40 ft deep, have passages radiating outwards from their base. The Stone Age and Bronze Age miners took flint from the walls of the shaft and from the seams of flint that the passages followed. The flint was probably roughly shaped nearby and then traded over most of southern England to be used to make axes.

The ruins of Weeting Castle, a 12th-century fortified manor house, stand in a moated rectangular enclosure about 1 mile north of Brandon. The castle was probably founded by William de Warenne, a friend of William the Conqueror, and was at one time owned by the Howard family (who were to become the Dukes of Norfolk).

Two miles northeast of Brandon, at the heart of Thetford Forest, is Santon Downham, which has a 2 mile walk through forest plantations.

BRENTWOOD
Essex
11 miles southwest of Chelmsford

Despite increasing commuter development, Brentwood is an excellent centre for walks through unspoilt rural country and spacious parklands within 25 miles of St Paul's Cathedral. Deer roam by the lakes in the 428 acre park at South Weald, part of Brentwood's attractive 'green belt'.

The town – now a dormitory for London – grew up in the late 12th century, around a forest clearing, as a convenient stopping place for pilgrims from East Anglia and the Midlands on their way to St Thomas Becket's shrine at Canterbury. The town later developed as a staging post with good inns. In the 1840s, its modern growth came with the railways.

BRESSINGHAM
Norfolk
3 miles west of Diss

Bressingham contains the most comprehensive museum of steam power in Britain, with 14 traction and road engines, and rail locomotives – including 18 standard gauge, main line and industrial locomotives.

Steam-hauled rides are given on miniature and narrow-gauge trains through 5 miles of the Bressingham Hall estates, which also include steam-driven fairground roundabouts with organs, and 6 acres of informal gardens of alpine plants and perennials.

About 5 miles to the west is the large village of Redgrave, with its Decorated and Perpendicular Church of St Mary, containing some fine monuments.

BRESSINGHAM GARDENS *The tranquillity of this lily pond hardly suggests one of the foremost commercial nurseries in Britain.*

BRIGHTLINGSEA

Essex
8 miles southeast of Colchester

The old fishing and yachting port of Brightlingsea on the mouth of the Colne Estuary is the only town outside Kent and Sussex which is a member of the Cinque Ports – ports on the southeast coast with ancient privileges. It is described in an Elizabethan charter as being 'a Limb of the Cinque Port of Sandwich' and on the first Monday in December a Deputy of the Cinque Port Liberty is elected from among the Freemen of the town.

Jacobes Hall, the best medieval house in the town, is now a hotel. The splendid church tower, 94 ft high, is one of the finest in East Anglia. Inside the Perpendicular church is a series of wall plaques dedicated to sailors killed at sea.

BUCKDEN

Cambridgeshire
4 miles southwest of Huntingdon

Two coaching inns, the black-and-white 16th-century Lion and the red-brick 17th-century George, face each other across Buckden's wide High Street – a reminder that this quiet thoroughfare was once part of the main road from London to the north. Most of the houses are brick; many are of the Jacobean and Georgian periods, but the village is dominated by the 15th-century palace of the Bishops of Lincoln. Catherine of Aragon, first wife of Henry VIII, lived here from 1534–5 before she was removed to Kimbolton Castle where she died. Behind the palace's red-brick walls stand a Tudor gatehouse and massive, turreted tower, all that remains of the original building used by the bishops from the early Middle Ages until 1838.

Adjoining Buckden Palace is the contrasting grey-stone church where Laurence Sterne, author of *Tristram Shandy*, was ordained in 1736. In the churchyard are buried two uncles of the nine-day queen, Lady Jane Grey.

Eastwards up a sweeping arc of road from the A1 at Buckden is the reservoir, Grafham Water. It covers 6 square miles and supplies towns within a 20 mile radius. There are extensive picnic areas, and some grassy walks round the lake.

About 4 miles south of the reservoir is Great Stoughton, whose village cross, erected in 1637, has a complicated sundial on three of its four faces.

BUNGAY

Suffolk
14 miles southwest of Norwich

The odd name of little Bungay in Waveney Valley possibly derives from 'bongue', a good ford, or 'le bon eye', a spit of land thrusting out into the river. Bungay is mainly 18th century in character, for a fire in 1688 destroyed most of the original houses and melted St Mary's church bells. Castle ruins seep through part of the town as alley walls and fragmentary lumps of masonry, and the White Lion stands on part of the old fortifications.

The castle was built by the Bigods in the 12th century and was already ruinous in the late 14th century. In the market place, the Butter Cross of 1689

replaced an older one destroyed by the raging fire.

At Earsham, $1\frac{1}{2}$ miles southwest of Bungay, is an Otter Trust, where one of the largest colonies of otters in the world can be seen.

BURES

Essex and Suffolk
5 miles southeast of Sudbury

A diminutive township, Bures straddles the River Stour and is partly in Essex and partly in Suffolk. The Church of St Mary is of the 13th to 16th centuries. It has a Perpendicular font with carved angels and heraldry. Edmund, East Anglian king and martyr, was crowned at the age of 15 on Christmas Day, AD 855, in a chapel above Bures. The chapel, consecrated by Archbishop Langton in 1218 and well restored in this century, stands not on St Edmund's Hill but on a crest at the end of a lane signposted 'Chapel', half a mile out of Bures on the road that leads to Boxford.

BURGH LE MARSH

Lincolnshire
5 miles west of Skegness

Burgh le Marsh is notable for the discovery, in the 1930s, of a superbly worked pre-Bronze Age axehead, one of only five similar heads which have been unearthed in Britain.

The village grew to the size of a small town at the end of the 19th century, with a brisk cattle market and annual foal fair, a number of inns and two breweries. The cattle market site is now occupied by modern flats called Market Close, leading to old people's flats in Dobson's Court, named after the last miller to operate the windmill on the side of the road. This splendid brick-tower mill, built in 1833, still works and has an unusual feature – its five sails turn clockwise instead of anticlockwise. It stands five storeys high.

The church has an elegant buttressed and pinnacled tower, built of Portland stone, with a brightly painted clockface on one side which bears the faintly ominous message 'Watch and Pray, For Ye Know Not When the Time Is'. Inside are an impressive Jacobean pulpit, traces of medieval wall paintings and a lectern made in 1875 by the local barber, Jabez Good.

To the west of the church, alongside the road leading to Lincoln, is Cock Hill, an ancient tumulus from which the remains of a Saxon burial have been excavated. Clay pipes and slate pencils unearthed from a depression in the summit suggest that the mound was once used as a cockpit, hence its name. The soil also contains pieces of Roman pottery and coins. A Roman road from Lincoln ended abruptly at Burgh and it is thought that a Roman ferry ran from nearby, taking travellers across The Wash to the junction of Peddars' Way and the Icknield Way on the Norfolk shore. Burgh may also have supported a small Roman fort or signal station.

In parkland about 3 miles northwest of the village is Gunby Hall, a manor house built in 1700 in the style of Christopher Wren. It is now administered by the National Trust and is open occasionally in summer.

GUNBY HALL *A fine example of William and Mary architecture, the mellow brick house has superbly panelled rooms.*

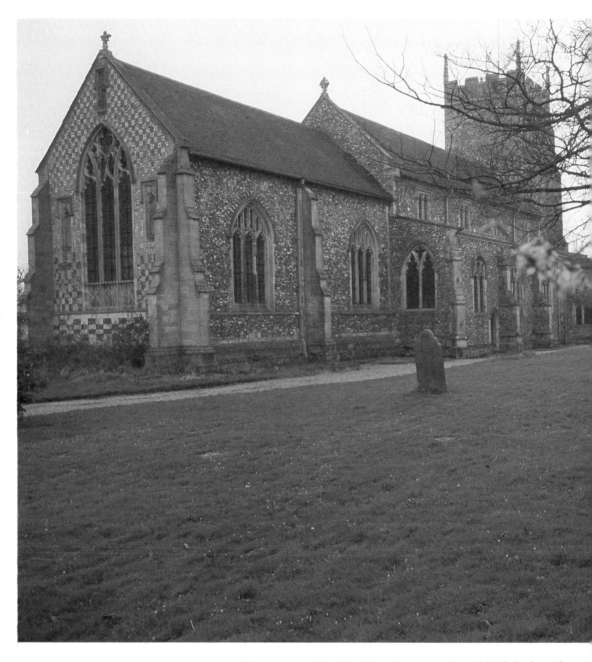

BURGHLEY HOUSE
Cambridgeshire
1 mile southeast of Stamford

The house, begun in c.1552 by Sir William Cecil, is square, built around a central courtyard with rounded corner towers topped by turrets. Burghley House is one of England's greatest Elizabethan houses, and the home of the Exeter and Cecil families for more than four centuries. The grandest room in the earliest part is the Great Hall, with a double hammerbeam roof and a large fireplace. The Marble Hall and the Andromeda Hall were completed in 1587, after Cecil had become Lord Burghley and Lord High Treasurer.

Little of the original decoration remains, but there is carved woodwork by Grinling Gibbons, and much wall-painting, the subjects of which give their names to the Hell Room and the Heaven Room. There are more than 700 works of art, and the house is also noted for its painted ceilings, fine furniture and tapestries, silver fireplaces and a rose garden.

Burghley House is open to the public daily throughout the summer. The house and grounds have been connected in the popular imagination with horses ever since the late 6th Marquis of Exeter won an Olympic Gold Medal in the 400 metres hurdles in 1928. The Burghley Three Day Equestrian Event takes place in the park each September.

BURNHAM-ON-CROUCH
Essex
9 miles southeast of Maldon

The town of Burnham-on-Crouch, which lies on the north bank of the Crouch 6 miles from the sea, is homely despite its five yacht clubs and the description 'the Cowes of the East Coast'. At the height of the summer sailing season, 2000 or more yachts and other craft crowd the anchorage.

Burnham-on-Crouch is not only famous for yachting, but for oysters, smuggling yarns and long sea-wall

was born. His father, Edmund, was the rector of Burnham Thorpe until his death in 1802; in the following year, the admiral's birthplace was demolished and replaced by the present rectory. Horatio returned to live in the village with his wife from 1787 until 1793, when he was given command of HMS *Agamemnon*.

The village has a wide green overlooked by brick-and-flint Georgian buildings and the 13th-century Church of All Saints. The church was restored in Nelson's honour in the 19th century, and there is a marble bust of the hero above his father's tomb.

The naval theme is maintained in the east end of the church where the flags flown by the battle-cruiser HMS *Indomitable* at the Battle of Jutland are displayed at the chancel crossing. On the west wall is the crest of the Second World War battleship HMS *Nelson*, and her white ensigns are in the western arch of the tower. There is a fine 15th-century brass in the chancel floor to Sir William Calthorp, who lived at the Manor House.

At one time Burnham Thorpe was one of seven Burnham parishes and the largest remaining one, Burnham Market, lies a little over a mile to the northwest. It has a large green enclosed by gracious 18th-century houses. Burnham Overy, to the northwest, has an early-18th-century watermill by the River Burn and a group of cottages, now owned by the National Trust, and a church, St Clement's, with a Norman central tower. Burnham Norton, also to the northwest, has the 13th- to 15th-century Church of St Margaret, with a round tower which may be of Saxon origin. The rood screen is dated 1458, there is a fine pulpit with painted panels of the donor and the Latin Fathers of the Church, and a Norman font.

BURWELL
Cambridgeshire
4 miles northwest of Newmarket

Among the trim lawns of Burwell's churchyard stands a poignant memorial to a sad episode in the long history of the fenland village. A tombstone, carved with a flaming heart, marks the grave of 82 people who died when what had begun as a joyous occasion ended in tragedy. On September 8, 1727, a travelling puppet showman set up his theatre in a barn, and people came from far and wide to enjoy the entertainment. But there were more spectators than the barn could hold, so the doors were closed. A few moments later a fire started which quickly engulfed the trapped audience. The doors were found to have been nailed shut, and later a man was accused of starting the fire. He was acquitted at Cambridge Assizes, but in 1774 the local press reported that a man from Fordham, $4\frac{1}{2}$ miles northeast of Burwell, had confessed to the crime on his deathbed, saying that he had set fire to the barn to spite the showman.

The soaring 100 ft tower of St Mary is an unmistakable landmark above the fenland fringes, its octagonal upper section clearly influenced by the tower of Ely Cathedral. It is one of the best examples of English Perpendicular style. There are also hints of the earlier Romanesque church, which was incorporated in the later building. These include the buttresses and some blocked windows.

walks. The Quay is a mixture of red, white and yellow colour-washed houses and cottages of former sea captains. There are boat-builders' yards, weather-boarded cottages, old inns and a smell of ropes, tar and salt water. The church, lonely on a farmyard, has an early Tudor porch and four fine late medieval stone heraldic shields.

THE BURNHAMS
Norfolk
2 miles around Burnham Market

The village inn at Burnham Thorpe is called the Lord Nelson. The village hall also bears the great admiral's name, while in the church, a cross in the chancel arch and a lectern are both made from timbers taken from HMS *Victory*. In this way Burnham Thorpe pays tribute to Horatio Nelson, who was born in the village in 1758.

A roadside plaque and a sign half a mile south of the village mark the site of the rectory where Nelson

BURWELL *The solitary post mill testifies to the importance of wind and water to local agriculture (left). The shops in the High Street display the typical pink and white exteriors which are such a feature throughout East Anglia (above).*

To the west of the church is the site of Burwell Castle, built during the 12th century by the villainous Geoffrey de Mandeville who used it as a base for his plundering exploits. But Geoffrey overstepped the mark when he rebelled against King Stephen, who gave him the choice of the gallows or surrender of the castle. Wisely he gave up the castle, but still continued to ransack the surrounding countryside until an arrow from Stephen's troops occupying the castle put an end to his infamous career. He is remembered in Burwell by a lane, The Mandeville, which leads from a dried-up moat — all that remains of the castle.

But Burwell's history stretches back far beyond the Middle Ages — back to the Dark Ages and the Devil's Dyke which ends at the village of Reach 1½ miles west of Burwell. The dyke was a massive earthwork defence system which included Fleam Dyke, the Brent Ditch and the Bran Ditch. Although these might have been Roman defences against Anglo-Saxon invaders, excavations carried out in 1924 showed that the dyke was built in the 8th century as an East Anglian defence against Mercia, to the west. There is also evidence of an Anglo-Saxon cemetery.

Burwell today is a sprawling village with a wide main street running for about 2 miles. Most of its buildings date from the 17th and 18th centuries, but in High Street a building numbered 4 and 6 was originally a hospice built in the 14th century by the Knights Hospitaller for travellers journeying to the Crusades. It is now a private residence. At Malting Corner, at the southern end of the village, a stone barn and malt house probably served the Priory of St John, established around 1100, where the vicarage now stands.

BURY ST EDMUNDS
Suffolk
23 miles northwest of Ipswich

Originally a Saxon homestead, known as Beodericsworth, today's Bury was chosen in 630 as a suitable place for a monastery. In 870, King Edmund was brutally killed by the Danes during their raids on eastern England. His mutilated body was buried at Hoxne, 4 miles southeast of Diss, where it lay for 33 years. Miracles were attributed to the king; he was canonised, and his body was removed to Beodericsworth Monastery. The name of the town was changed to St Edmund's Bury. The monastery was granted abbey status in 1032 by the Danish-born king, Knut (Canute), who conquered all England in 1016. At the great altar of the abbey church in 1214 the barons vowed to extract from King John the concessions set out in Magna Carta — thus the town's claim to be the 'Cradle of the Law'.

Cathedral extensions among the abbey ruins were completed in 1970, to mark the 1100th anniversary of Edmund's death. There is still controversy over the future of the west front, which has Tudor, Georgian and Victorian houses built into its remains.

The town plan is based on the medieval formula of a square for God and a square for man. The former — just outside the abbey — is now known as Angel Hill; the latter is the market place, still the commercial heart of the town. On Angel Hill is a Queen Anne house, owned by the National Trust, which has a collection of clocks given by Frederic Gershom-Parkington, a musician known for early radio broadcasts, in memory of a son who was killed in the Second World War.

Moyse's Hall is a Norman building dating from the 12th century, and is possibly the oldest domestic building in East Anglia. It escaped conversion into a fire station in the late 19th century and is now an unusual

ICKWORTH *The rotunda is the centrepiece of the late 15th-century former home of the Earls and Marquesses of Bristol.*

museum with the death mask of William Corder, Maria Marten's murderer in the Red Barn at Polstead in 1828, and a book bound in his skin. The Nutshell is one of the smallest inns in the country, and has a collection of Victoriana and other bric-a-brac.

Ickworth, a freakish rotunda 3 miles southwest, is owned by the National Trust and houses an impressive array of silverware and Regency and 18th-century French furniture. Its park was landscaped by the celebrated gardener 'Capability' Brown.

BUTLEY PRIORY
Suffolk
4 miles west of Orford

Butley Priory lays claim to be the second greatest medieval gatehouse in Suffolk, and the first in Europe with a heraldic display in stone. The 14th-century gatehouse was once part of the Augustinian priory founded by Ranulf de Glanville in 1171, who travelled with Richard the Lionheart on the Third Crusade. Above this huge gateway are cut in stone the Arms of England and France, the three crowns of East Anglia, the Passion, and the Arms of the Holy Roman Empire, with Leon and Castile. Below them is the blazonry of many great East Anglian families. The central block of ashlar and blue-grey flints is flanked by huge buttresses. Lancet windows, pierced and foliated, give grace and light.

The gatehouse is surrounded by one of the oldest forests in England; the pre-Druidic Staverton Forest. Behind it, in the farmyard somewhere beneath the ruins of the priory, is said to be the silver coffin of Michael de la Pole, Earl of Suffolk killed at Agincourt.

CAISTOR
Lincolnshire
8 miles north of Market Rasen

The small market town of Caistor was once a Roman settlement, the remains of which can still be seen. The Church of St Peter and St Paul is partly Saxon, and has a tower with Norman work in it. Among the interesting monuments in the church is one in the vestry to Sir Edmund Maddison, who died in 1553 at the age of 100. There are some 13th- and 14th-century stone effigies and a 15th-century brass on the chancel floor. The 19th-century stained-glass windows include some by C. E. Kempe.

To the south of Caistor, a mile away, is Nettleton Hill, known locally as Nettleton Bump, because of its modest height of 370 ft. The deep-channelled Nettleton Beck rises in the Wolds to the southeast of the village of Nettleton. It winds its way down to the foot of the Wolds, and on to the Ancholme valley.

About 2 miles to the southeast is Rothwell, whose Church of St Mary Magdalene has an interesting Saxon west tower and Norman work inside – nave arcades with sturdy round columns and arches with zigzag ornament.

CALCEBY
Lincolnshire
2 miles west of Ulceby Cross

A lost village of the Wolds, Calceby lies in a lovely, little-known area of secluded villages and wooded parkland. Near the south end of the Bluestone Heath Road, an ivy-covered chalk-stone ruin on a hilly outcrop springs dramatically into view. This was once the parish church of Calceby. As the *-by* in its name suggests, Calceby was probably founded by Danish settlers in the 9th or 10th centuries, and in medieval times was a busy community. According to the Domesday Book, it received income, with four other villages, from salt-pan holdings on the coast.

Why the village was deserted is uncertain. It survived for some 200 years after the Black Death. There were still 18 families living there in 1563, but with the death of the last vicar in 1621 the village dwindled to the present farmhouse and a handful of scattered cottages.

A Norman doorway from Calceby church is now incorporated in the south aisle of the church at South Ormsby village, tucked away in tree-shaded surroundings a mile westwards. Southwards from Calceby, a field footpath leads to the cul-de-sac hamlet of Driby, and onwards to the southwest there is a bridle-path to Brinkhill.

Northwards from South Ormsby, the wooded parklands of Ormsby Hall (not open to the public) border the west side of the road. The Great Eau (from the Old English *ea*, 'a stream'), which rises high in the Wolds beyond, powered the old water mill at Ketsby further north. It stands just off the minor road beside a new trout farm, its water wheel still in position.

CAMBRIDGE
Cambridgeshire
49 miles north of London

A Roman town was established by AD 70 on a hill overlooking the River Cam, which the Romans knew as Granta. The name of the site, where the Saxons settled after the Romans had left, evolved gradually from Grantacaester to Grantabric, Cantabridge and finally to the modern Cambridge. Part of the Cam near the city is still called locally by its old Roman name.

When the university was established early in the 13th century, students made their own lodging arrangements and grouped around the religious and lay-teachers whose ideas most appealed to them. Discipline was slack and the behaviour of students led to a 'town and gown' conflict which went on into the 18th century.

Cambridge was a busy commercial centre before the university was established, and today its industries include radio and electronics, cement-making, printing, and the manufacture of scientific instruments. Even so the university is the heart of Cambridge. Its colleges, churches and museums cover much of the city centre. The university is also a major scientific research centre with its Cavendish Laboratory, the Observatories, the Scott Polar Research Institute and the University Chemical Laboratory.

Visitors can go into college courtyards, chapels, dining halls and certain gardens at most times. A good place to start a tour would be Trumpington Street, which enters Cambridge from the south. The deep gutters which line Trumpington Street survive from a 17th-century scheme for bringing water into the city. Hobson's conduit, an ornate fountain-head on the west side of the road, is named after Thomas Hobson (1544–1631), a livery-stable owner who contributed to the scheme. He is immortalised in the expression 'Hobson's choice', after his custom of offering his patrons a horse of his own choice or none at all. Also in Trumpington Street is the Fitzwilliam Museum, which was founded in 1816 by Viscount Fitzwilliam. One of the world's greatest museums, its exhibits include Egyptian, Greek and Roman antiquities; illuminated manuscripts; ceramics; coins; arms and armour; and an outstanding collection of paintings, including works by Rembrandt, Titian, Constable and Turner.

Beyond the museum lies the university's oldest college, Peterhouse, endowed by Hugh de Balsham, Bishop of Ely, in 1284. The first students had settled in Cambridge 75 years earlier, after fleeing from riot-torn Oxford in 1209. The construction of the 17th-century Front Court meant the demolition of the original 13th-century student hostels on the site. Peterhouse is one of 12 colleges founded between the 13th and 15th centuries. Since then, another 18 have been established. The members of these 30 colleges compose the university today.

Pembroke College, a little way up the street from Peterhouse, was founded in 1347 by the Earl of Pembroke's widow, Lady Mary de Valence. Some of the medieval building survives. The chapel, built in 1666, was the first completed design of Sir Christopher Wren, England's greatest architect.

On the corner of Silver Street, which leads from Trumpington Street to the river, is St Catharine's College which was founded in 1473. None of the original buildings remain, but there is a handsome open court, built between 1674 and 1780.

Queens' College, in Silver Street, is named after the two queens who founded it in the mid-15th century: Henry VI's wife, Margaret of Anjou, and Edward IV's wife, Elizabeth Woodville. Most of the original 15th-century building survives. The Dutch theologian Erasmus stayed at the college in 1511 and imported his own wine rather than drink the local beer.

Leading from Queens' over the river is the wooden Mathematical Bridge, erected to the design of William Etheridge in 1749 without metal fastenings. It was dismantled by inquisitive Victorians to see how it was made, but they could only put it together again with iron bolts.

Opposite St Catharine's, in Trumpington Street, is Corpus Christi College, founded by the townspeople in 1352. On one wall of the Old Court is a tablet commemorating two of the college's most famous students, the Elizabethan dramatists Christopher Marlowe and John Fletcher. A 16th-century passage links the college's Old Court to the city's oldest building, the Saxon Church of St Bene't, which dates from the early 11th century.

Beyond Bene't Street, Trumpington Street gives way to King's Parade, with King's College set back to the west. Founded in 1441 by Henry VI, it is best known for its chapel which was built between 1446 and 1515. It is one of the supreme achievements of the English

Gothic or Perpendicular style of architecture. The 16th-century stained-glass windows are a glory of coloured light; and the wooden screen and the choir stalls are richly carved. Behind the altar is Rubens' masterpiece the *Adoration of the Magi*.

Further up King's Parade is the 18th-century Senate House, where the Senate, the university's 'parliament', meets fortnightly to supervise the running of the university. Successful students gather here at the end of June to receive their degrees.

On the opposite side of the road is Great St Mary's Church, the official university church. Visitors can climb the 17th-century tower, which provides sweeping views of the town and surrounding countryside. St Mary's clock chimes a tune specially written for it in 1793 which was later copied for Big Ben in London.

Next to the Senate House is Gonville and Caius (pronounced Keys) College, founded in 1348 by the priest Edmund Gonville and further endowed in 1557 by Dr John Caius, a former student who became physician to Edward VI and Mary I. Ancient Gonville Court is disguised by an 18th-century facade. Dr Caius added a second court with the gates to symbolise his students' progress. Two can still be seen: 'Virtue' leads into Caius' Court, and 'Honour' marks the way out for successful students.

Backing the river behind these buildings on the left of King's Parade are Clare College and Trinity Hall. Clare, founded in the 14th century, was re-built

WREN LIBRARY *Trinity College's famous library contains ancient manuscripts in rooms decorated by Grinling Gibbons (below).*
THE BRIDGE OF SIGHS *Inspired by its Venetian namesake, the bridge spans the Cam at St John's College (overleaf).*

between 1638 and 1715. Graceful wrought-iron gates give access to the oldest bridge in the city, built in 1640. This leads to the Masters' and Fellows' gardens across the river. Trinity Hall was founded in 1350 as a training college for priests. It has an Elizabethan library, where the books are chained to the shelves.

King's Parade gives way to Trinity Street, on the left of which is Trinity College, established by Henry VIII in 1546 and now the university's largest college. Thomas Nevile, Master of the college in Elizabeth I's time, built the Great Court, the largest university courtyard in the world. The college chapel, which was built between 1555 and 1567, contains memorials to Isaac Newton, Francis Bacon, Lord Macaulay, Lord Tennyson and other former Trinity undergraduates who made their mark on the world.

Beyond Trinity is St John's College. It is entered through a Tudor gateway surmounted by gilded heraldry, including the arms of Henry VIII's mother, Lady Margaret Beaufort, who founded the college in 1511. The Hall has a fine Tudor roof and is hung with portraits of famous men who studied at the college, including William Wordsworth, William Wilberforce and Lord Palmerston. Behind St John's the river is spanned by the charming New Bridge, built in 1831. It is known as the Bridge of Sighs because it resembles the Venetian bridge of that name.

To the north, across Magdalene (pronounced Maudlin) Street, is Magdalene College. This was founded in 1542. The diarist Samuel Pepys was a student here, and he left his library of 3000 books, including the shorthand manuscripts of his diaries, to the college. Southwards, Magdalene Street becomes Bridge Street where the Church of the Holy Sepulchre, known as 'The Round Church', stands. It is one of the few circular churches in England.

Set well back from Jesus Lane, a turning off Bridge Street, is Jesus College. It was founded in 1497 by John Alcock, Bishop of Ely, on the site of a 12th-century convent, whose chapel, cloister and other buildings were retained.

Bridge Street continues into Sidney Street, with Sidney Sussex College on the left. This was founded in 1596 by Lady Frances Sidney, widow of the Earl of Sussex. Oliver Cromwell was a student there in 1616. What is believed to be his embalmed head was buried in the ante-chapel in 1960.

Further down the street, in the angle with Hobson Street, is Christ's College, which originated in the mid-15th century as a teachers' college known as God's House. It was reformed in 1505 by Lady Margaret Beaufort, whose arms and statue are displayed on the main gate. In the chapel there is an oriel window through which Lady Beaufort joined the services from her rooms in the Master's Lodge. John Milton, who was a student at the college, is reputed to have written his poem *Lycidas* under the ancient mulberry tree in the grounds.

Further down the main thoroughfare, where it becomes St Andrew's Street, is Emmanuel College, founded in 1584 by Sir Walter Mildmay, Chancellor of the Exchequer to Elizabeth I. Sir Christopher Wren designed the chapel and its colonnade in 1666.

The Scott Polar Research Institute in Lensfield Road was founded in 1920, as a memorial to Captain Scott and his companions, who perished in Antarctica in 1912, after reaching the South Pole. Letters, diaries and photographs from their journey are on display, together with records of other polar expeditions.

Across the river, behind the colleges, are the Backs – lawns and gardens sloping down to the river's edge. Downstream from the Backs is Midsummer Common, where the Midsummer Fair has been held since the Middle Ages. At the opening the mayor distributes pennies to children. The stretch of river by the common is where the colleges and local clubs go for rowing practice. The river is not wide enough for conventional racing, and the university eight practises for the Boat Race against Oxford at Ely where conditions are similar to those on the Thames.

CASTLE ACRE
Norfolk
4 miles north of Swaffham

Set between the ruins of castle and priory, and built largely of flint quarried from both, Castle Acre is a severely attractive village. In the Domesday Book, Castle Acre and the neighbouring villages of South and West Acre are referred to collectively as 'Acra', from the Saxon word *aecer* – 'a field'.

Castle Acre commands the point where the Roman or prehistoric Peddars' Way crosses the River Nar, and must have been of considerable importance from very early times. The present village owes its form to William de Warenne, William the Conqueror's son-in-law, who reared up the great motte or mound that still looms over the village, and set on top of it his huge flint keep. Much of Castle Acre, at least as far as the church, is contained within the outer fortification of the bailey. The remains of the castle, a ruin since the de Warenne line petered out in the 14th century, are now in the guardianship of the Department of the Environment. The well-maintained gatehouse is at the top of Bailey Street, which runs down to the river.

Both the street and the green are a pleasant blend of brick and flint. Even the modern houses are built of the same materials, and rapidly weather into the general harmony. Many houses are of considerable age, but others belong to the mid-19th century, when, during the agricultural depression of the period, Castle Acre was declared an open village. This permitted the poor, the homeless and the unemployed to use it as a base for seeking work, and to build houses there.

The Church of St James, built mainly between the 13th and 15th centuries, stands at the end of the green, a vast, airy building filled with golden light from the tinted windows. There are some panes of medieval stained glass in the south aisle, and a marvellous screen and pulpit bearing medieval painted panels of saints in deep reds, blues and gold. The font cover, too, is remarkable – a gilt, green and red spire towering some 20 ft to the golden dove at its peak.

The priory ruins lie behind the church, a range of jagged crags set among decorous paths and lawns. Like the castle, the priory was founded by the de Warennes. Shortly after the Conquest, they brought 25 Cluniac monks first to their lands near Lewes, and then to Castle Acre. The west front of the church is especially lovely, standing as it does against a soaring background of uplands and sky. The Prior's Lodging, the only part that is still roofed, was a farm building until recently, and now contains a small museum.

BESIDE PEDDARS' WAY *Castle Acre stands guard on a hill, with the prehistoric trade route running through it.*

CASTLE HEDINGHAM *The solid keep of the de Vere family is all that remains of the 12th-century castle.*

CASTLE HEDINGHAM
Essex
4 miles northwest of Halstead

For more than 500 years the powerful de Vere family, Earls of Oxford, were lords of the manor at Castle Hedingham. Their 12th-century castle was built to dominate the Colne Valley and was once one of the strongest castles in England. The Norman keep, almost 150 ft high, still stands on a mound above the village. It is four storeys high, with square turrets, and walls averaging 11 ft thick.

King John granted Castle Hedingham a market charter in the 13th century. The market has long since ceased to be held, but there are reminders of the days when this was a prosperous little town; from the 15th-century Moot House in St James Street to the elegant Georgian houses of the wealthy wool merchants in King Street and Queen Street.

The castle was partly demolished in the 16th century by the 17th Earl of Oxford. Robert Ashurst, who bought the castle from the widow of Henry, the 18th and last Earl of Oxford, built a Georgian house in 1719 in the grounds of the keep from the castle ruins. The keep is open to the public all day, every day from May to October.

Parts of the Church of St Nicholas are possibly as old as the castle, but much of it is Tudor and an inscription on the tower says that it was 'renovated in 1616'. The war memorial in the churchyard is Norman.

Set 2 miles southeast of Castle Hedingham is the village of Little Maplestead. Its main feature is the 14th-century round church of the Knights Hospitaller. There are only four others like it in England.

CASTLE RISING
Norfolk
4 miles northeast of King's Lynn

According to a centuries-old legend, the ghostly screams of an imprisoned queen echo through the keep of the now-ruined Norman castle from which the village of Castle Rising takes the first part of its name.

In 1330 Edward III sent his mother, Queen Isabella, to Castle Rising after her part in the downfall and murder of her husband, Edward II. Despite the stories of her screams of loneliness and remorse, however, she lived a fairly comfortable life in the castle and was often visited by her son.

'Rising' probably comes from the Anglo-Saxon, meaning 'people of the brushwood', or Old German, meaning 'Risa's people'. The castle was built there in 1150 by William de Albini, who married the widow of Henry I and became Earl of Arundel. It passed to the Howard family in 1544. Henry Howard, Earl of Northampton, founded the attractive almshouses to the east of the church in 1614.

The single-storey, red-brick houses were rebuilt in 1807, but behind the leaded windows are rooms containing the original 17th-century furniture. The almshouses are occupied by elderly ladies who, on special occasions, wear red cloaks bearing the Howard badge and tall, pointed hats.

Surrounding the castle is a ditch, which is crossed by a 13th-century bridge. The keep is one of the largest in England and stands 50 ft high. A stone staircase leads to the first floor and a splendid Norman arch, which was the original entrance to the great hall.

St Lawrence's Church, though greatly restored, retains its Norman character, particularly at the west end which has a decorated doorway and windows. To the west of the church is the village green with a 15th-century cross.

Castle Rising was a port on the River Babingley until the 15th century, when ships became too large to navigate the receding river.

CAVENDISH
Suffolk
4 miles west of Long Melford

Thatched cottages with pink-washed walls huddle beneath the tower of St Mary's Church on the edge of Cavendish village green. The cottages, whose origins go back 400 years, have been rebuilt twice since the Second World War because of dilapidation and fire, but none of their charm has been lost. They stand by a spot known as Hyde Park Corner, near the Stour.

The village name comes from *Cafa's Edisc*, an Anglo-Saxon settlement of 'Cafa's people' where *Edisc* meant an 'enclosure'. From there came the family of the Dukes of Devonshire and that of Thomas Cavendish of Trimley, a parish in the southeast of the county. He sailed around the world in the 1580s, and died at sea on his second attempt in 1592. Another Cavendish – Sir John – was Chief Justice of the King's Bench, and was with Richard II in 1381 when he confronted Wat Tyler, leader of the Peasants' Revolt, at Smithfield. Angered by the killing of their leader by Sir John's son, some of Tyler's followers pursued Sir John to Cavendish, where he hid his valuables in the church belfry before fleeing. He was later caught near Bury St Edmunds and beheaded.

Sir John left £40 in his will for a new chancel in St Mary's Church. Its 14th-century tower dominates the village and contains a chimney in the ringing chamber, which was formerly a priest's room. At a fork in the road beyond the church stands Nether Hall, a fine early Tudor house. The present owner's family has farmed here since the 17th century. The timber-framed house near the pond was built in the 16th century. It is now the home of the Sue Ryder Foundation for the Sick and Disabled, founded by the philanthropist Lady Ryder. It contains a museum and gift shop, open daily.

CAWSTON
Norfolk
11½ miles northwest of Norwich

Cawston's Church of St Agnes was built in the 14th and 15th centuries, when the wool trade flourished in East Anglia. The fine hammerbeam roof has carved figures on its projecting beams. In the north aisle stands a plough – souvenir of a past ritual when a plough was dragged through the parish by locals, begging for 'plough money' to spend in the inn.

About 2 miles to the northwest is Sall, which has an early 15th-century church with a later 15th-century north transept. The Boleyns were among those who contributed to its construction. Both north and south porches are two-storeyed, and the carved bosses in the chancel are decorated with angels. The carved stalls have poppy-heads and misericords. There are many monumental brasses, including a shroud brass, unusual in that the figure is not a skeleton.

CAXTON
Cambridgeshire
9 miles west of Cambridge

Two miles north of the village of Caxton, at the junction of the A14 and A45, stands the sinister Caxton Gibbet. According to legend it marks the spot where a murderer was hanged alive in an iron cage, to starve to death. A baker, who took pity on him and gave him a loaf, supposedly was hanged from the same gibbet. In fact, the gibbet was probably erected to carry the body of a highwayman named Gatwood, who was executed in 1753 for robbing mail coaches on the Great North Road.

The small post-mill just outside Caxton is one of the country's oldest surviving mills – a type common in the Middle Ages – with a pitched roof, a small body and a pair of millstones driven by two pairs of sails.

The mill, re-equipped in the 19th century, is open to the public but not working.

CHELMSFORD
Essex
30 miles northeast of London

The county town of Essex, Chelmsford is set in heavily cultivated farmland dotted with unspoilt villages. Although Chelmsford has lost much of its rural peace through the demands of industry, its roots are still in

TIMELESS CAVENDISH *Thatched cottages clustering under St Mary's 14th-century tower have been sympathetically restored.*

the soil. Its livestock market, which began about AD 1200, is one of the most important in East Anglia.

The Romans built a small town, which they called Caesaromagus, halfway along the road from London to Colchester in the 1st century AD. Traces of it have been found in the Moulsham area of Chelmsford. The present town grew from the medieval manors of Moulsham and Celmeresfort, which were linked in about 1100 by a wooden bridge across the River Can. The present bridge was designed in 1787 by John Johnson, who also built the Classical Shire Hall in the High Street. Bridge and Hall are among Chelmsford's oldest buildings, for many earlier ones have been pulled down since 1800, as the town has grown.

Johnson helped to restore the Church of St Mary the Virgin, St Peter and St Cedd, at the top of the High Street, which has been Chelmsford Cathedral since 1914. It is basically a 15th-century parish church with many old tombs and monuments. But there are some striking later additions, such as the 20th-century figure of St Peter on the South Chapel, which depicts the saint dressed as a modern fisherman and holding a Yale key.

All Saints' Church, in the Springfield district, has a Norman base to its tower and fragments of Roman tiles and bricks built into its walls.

The construction of the Chelmer and Blackwater Navigation in 1797, and the arrival of the railway in 1843, made Chelmsford a suitable centre for industrial development. The growth of the town's industry is traced in the Chelmsford and Essex Museum in Oaklands Park, which also has a collection of birds, fossils, costumes, paintings and drawings.

CHIGWELL

Essex
12 miles northeast of London

Captain Eliab Harvey, who fought alongside Nelson at Trafalgar, lived at Chigwell. Two chairs in the garden of Rolls Park, his family home, are said to have been made from the timbers of his ship, the *Temeraire*, immortalised by the artist J. M. W. Turner in his picture the *Fighting Temeraire*.

Chigwell School in High Road was founded in 1629 by Samuel Harsnett, Archbishop of York. Among its former pupils was William Penn, the Quaker who gave his name to the state of Pennsylvania in America, where he had established a colony.

CHIPPENHAM

Cambridge
4 miles north of Newmarket

Chippenham has a splendid example of a squire's model village, with attractive cottages and larger houses, many dating from c. 1800. Chippenham Park Mansion, rebuilt in 1886, replaced the earlier 17th-century mansion of the Earl of Orford. The church at Badingham Manor has attractive early wall-paintings.

At Isleham, about 4 miles north, is the Church of St Andrew, a spacious, cruciform, 14th- and 15th-century building. The hammerbeam roof of 1495 is embellished with angels. Inside are stalls with misericords of c. 1350, a font, brasses and effigies of knights. There are two big monuments of c. 1590 and 1616 and an eagle lectern of the 15th century.

CHIPPING ONGAR

Essex
6 miles northwest of Brentwood

Round the town of Chipping Ongar lies pleasant farming country – *ongar* is an Anglo-Saxon word meaning 'grazing land'. The wide High Street has houses dating from 1642, and the 50 ft high castle mound northeast of the church is impressive.

The little Church of St Andrew, a mile west at Greensted, dating from 1013, is the only surviving Saxon church with a nave wall built of logs. It is, in fact, the oldest timber building in Europe. The nave is made of tree trunks split in half and stood on end.

A mile northeast is Ongar Castle, founded in the 11th century by Eustace, Count of Boulogne. Today only a substantial mound and ditches remain.

The 19th-century Tolpuddle Martyrs, who were transported to Australia for forming an agricultural trade union, were resettled in Greensted after they had been granted a pardon.

CLACTON-ON-SEA

Essex
13 miles southeast of Colchester

A century ago the quiet east coast village of Great Clacton awoke to the then novel craze for sun, sea and sand, and became Clacton-on-Sea. The town takes its name from a Viking settler called Clak. Today it is a typically boisterous English seaside resort with pier, funfair, pavilion, holiday camp, scenic railway and other traditional amusements. It is spacious, with wide tree-lined streets, Victorian and Edwardian houses and attractive public gardens.

Moot Hall is a mock-medieval barn reconstructed from one originally built in a Sussex village in 1490. The martello towers on the seafront are two of many built around the south and east coasts when Napoleon was threatening to invade Britain at the beginning of the 19th century.

Great Clacton's church dates from Norman times. Although it has been restored, it retains a 15th-century tower.

CLARE

Suffolk
7 miles northwest of Sudbury

The 100 ft high motte on which Clare Castle stands is believed to be Saxon. The Normans built a wooden tower on it, and converted that to a stone shell-keep in the 12th century. It lies between two baileys, one of which was used as the station yard when the railway came to Clare. But the station has, in its turn, been abandoned, and the site is now a country park.

The 15th-century priest's house at the churchyard corner has an exuberant flourish of pargetting, and there is a colourful swan and foliage sign outside the Swan Inn. Bridewell Street leads to Upper Common and to an enclosure of earthworks identified by some authorities as an Iron Age fort and by others as a Danish stronghold.

Clare Priory, converted into a house in 1604, is now again the property of the Augustinian Friars. Clare College, Cambridge, was named after the family of the Earl of Clare; Elizabeth de Burgh, sister of the 10th Earl,

gave money to help refound the college in the 14th century.

Neighbouring Stoke-by-Clare once had a Benedictine priory, the remains of which are now incorporated in a private school. The Tudor tower on the curve of the village street looks like a decorative gatehouse but is, in fact, a dovecote.

PRIEST'S HOUSE *An extravagant wealth of pargetting lends distinction to the home of Clare's medieval clergy.*

century chimney. The five cottages in the chestnut-shaded Church End were built as one house in the 15th century; between the 1750s and 1836 it was the local workhouse.

CLAVERING
Essex
7 miles north of Bishop's Stortford

The parish of Clavering, some 14 miles in circumference, consists of seven 'greens' – Deer Green, Stickling Green, and so on – many of which are hamlets of considerable charm. But the main part of the village is gathered about the church, and it is this portion that owes its existence to what is now a tussocky field surrounded by a still impressive moat and bordered by the mini-ravine of the River Stort. This is all that remains of the castle built in 1052 by Robert Fitz-wimarc, a French adventurer who was sufficiently adroit to hold high office under both Edward the Confessor and William the Conqueror. Edward himself is said to have visited the village in order to dedicate a chapel to St John the Evangelist. On that occasion, according to legend, he presented his ring to a beggar by the chapel door. The ring was returned to him many years later by a pilgrim from the Holy Land with the news that the beggar had been none other than St John, and that the king would shortly be joining him in paradise.

Clavering's inhabitants have gently adapted their village to their changing needs over the centuries; this is apparent in the mingling of architectural styles that occurs in most of the older houses. The Old Post Office, for example, one of the colour-washed houses in Middle Street, shows much 19th- and 20th-century work, yet the roof still contains the blackened timbers of the 15th-century smoke hole alongside the 16th-

CLEY NEXT THE SEA
Norfolk
4 miles northwest of Holt

In the Middle Ages Cley next the Sea was a busy seaport at the mouth of the River Glaven. Its ships carried wool to the Low Countries and brought back Dutch tiles that still turn up in old Norfolk cottages. However, the village has not been 'next the sea' since the 17th century, when land reclamation for pasture left it 1 mile inland. Traces of the old quay remain, dominated by an early-18th-century windmill which has been converted into a private house. It looks across a landscape of marshes, creeks, gullies and mud-flats – and beyond is Cley's beach, a deeply shelving expanse of shingle and the site of a coastguard look-out.

Behind the old quay the main street of Cley, pronounced 'Cly', winds between flint-built houses. One of the shops, called Whalebone of Cley, has some unusual flint panels outlined in animal bones.

The church stands on Newgate Green, a patch of high ground south of the village and near meadows that were once the harbour. St Margaret's Church reflects Cley's former prosperity; it was rebuilt on a large scale in the 14th century, though the transepts fell into disrepair in the 16th century and are now roofless.

CLEY *Reclaimed marshes and windmills emphasise Norfolk's long-time ties to the Netherlands (overleaf).*

In 1926 some of the reclaimed marshes between Cley and Salthouse, to the east, were acquired by the Norfolk Naturalists' Trust and established as one of Britain's first nature reserves. They can be visited by applying to the warden, in Cley, or to the Trust's headquarters at 72 Cathedral Close, Norwich.

CODDENHAM
Suffolk
6 miles north of Ipswich

Tucked snugly away in a wooded hollow amid rolling acres of wheat, barley, sugar beet and pastureland, Coddenham has a Saxon name but an older ancestry. It was the Roman settlement of Combretovium, guarding an important road junction from Cambridge towards the east coast, and from London by way of Colchester to Caistor St Edmund. Traces of small Roman villages have been found in the neighbourhood, but none has yet been thoroughly excavated, and outlines of the Roman fort have been revealed only by aerial photography in this century.

The parish church of St Mary is a typical Suffolk rough flint building, tilted gently upwards to the east by the slope of the knoll on which it stands. The 15th-century timbered roof was restored in the 19th century and is decorated with flights of angels.

The narrow main street also slopes, though a lot more steeply, through an almost unspoilt ascent of imposing old houses, some with overhanging upper storeys. No two are the same and each is lovingly painted, plastered and cared for. Gryffon House at the bottom was once part of an inn, licensed in the early 17th century. It is said to be the home of an archer named Wodehouse, who was knighted by Henry V after the Battle of Agincourt. A few steps up the hill is another inn, built in about 1500 and now the post office, with a frontage of timber and pink-washed plaster adorned with 17th-century geometrical pargetting – a technique of raising or indenting designs by means of a comb or trowel. The regional colour, known as Suffolk pink, was obtained by mixing white plaster with pig's blood or the juice of sloes.

COGGESHALL
Essex
6 miles east of Braintree

One of England's finest half-timbered buildings, the house in West Street called Paycocke's, is probably more famous than Coggeshall itself, but visitors find much else to admire in this large village. Wool and lace-making gave Coggeshall its prosperity in medieval times, and wool merchant John Paycocke built his house here in the 16th century. It was first mentioned in 1505, when John Paycocke willed it to his son Thomas, whose initials together with those of his wife, Margaret Herrold, can still be seen carved on a breast beam.

The house has had a chequered history, passing from the Paycockes in 1584 to a series of owners over the next three centuries. It was allowed to deteriorate so badly that in 1890 it was sold for demolition. But it was saved from this fate by a Coggeshall antiquary, Mr G. F. Beaumont, who managed to cancel the sale. In 1904 it was bought by Edward Noel – later Lord Noel-Buxton – and restored to plans approved by the architect Sir Edwin Lutyens. It is now owned by the National Trust and is open to the public three days a week. Heavily beamed and panelled, with elaborate woodcarvings, the house contains a collection of period furniture.

THE PRIDE OF COGGESHALL *One of the finest half-timbered buildings in England overhangs West Street.*

Whipsnade Park Zoo

In the Castle Museum, Colchester

...mainly dating from 1746–47, ...on the site of an earlier Cistercian ...The interior decoration of the state ...was the work of Henry Holland (1802). The mansion is a treasure-house of art, with valuable furniture and ...and a richly stocked picture gallery (works by Holbein, Van Dyck, Rembrandt, Gainsborough, Reynolds, ...).

...southern foothills of the Chilterns ...Goring, where vines were formerly grown, as the place-name "Vineyards" indicates. Here, at the Goring Gap, the Thames has cut its way through the chalk. The Ickneild Way, the old strategic Roman highway along the northern slopes of the Chilterns, is crossed just N of Goring by the massive earthworks known as Grim's Dyke or Grim's Ditch, the purpose of which has not been established. Here is a hill named after St Birinus, the apostle of Wessex, who converted its king Cynegils in 634.

Colchester

...England. – County: Essex.
...107 ft. – Population: 80,000.
...dialling code: 0206.
Tourist Information Centre,
4 Trinity Street;
tel. 46379.

HOTELS. – George, High Street, 46 r.; Rose and Crown, 13 r.; Red Lion, 19 r.

RESTAURANT. – Wm Scragg's, 2 North Hill.

YOUTH HOSTEL. – East Bay House, 18 East Bay, etc.

EVENTS. – Oyster Feast (end of Oct.).

SPORT and RECREATION. – Golf, tennis.

Colchester, a Celtic capital even before the Romans came, can claim to be the oldest town in Britain. It is now famous for its fields of roses and its excellent oysters. It is an attractive town with many old buildings of different periods.

Colchester Castle, with a massive Norman keep, houses a very fine museum containing the main finds of Romano-British material; and the town has other impressive Roman remains, including the best preserved Roman town walls in the country.

HISTORY. – Some time before 43 B.C. Cunobelin (Shakespeare's Cymbeline), chief of the Catuvellauni, moved his capital from what is now St Albans to Colchester (Camulodunum). In A.D. 44, during the reign of Claudius, the Romans captured the town, but in 61–62 it was sacked by the Iceni under Boudica or Boadicea. When the Normans arrived Colchester had a population of some 2000 and several churches, and still preserved parts of its Roman walls. In modern times excavation has revealed the British town, the Roman camp and the later Roman city. – in 1648 the town surrendered to Fairfax after a 76 days' siege. Later it became an important centre of the wool and cloth trade.

SIGHTS. – The Roman walls, the best preserved in Britain, are some 9 ft thick and enclose an area 1000 yards by 500. The imposing *Balkerne Gate, the W gate of the Roman town, is still partly preserved. The walls and the gate date from about A.D. 140.

In the wide, well-built High Street is the Town Hall (by Sir John Belcher, 1898–1902). On the tower is a bronze figure of St Helen, who according to local tradition was the daughter of "Old King Cole" of Colchester. The king himself is said to be buried in a mound in the Dykes area on the outskirts of the town.

St Martin's Church in West Stockwell Street dates mainly from the 14th c.; the tower, now destroyed, was constructed partly of Roman bricks. The Castle, N of the High Street, built by William the Conqueror about 1080, also contains Roman bricks. It has the largest Norman keep in England, and now contains a notable Museum with a fine collection of Roman material.

P

Bus Stop

Bird Wood

26

Whipsnade Common

18

Chartley Paddock

25

24

P

23

22

from

Africa

| | 200 m |
| | 600 ft |

giraffes | 20 Avenue Café
lions | 21 Railway
aviary | 22 Rhinoceros
young animals | 23 Birds
hamsters | 24 Steam engine
cafeteria | 25 Children's
marine mammals | 26 Administration

...e on the N side of the park ...to aircraft. A narrow-gauge ...runs through part of the park.

...worth while making an excursion ...stable (pop. 31,800; hotels: ...man, 26 r.; Old Palace Lodge, ...foot of Dunstable Downs ...Whipsnade. The church of St Paul, originally belonging ...founded in 1131, has a Norman ...miles NW is *Woburn Abbey ...draws many thousands of visitors ...most of them attracted by the ...range of entertainments it offers ...and an aquarium, sports ...playgrounds, boating, cafés, ...market, etc. The house itself, ...Duke of Bedford, is a huge

Paycocke's is one of many old buildings in the village, including the 15th-century Woolpack, which has been an inn since the 17th century, and the 12th-century Grange Hill barn, used by monks who introduced sheep into the region and so started the wool trade upon which Coggeshall prosperity was built.

Coggeshall Abbey was founded in 1140 by King Stephen, then taken over by Cistercian monks, who learned the art of brick-making from sister houses on the Continent and thus re-established brick manufacture in England for the first time since the departure of the Romans. The arches of Long Bridge, in Bridge Street, are made of abbey bricks, and it is now claimed to be the oldest brick bridge in the country.

On the south side of the bridge is Monkwell, the lower portion of which served as the abbey brewery. Its brick-lined well is still there, in the garden. The house later became a silk works, and then the home of a French immigrant named Drago who introduced lace-making to Coggeshall early in the 19th century. The industry prospered until the First World War and Coggeshall lace is still made.

Coggeshall Church of St Peter ad Vincula stands on the site of a Norman building and was rebuilt in the 15th century. Much of the building was destroyed by a lone German bomb during the Second World War; repair work took six years to complete. Brasses of the Paycocke family survived, and in the south chapel is a monument to Mary Honywood who died in 1620 and left no fewer than 367 descendants.

The early Georgian Congregational church in Queen Street was opened about 1715. There are other attractive Georgian and later buildings in East Street, which follows the line of the Roman Stane Street; and round the corner in Stoneham Street is the hexagonal weatherboarded Clock Tower, which was built in 1787 and was then restored a century later.

COLCHESTER
Essex
51 miles northeast of London

Colchester derives its name from an encampment built by the Romans on the River Colne. Local tradition, however, associates the name with the legendary British king, Old King Cole. Geoffrey of Monmouth, the 12th-century historian, relates that King Cole was the father of the Roman Emperor Constantine, and gave his name to the town of Colchester.

Colchester Castle, built by the Normans in the last years of the 11th century, has a massive great tower similar to the White Tower of London, but larger. It was built largely of stone from local Roman ruins.

In the Middle Ages the town's livelihood depended on its market, fishery and cloth-making. The cloth trade declined in the 1550s, but two decades later 500 Flemish Protestant refugees gave it new life. The half-timbered and plastered houses of Stockwell Street are now known as the Dutch Quarter. By the early 19th century the cloth trade had disappeared. But it was soon supplanted by an engineering industry which revived the town's fortunes.

Holy Trinity is the only Saxon building in Colchester and is largely built from Roman materials. The west wall of the nave goes back even beyond Saxon times to an unknown date. A notable feature is the triangular-headed door in the west wall. The church is now a museum displaying rural crafts.

All that now stands of the Benedictine St John's Abbey, founded in 1096, is its imposing 15th-century gatehouse. Bourne Mill was built in 1591 of stone from St John's Abbey. Its most striking feature is its stepped, curved, pinnacled gables. Originally a fishing lodge, it was converted into a mill in the early 19th century. It is now owned by the National Trust.

The Town Hall, which was completed in 1902, dominates the broad High Street. Its tall clock-tower is topped by a figure of St Helena, holding a sceptre and cross and facing towards Jerusalem. She is said to have been the daughter of the mythical King Cole of Colchester. One of the bells in the tower dates from about 1400.

Colchester has long been famous for its oysters and the season is opened by a traditional festival in early September. In the main room of the Town Hall, the Moot Hall, the Oyster Feast, for the mayor and corporation, is held each October.

Roses, as well as oysters, have long been associated with the town. Cant's well-known horticultural nurseries were first established in 1766. Each July a great rose show is held.

The Holly Trees Museum, the centre for the Essex Archaeological Society, is in a fine Georgian house built in 1716–19. It contains collections of 18th and 19th-century domestic, craft and military objects. The Minories, another Georgian house, with an early-16th-century wing, is an art gallery that contains work by Constable. It also houses a collection of Georgian furniture, pictures, china and silver.

On the western side of Colchester is Lexden Tumulus, a low mound once thought to be the burial ground of Cunobelinus, king of the Belgae from about AD 5–40, or 'Old King Cole'. Research suggests, however, that it was that of one of his predecessors, Addedomarus, who was buried there in AD 1.

Colchester's harbour, the Hythe – which may have been used by the Romans – declined with the arrival of the railways in the 19th century. Since the Second World War, however, it has become busier, and now over 2000 ships in the coastal trade use it yearly.

COLSTERWORTH
Lincolnshire
7 miles south of Grantham

Limestone houses are strung out along a ridge in the large village of Colsterworth, with the infant River Witham flowing below. The straightness of the narrow main street provides a clue to its Roman origins. The Roman road, Ermine Street, leaves the line of the main modern highway near Colsterworth and runs straight north to Lincoln.

Colsterworth is the birthplace of Isaac Newton. The great scientist was born in the little 17th-century Woolsthorpe Manor adjoining Colsterworth on Christmas Day 1642. The record of his baptism is in the church register: 'Isaac, son of Isaac and Hanna Newton, January 1, 1642–3'. In the quiet orchard in front of the house Newton watched an apple fall to the ground; this is reputed to have led him to his universal law of gravitation. A descendant of the apple tree can be seen today. The house was built in the early 17th century. In 1665–6 the plague caused Newton to flee from Cambridge and return to Woolsthorpe Manor for a stay of 20 months. The manor is now maintained by the National Trust and is open in the afternoon,

Sunday to Wednesday from April to October – when the public can see the study in which Newton did much of his most important scientific work during his stay.

The Church of St John the Baptist, part of which dates back to the 12th century, contains a sun-dial cut by Newton at the age of nine. It is set into the wall behind the organ.

COPFORD GREEN
Essex
5 miles west of Colchester

The remote Norman church, St Michael and All Angels in Copford Green, is one of the most impressive in Essex. Its nave, chancel and apse are original. A south aisle was added later. The remains of 12th-century paintings which once covered all the walls – Christ in Glory and the signs of the zodiac, among others – are considered the best medieval wall-paintings in this part of the country. In the 16th century the paintings were obliterated with whitewash by the Puritans, who wanted to banish 'superstitious imagery'. They were further covered in 1710, during repairs. Finally, in 1871, they were revealed and restored in all their beauty.

The church also has a 12th-century font, a 14th-century oak chest, and – framed on a wall – fragments of human skin originally fixed to the south or Dane Skin, door. It was the practice in parts of Essex, during the 9th and 10th centuries, to punish sacrilegious Danes by flaying them alive and fixing their skin to the south door as a dire warning to others.

COVEHITHE
Suffolk
4 miles northeast of Southwold

A ten-minute walk along a footpath from the village of Covehithe leads to one of the most rewarding views on the entire Suffolk coast. Low cliffs topped with gorse and broom-dappled heathland shelter a beach of pale yellow sand and grey shingle.

Covehithe is a village with a startling landmark – the gaunt ruin of St Andrew's Church that dominates the landscape for miles around. It was originally built in the 15th century, but in 1672 the parishioners found that they could no longer afford the upkeep of such a huge building. They were given permission to build a new church using the fabric of the old. So they constructed it, with a thatched roof to its nave, inside the shell of the partly demolished building, though the original tower was retained. The church towers at Covehithe and at Kessingland, 3 miles to the north, have long been navigational marks for mariners.

CRANWELL
Lincolnshire
4 miles northwest of Sleaford

Three sets of horseshoes in the turf where Ermine Street crosses the A17 just west of the RAF College at Cranwell commemorate the wild leaps of a blind horse called Bayard, as it struggled to unseat Old Meg, a wicked local witch, as she fought on Bayard's back with Abner, the owner of the horse. Abner cut off one of Old Meg's breasts, but still she clung on, her long

talons sunk deeply into Bayard's flanks. The dreadful battle ended when Abner plunged his sword through the witch, but he stabbed his horse as well, and Meg and Bayard died together.

THE CREAKES
Norfolk
6 and 7 miles northwest of Fakenham

Both the Creake villages, North and South, have churches named after St Mary. That at North Creake was built *c.* 1330. It has an elaborate Easter Sepulchre, sedilia, and piscina. The Perpendicular additions are the clerestory, nave windows, hammerbeam roofs and the tower. Above the chancel arch there is a faded 'Doom' painting, and internally, above the north door, the Royal Arms of Charles I. On the sanctuary floor there is the Calthorpe Brass, depicting the 15th-century donor holding a model of the church he restored. It may be the work of a Flemish craftsman.

The Church of St Mary at South Creake is one of the finest village churches in East Anglia, dating mainly from the 13th and 14th centuries. The hammerbeam roof is decorated with medieval carved angels which have recently been restored. The bases of the nave pillars form seats and the larger of the two brasses is unusual in that it depicts a priest lying between his mother and father. With its glorious nave, 15th-century rood screen and pulpit, St Mary's is one of the most impressive of Norfolk's churches.

CRESSING
Essex
3 miles southeast of Braintree

The village of Cressing takes its name from the watercress that provided a thriving industry until about 200 years ago. It is probably known best, however, for the huge, ancient barns in the grounds of Cressing Temple, part of a farmhouse on the road towards Witham. This land once belonged to the Knights Templar. When their order was outlawed in 1312 – on the grounds of heresy, blasphemy and immoral practices – the place was handed to the Knights Hospitaller.

Evidence of the Hospitallers' vast wealth is displayed in the magnificence of the great barns. The huge-aisled barley barn is weatherboarded and 120 ft long; the narrower, 140 ft long wheat barn has brick infilling around its massive timbers.

For many years the barns were thought to be 14th or 15th century, but radiocarbon dating has proved that timber in the barley barn is more than 800 years old, and that in the wheat barn about 700.

In 1623 a third barn was added, and this one is whitewashed. Although the barns are on private ground, admission is obtained by arrangement with the farm manager.

But Cressing has more than its barns to be proud of – it has a hero, Sir Henry Evelyn Wood, whose exploits in numerous wars were the stuff that Victorian imperialism was made of. Born in 1838, Wood joined the navy as a midshipman at the age of 14 and served on HMS *Queen* during the Crimean War. Despite being wounded while with a landing party, Wood decided that fighting on land was more to his liking than a life at sea and in 1855 he transferred to the army. As a

lieutenant with the 17th Lancers he was mentioned in dispatches many times for his gallantry and zeal during the Indian Mutiny, and in 1860 received the supreme award, the Victoria Cross, for defeating, the year before, a band of some 80 rebels in dense jungle with a force of just 11 men.

During the Zulu Wars, Wood distinguished himself again when a column he was leading was attacked by the Zulu army. The battle raged for $5\frac{1}{2}$ hours and, although outnumbered by 12 to 1, Wood's men put the Zulus to flight. In 1879 Wood's commander, Sir Garnet Wolseley, wrote of his 'genius for war' – a genius that was to serve him well during the Egyptian campaign of 1882 when he commanded a brigade and stayed on to become the first British Sirdar (commander-in-chief) of the Egyptian army.

In 1903 Sir Henry Evelyn Wood, VC, CM, GCB, GCMG, became Field-Marshal. He died in 1919 and has a fittingly impressive memorial in Cressing's All Saints' Church. All Saints stands on a site where there was once a pre-Roman tribal settlement and then a Saxon building. A wooden bell turret tops the small, flinty church which has a part-Norman nave, 12th-century chancel and early 15th-century roof.

CROMER
Norfolk
21 miles north of Norwich

A bustling family holiday resort, Cromer has a zoo, a pier, a boating lake, a good sandy beach, and large hotels and boarding houses. The narrow streets of the old town twist around the 160 ft tower of St Peter and St Paul, the tallest church tower in Norfolk.

A cliff path leads half a mile east to the 58 ft lighthouse. It was built in 1833 half a mile from the cliff edge, to avoid the fate of its predecessor. The original lighthouse was built near the cliff in 1719, but after numerous landslips it was declared unsafe, and in 1866 it was carried away by a cliff fall.

Two miles inland are the earthworks of a Roman camp near Beacon Hill, the highest point in Norfolk.

DOWN TO THE SEA IN SHIPS *Not just a resort town, Cromer still has a sizable fishing and crabbing community.*

Overstrand, a holiday resort with a good sandy beach, is set 2 miles east of Cromer, built near crumbling cliffs. In the 14th century its church fell into the sea and the present Church of St Martin was built – although this, too, had to be restored after the roof collapsed in the 18th century. At Sidestrand, a mile further east, the 15th-century church was in danger of falling over the cliff as well; so in 1881 it was taken down and rebuilt inland, on its present site.

CROWLAND
Lincolnshire
8 miles south of Spalding

The village of Crowland has two particularly interesting features. The abbey, founded in 716 by King Ethelbald, was built in memory of St Guthlac, who had built a cell on the Fen island. The abbey was burnt by the Danes, rebuilt c. 930, burnt again in 1091, rebuilt in 1114, shaken by an earthquake in 1117, partly burnt in 1146, completed in 1190 and remodelled c. 1281. The relics of St Guthlac were taken there in 1195. His cell, at the west end of the south aisle, was excavated in 1908, but filled in again. The abbey is now the parish church; the west front is sculptured, and inside there is a 15th-century oak screen. Hereward the Wake is said to be buried here.

The second feature is a triangular bridge, probably unique in Europe. The bridge consists of three 14th-century stone arches meeting at an angle of 120 degrees. They originally spanned three streams of the River Welland, but now stand over dry land. The carved figure on the bridge was put in position in 1720, and probably came from the abbey.

D

DALHAM
Suffolk
5 miles east of Newmarket

At Dalham the River Kennett meanders between the grass-fringed village street and a cluster of thatched and white-plastered cottages with trim gardens, reached by smart little white footbridges and sometimes backed by orchards. A footpath from an inn, the Affleck Arms, leads to stepping stones through the water.

The 14th-century Church of St Mary stands in manorial grounds, up a steep avenue of overarching yews and on the site of an earlier Saxon church. In 1303 the manor was presented by Edward I to his second wife, Margaret, daughter of Philip the Bold, King of France. She appealed formally to him at the church door for the manor as a marriage settlement – though they had been wedded for four years.

The tower was rebuilt in 1627, with the injunction 'Keep my Sabbaths' carved on the parapet. It has a wooden steeple which blew down in a storm on September 3, 1658 – the night Oliver Cromwell died. Within the church are memorials to the Stuteville family, who owned the manor for nearly 300 years. There is one to Sir Martin Stuteville, who 'visited the American world with Francis Drake'.

The last Stuteville sold the manor to Simon Patrick, Bishop of Ely, who between 1704–5 built a new red-brick mansion, Dalham Hall, in the adjoining parkland, on medieval foundations whose stone vaults remain below the house. He added an extra storey from which he may have been able to see his cathedral at Ely, some 16 miles away. Although the hall burnt down and was rebuilt with only two storeys, it is still the highest point in the county, looking across the Kennett Valley to a ridge topped by a white windmill.

In the late 18th and 19th centuries, the Affleck family were the landowners, giving their name and coat of arms to the inn sign. The estate was bought in 1900 by the statesman Cecil Rhodes (Rhodesia, now Zambia and Zimbabwe, was named after him) for his retirement. But he died in 1902, without returning to England. His brother inherited, brought home Rhode's horse, and built a village hall in his memory.

Linked to Dalham, by the River Kennett, is the village of Moulton. It has a packhorse bridge so narrow and hump-backed that traffic must now follow the by-road through a ford which is sometimes swirling with water.

North from Moulton about 2 miles is Kentford, whose crossroads on the way to Bury St Edmunds road has a grave which is still kept colourful with fresh flowers. Known as 'The Boy's Grave', it is supposedly the burial place of a young shepherd who hanged himself when accused of sheep-stealing. It was the custom, until the early 1800s, to bury suicides at a crossroads. The Church of St Mary is Decorated, except for the top of the tower. The five-petalled rose window is distinctive, and the late 14th-century wall-paintings, though difficult to see, deserve attention. They include St Christopher, the Seven Deadly Sins, and the Seven Works of Mercy.

DANBURY
Essex
5 miles east of Chelmsford

The town of Danbury crowns a 400 ft hill, with wide views over gorse-clad commons and, to the east, the sails of barges and yachts on the Blackwater Estuary. The stately church is 600 years old and has some notable wooden effigies of knights. Two centuries ago, the embalmed body of a 13th-century knight was found perfectly preserved in a lead coffin in the church. Danbury Palace, built in 1832, stands in grounds that contain a 39 acre country park.

DEBENHAM
Suffolk
11 miles north of Ipswich

The first trickles of the River Deben run beside the gently sloping main street of Debenham and then weave in and out of the town. The appropriately named Water Lane is almost permanently submerged. Rush-weaving is carried on in a building beside the bridge, and looms can be seen through the street window. The surrounding farmlands are sometimes desolate at first sight, but time and familiarity add lustre to the hamlets, including Wetheringsett, where Richard Hakluyt, a 16th-century rector and geography lecturer, wrote his scientific and patriotic book, *Principall Navigations, Voiages and Discoveries of the English Nation*, first published in 1589.

Four miles north is Bedingfield, with its Flemings Hall, a moated building of *c*. 1380 with later additions.

DEDHAM
Essex
6 miles northeast of Colchester

At Dedham, beside the River Stour, the painter John Constable's father had a watermill, now replaced by one of Victorian red brick. Dedham Vale was 'Constable Country', and Dedham church tower featured in many of the painter's works.

The road into the village winds past houses of brick and plaster with luxuriant gardens, to a junction where the main street opens out and the battlemented church tower rises above shops, Georgian-fronted houses and old inns. The Sun has a coaching archway leading into its yard, where a Tudor stairway climbs to a rear wing. The Marlborough Head was the home and workshop of a clothier and then a dyer in medieval times, and became an inn only in 1702.

Diagonally opposite the Marlborough Head stands what was once the grammar school, attended by John Constable in the 1780s. It is now two private houses. Sherman's Hall, opposite the church in the High

DANBURY *A peaked wood cap tops the 346 ft church spire of this estuary church.*

Street, derives its name from the Sherman family, ancestors of the American Civil War general, who were wool merchants in the 15th century.

The 15th-century Church of St Mary the Virgin has heraldic symbols in the nave roof. Among other things, they depict the mark of Thomas Webbe, a wool merchant who financed the building of the church. A pew bears a medallion commemorating the first landing on the moon in July 1969.

South of the village the road passes Castle House, the home of the 20th-century artist Sir Alfred Munnings, who specialised in painting horses. Some of his paintings are on view in the house, and can be seen on Bank Holidays, Wednesday and Sunday afternoons from May until October.

Just north of Dedham is the village of Stratford St Mary. The main London to Yarmouth road bypasses the village, leaving its church isolated on a mound on the far side of the dual carriageway. A white, tomb-like building is a pumping station, but otherwise the buildings, which include old coaching inns, are mellow and welcoming.

DENNINGTON

Suffolk
2 miles north of Framlingham

A farming community in the middle of fertile, heavy clay lands, Dennington was for generations a centre for horse and cattle dealers. Until some years after the Second World War there were regular parades of Suffolk heavy horses and horse-drawing team contests on the village green. This became so trampled by horse and man that all traces of green vanished and its bare surface has become known simply as 'The Square'.

Behind it, The Queen's Head Inn, bought by the parish in 1694, has records dating back to 1483. Only the addition of a porch in 1961 and tiles instead of a once thatched roof have changed its original appearance.

The flint Perpendicular Church of St Mary the Virgin has a sturdy tower with a turret on top, and a superb interior. Over the main altar is an extremely rare pyx canopy, made from a single piece of wood, and two lavish 15th-century parclose screens. The 15th-century bench-ends have interesting geometrically designed patterns, broken only in the centre aisle by one depicting a Sciapod, a mythical creature supposed to have lived in the desert. It hopped about on its single foot until, wearying, it lay down and used that huge foot as a sunshade. This is the only known representation of the creature in Britain.

Armrests are fashioned into other mythical figures and more ordinary beasts, including a hare, a pelican and a mermaid. In front of the benches are Georgian box-pews, watched over by a 1625 pulpit later converted into a three-decker. The church houses two ornately screened chapels. The one dedicated to St Margaret of Antioch was lengthened between 1440 and 1450 to accommodate the Bardolph tomb. An alabaster effigy of Lord Bardolph, who fought with Henry V at Agincourt, lies with its feet on a hawk, while beside him the feet of his wife's effigy rest on a wyvern, a two-legged dragon with wings.

In the north aisle a 19th-century sand table is preserved. Here, schoolchildren practised writing and sums by making marks in the sand with their fingers.

Beside the table is an 18th-century bier (on which coffins used to be placed before burial), a 19th-century reading desk for use in the choir, and the mechanism of a 17th-century clock which was replaced in 1948 by a memorial clock in honour of those who died during the Second World War.

DENTON

Lincolnshire
4 miles southwest of Grantham

Two 19th-century gatehouses of the former manor make an impressive entry to the village of Denton. They stand by the road close to a junction that leads to the village centre, where every building seems to be made of golden ironstone. They include the imposing double-fronted inn, the Welby Arms, and the church overlooking a lake.

The present manor house was extended in 1962, and is the home of the Welby family, whose ancestors came to the village in the 16th century. Welbys also occupy Welby House, the former school built by William Welby in the 18th century. The Church of St Andrew is early 14th century, with a tall tower which rises in five stages. The lake in the grounds of the manor is fed by a spring called St Christopher's Well.

A little more than 1 mile from Denton is Harlaxton, with its bizarre 19th-century manor – a monument to Victorian architectural exuberance. It is large and rambling, with turrets, cupolas, pinnacles and tall chimney-stacks in styles ranging from Baroque to Gothic. The village, by comparison, is small and pretty with timber-framed cottages near the church and a 17th-century mansion, Nether House.

DEVIL'S DYKE

Cambridgeshire
Reach to Newmarket Heath, 3 miles south of Newmarket

The remarkable bank and ditch known as Devil's Dyke runs straight across country for a distance of some $7\frac{1}{2}$ miles. It faces southwest and straddles the main road, the A11, which here overlies the Icknield Way, a prehistoric trackway which has served East Anglia for more than 2000 years. The Dyke's north-west end rests on the Fen-edge, and its southeast end would originally have reached the virgin forest which at that time lay around the River Stour basin.

Some 6 miles to the southwest, the smaller Fleam Dyke served a similar purpose; it is almost certain that these defences were erected early in the 7th century when East Anglia began to be threatened by its neighbour, the midland kingdom of Mercia.

DISS

Norfolk
19 miles southwest of Norwich

Diss is an attractive place with a mixture of Tudor, Georgian and Victorian houses stacked up around a wide mere, with streets twisting out narrowly at the head of the sloping market place.

Scole, 2 miles east, possesses one of the finest old coaching inns in England. Built of red brick in 1655, and resembling a mansion rather than an inn, it is

crowned with five Dutch gables in front and more at the back. It has giant angle pilasters, square chimney-stacks with arched panels and, inside, a magnificent staircase, carved in oak.

DODDINGTON

Lincolnshire
5 miles west of Lincoln

The main attraction at Doddington is 17th-century Doddington Hall, but the village has its charm too. Groups of red-brick cottages, mostly 19th century, and farmland alternate along the main road. Doddington Hall stands close to the road behind a Tudor-style gatehouse and high brick walls.

The hall has been the home of the Jarvis family since the middle of the 19th century, and is open to the public on Wednesday and Sunday afternoons, from May to September. The rooms and furnishings are mostly 18th century, with outstanding tapestries and collections of china. From the outside the house is plain and symmetrical, with three jutting bays of red brick, each topped by a small dome. It is believed to have been designed by Robert Smythson in 1600, for Thomas Taylor, Recorder to the Bishop of Lincoln.

The Church of St Peter stands beside Doddington Hall. It was rebuilt in 1770 by Sir John Deleval, then owner of the hall, as a fitting burial place for his daughter who had died suddenly. Later, when Sir John's only son died, the church was painted black for the funeral, and traces of the paint can still be seen.

DODDINGTON HALL *The late Tudor, red-brick facade belies the largely 18th-century interior.*

DOGDYKE

Lincolnshire
3 miles east of Billinghay

A late 18th-century drainage pump still works on open days at Dogdyke in Lincolnshire. The pump was built in 1796 to drain water from the Fen peatlands into the River Witham, and was originally powered by a wind-mill. A 28 ft diameter scoop wheel, powered by a steam-operated beam engine and capable of moving 25 tons of water a minute, was installed in 1855.

DONINGTON ON BAIN

Lincolnshire
6 miles southwest of Louth

The banks of the attractive but elusive River Bain, that flows for 20 miles or so below the western edge of the Wolds, are not easily accessible except at Donington. From the picturesque, white-painted old water-mill by the weir at Donington, the Viking Way goes through farm and parkland and the sites of lost villages. The Way is a way-marked long-distance foot-

DONINGTON ON BAIN *The little River Bain courses over weir and waterspill by the old whitewashed mill* (overleaf).

ELY

Cambridgeshire

14 miles northeast of Cambridge

ELY CATHEDRAL *Dominating towers give the 900-year-old edifice the feeling of a stone island in a sea of fens.*

Ely Cathedral has dominated the flat fen country that surrounds it for some 1300 years, and can be seen for miles around. Ely began as a religious community founded by St Etheldreda, the daughter of a king of the East Angles, who built an abbey here about AD 670. The cathedral was built 400 years later and most of the original Norman work survives in the west front, nave and transepts. The nave is 248 ft long.

In 1322 the original central tower collapsed and was replaced by a unique octagonal lantern tower. The octagon consists of eight large piers, soaring up to form four 72 ft high arches. From the piers sprout ribs of vaulting that form the octagonal-shaped opening on which the lantern sits. The lantern has a framework of eight massive oak uprights, each nearly 3 ft thick and 63 ft long, tapering to 12 in. thick at the apex.

For most of its history, the 68 ft high mound of Ely was an island surrounded by mile upon mile of swamp and fen, and known as 'Eel Island' because of the abundance of eels. It made an ideal hide-out for Hereward the Wake, the Anglo-Saxon patriot who led resistance to William the Conqueror until 1071.

The Ely Porta is a 14th-century three-storey gate-house to the original abbey. King's School, founded in AD 970, is one of England's oldest schools. Edward the Confessor, while Prince Edward, entered the school in 1010 and as king, granted a charter to the town.

Ely's marshes were drained in the 17th century, leaving a flat and curious landscape of fertile black-earthed fields and rivers banked higher than the roads.

EUSTON HALL *The wide, grassy parkland is watered by a stream which joins the Little Ouse.*

EUSTON
Suffolk
3 miles southeast of Thetford

When Charles II visited Euston Hall it is said that he was much taken by the horse-racing in the park. He was also much taken, it seems, with his host Lord Arlington's five-year-old daughter, Isabella, whom he considered a suitable wife for his illegitimate son by Barbara Castlemaine – the eight-year-old Henry Fitz-roy. Later in life, Henry became Earl of Euston and Duke of Grafton.

Black-and-white cottages, some thatched, and flint-and-brick houses line Euston's pretty main street.

Euston Hall is still the seat of the Dukes of Grafton. It is approached on one side by a parapeted bridge cross-ing a stream which flows through the grounds to join the Little Ouse. Back from the road is a red-brick mill disguised as a church, complete with a battlemented tower. It is probably Georgian, as the grounds were laid out in the 18th century by William Kent, the architect of London's Horse Guards. Kent also designed an Italian temple above an underground ice-house in the grounds.

Euston Hall was originally built for Lord Arlington in 1666–67. It was enlarged and altered in 1750, but had to be largely rebuilt in 1902 after a disastrous fire. It was reduced to its present size in 1951. The main attractions in the house are the paintings by Stubbs, Van Dyck, Kneller and Lely.

Euston's church, dedicated to St Genevieve, is in the grounds of the hall. Although there are traces of

medieval work in the tower and walls, the church dates mostly from 1676. The architect is unknown, but he was obviously familiar with Wren's City of London churches. Inside the church are woodcarvings on the pulpit and screen, whose excellence supports the claim that they are the work of Grinling Gibbons.

EYE
Suffolk
4 miles southeast of Diss

The agricultural town of Eye was once surrounded by water, and named after the old Saxon word for island. Its Norman castle reverted to the Crown five times, and was finally demolished by Cromwell's army in 1655. Stones from the castle were used to make a castellated folly on the original site in the 19th century. The west tower of the 15th-century Church of St Peter and St Paul is one of the best in the county. There is flint and stone panelled decoration from ground to battlements. The fine 15th-century rood screen, with painted figures, was restored in 1925.

The railway between Stowmarket and Norwich, opened in 1849, was to have gone through Eye. But it went to Diss, across the border in Norfolk, when Eye's local squires refused to have it on their land.

Two miles west is Yaxley, with its 700-year-old Church of St Mary. Over the door hangs a Sexton's Wheel, one of two which survive in England. It consists of a pair of iron wheels on one axle, and was used in the Middle Ages to choose the days of Lady Fasts, periods of abstinence. When both wheels were spun, strings attached to the outer one eventually caught on the inner, braking both to denote the fast day.

F

FELBRIGG

Norfolk
2 miles south of Cromer

Historians believe that the original village of Felbrigg clustered around its Perpendicular church, in the grounds of Felbrigg Hall, 1 mile to the east of the present village. In the church are some fine 14th-century brasses of Simon De Felbrigg and his wife, the first owners of the original hall. Other features of the Church of St Margaret are a 14th-century octagonal font, box-pews and a wall oven in the vestry.

The present Jacobean mansion was built in the early 17th century. It was added to in 1680, and substantially altered during the 1750s by James Paine. The library, in the Gothic Revival style, has books that belonged to Dr Johnson.

There is a walled garden – which in the 17th and 18th centuries provided fruit, flowers, herbs and vegetables for the household.

Felbrigg Great Wood, the wood adjoining Felbrigg Hall, is part of the great belt of trees that extends along the Cromer Ridge. It is believed that there have been beechwoods on the site since the end of the last Ice Age, and that some of the ground has never been cultivated to this day.

FELIXSTOWE

Suffolk
11 miles southeast of Ipswich

There are no historic mansions, no pretensions here, but much brash good cheer. Felixstowe is one of the largest 'roll-on, roll-off' cargo and container ports in Britain and a ferry port to the Continent.

The wide arc of the seafront road stretches right round the bay for more than 2 miles and is separated from the promenade by floral gardens and lawns. With its multi-storeyed houses, it is a familiar sight to voyagers bound from Harwich for the Hook of Holland or Denmark. The cranes and activity of neighbouring Harwich form part of wide panoramas seen from old fortifications below The Dooley, a historic inn with many doors to facilitate escape from press gangs and Revenue men.

FINCHINGFIELD

Essex
8 miles northwest of Braintree

Winding roads and lanes plunge down into Finchingfield through divided greens. Above the greens stand white-painted cottages and houses. Chief among them is the gabled and bargeboarded Finchingfield House, facing a row of Georgian houses and 16th-century cottages. The 17th-century house with a four-stack chimney beside the footbridge over the nearby pond – known as Bridge House – was once the village workhouse.

Crowning the curve of the hill is the Church of St

John the Baptist with its Norman tower and Georgian-style bell-cote. The entrance to the churchyard is through the arch of the timbered 15th-century Guildhall, which contains four almshouses, a meeting room and a small museum of local bygones. Across the road is a house with plasterwork panels of animals, horse-shoes, clover and other reliefs.

Just north of the village stands a windmill, dating from the 18th century, though a mill has stood on the site since 1100. A little further on is a six-sided thatched cottage called the Round House. It was built in the late 18th century by the local squire who lived at Spains Hall, 1 mile northwest of Finchingfield.

The hall dates from the 16th century and is built of red brick and stone, with carved gables, tall chimneys and mullioned windows. One of its 17th-century owners, William Kempe, remained silent for seven years as a penance for unjustly accusing his wife of infidelity. There are seven ponds in the grounds of Spains Hall, said to have been dug by Kempe to mark each year of his penance, which is recorded on a memorial shield in the church.

The hall was bought by the Ruggles-Brise family in 1760 and remains in their possession.

Two miles southeast is Wethersfield and the Church of St Mary Magdalene. Mainly of the 13th and 14th centuries, the church has a 15th-century nave and clerestory. Fragments of medieval stained glass exist. Monuments with effigies date from the 15th century, tablets from the 18th century.

FOLKINGHAM

Lincolnshire
8 miles south of Sleaford

Folkingham's broad main road climbs as it enters the village, and widens still further to form the Market Square, which is lined with brick and stone-built houses standing well back. At the summit a 17th-century coaching inn, the Greyhound, faces down the road, giving the centre of the village a most elegant and spacious air. At the bottom of the road is a manor house, in Restoration style, with an early 18th-century doorway. The roof is steep and the windows are leaded two-lights.

Folkingham, now merely a large village, was once an important place in the county. It was the seat of the Quarter Sessions Court, and its austere former House of Correction, or prison, stands to the east of the village. The building consists of the original 19th-century gateway and Governor's House, faced in cold-looking grey stone and with arched windows half blanked off and half grilled. It occupies the site of Folkingham Castle, built by Henry de Beaumont in Norman times and destroyed by Cromwell during the Civil War.

Justice was undoubtedly swift and severe in Folkingham at one time; the stocks and whipping post are preserved in the church.

The Church of St Andrew lies at the northwest corner of the village and has an outstanding Per-

FOLKINGHAM *The Greyhound is an elegant example of a 17th-century coaching inn and post stop.*

pendicular tower. Inside are 14th-century arcades, early 15th-century windows, a good screen, and an Early English chancel.

Some 3½ to 4 miles north of Folkingham is Osbournby, whose Church of St Peter and St Paul is mainly Decorated, and has a Norman font. It contains much 15th-century woodwork, including a set of carved bench-ends and poppy-heads.

FOSSDYKE CANAL

Lincolnshire
River Trent at Torksey to River Witham at Lincoln

Fossdyke Canal is still navigable, with a tow-path which can be walked from end to end. The waterway links the River Witham at Lincoln with the River Trent at Torksey. It formed part of a system of water-transport designed by the Romans, probably to convey the corn of East Anglia to the garrison at York and thence north by road.

Much of the first part of that system, the Car Dyke, which ran from the River Cam near Cambridge to the central river-system of the Fens and then from the Nene to the Witham, is now filled in or incorporated in the Fenland dyke-drainage system. But the Fossdyke was reconditioned in post-Roman times and still provides a route by water from Lincoln to the Trent and so down to the Humber and up the Yorkshire Ouse.

FRAMLINGHAM

Suffolk
9 miles north of Woodbridge

Framlingham Castle, built in the 12th century by Roger Bigod, Earl of Norfolk, stands a little way outside the town, but its rugged walls and battlements dominate the area. The most notable of its towers is the Prison Tower, which has no outside entrance to its ground floor. The only way in is by a door on the first floor of the west wall, then down through a trapdoor to the dungeon-like room below.

The original Great Hall, once the scene of splendid banquets, was razed in the early 18th century and replaced by a poorhouse – which still stands. Framlingham spreads between the castle and Mills Almshouses, named after Thomas Mills, a wealthy wheelwright who left the money to build them when he died in 1703. The almshouses stand back from Station Road – the station is now a garage and the railway was closed to passengers in 1952. The town's other group of almshouses, Hitcham's Almshouses, was built in 1654 with money bequeathed by Sir Robert Hitcham, the Attorney-General to Anne of Denmark, wife of James I. Sir Robert, who died in 1636, is buried in a black marble tomb in St Michael's Church.

On the east side of Market Hill is the Mansion House, built in the 16th century and later faced with special tiles – known as mathematical tiles – that look

FRAMLINGHAM *The massive castle walls are a vivid monument to medieval bids for power* (overleaf).

like bricks. They are also on the house next door. At the top of Market Hill a narrow lane called Queen's Head Passage runs down to Fore Street. The monarch concerned was Mary Tudor (1516–58), who owned the castle and was staying there when she heard that she had been declared queen in July 1553. Later she paid a state visit to the town with her husband, Philip II of Spain.

The parish church of St Michael, built between the 14th and 16th centuries, has one of the few pre-Civil War organ-cases in England that escaped destruction by Oliver Cromwell's Commissioners. The organ itself, built in 1674, originally belonged to Pembroke College, Cambridge, who gave it to the church in 1708. The church also contains the tombs of several members of the Howard family, including that of Thomas Howard, the 3rd Duke of Norfolk, who in 1547 was sentenced to be executed for treason. His neck was saved by the death of Henry VIII the night before the execution, and the duke died seven years later in his bed. To the east of St Michael's is Double Street, with its early Victorian pillar box – one of two in the town. The street was the first in Framlingham to have houses and shops on either side – hence its name.

As a market town, Framlingham has a number of fine inns – once used by the farmers and their wives who came by horse and carriage on market days. The oldest of these which is still a pub is the Crown Hotel on Market Hill – now modernised, but with parts that date back to the mid-16th century.

FRINTON-ON-SEA AND WALTON-ON-THE-NAZE
Essex
5 and 7 miles northeast of Clacton-on-Sea

Two contrasting seaside resorts exist side by side on the East Coast. Frinton-on-Sea is sedate, with no pubs within the gates and no organised entertainment. Walton-on-the-Naze has an 800 ft long pier, amusement arcades and bustling crowds. But both have fine sandy beaches.

Frinton developed as a resort at the end of the last century, and has preserved an air of Victorian gentility. Walton's popularity began nearly 100 years earlier, and its Marine Parade was completed in 1832. The Naze, or Ness, is a headland jutting into the sea with its great Naze Tower to warn mariners of the West Rocks offshore. Behind it is a 1900 acre National Nature Reserve – a haven for birds.

FULBECK
Lincolnshire
9 miles north of Grantham

Part of Fulbeck village stands on rising ground overlooking the Brant Valley. To the west of the main Grantham to Lincoln road are narrow winding lanes bordered by old cottages nestling close together, and the Hare and Hounds Inn links the village and the main road. The inn sign depicts the master of the Per Ardua (RAF) Beagles in the hunt uniform, and was erected in 1961.

Fulbeck Hall dates from 1733 and stands at the end of an avenue of great lime trees. Its wrought-iron gates are believed to date from the early 18th century. The house and inn form a group with the 14th-century Church of St Nicholas, which has a tower with eight pinnacles. Inside are memorials to the Fane family, who have lived at Fulbeck Hall since it was built for Sir Francis Fane, who was a Fellow of the Royal Society. His son, another Francis, was knighted at the coronation of Charles II in 1661. He became known as a successful playwright – his *Love in the Dark or The Man in Business* was successfully performed at London's Theatre Royal in 1675.

About 5 miles to the northwest is Brant Broughton, whose Church of St Helen has a Decorated west tower. Its tall spire has crockets all the way up; the arcades are 14th century, and there is a Perpendicular clerestory. The church was restored and the chancel rebuilt in 1876 by Bodley, who also installed some wood carving and wrought iron.

FULBOURN
Cambridgeshire
5 miles southeast of Cambridge

A footpath leads east from Fulbourn village to the 3 mile long Fleam Dyke, a massive 17th-century earthwork built to defend East Anglia from the Mercians. Other footpaths go northeast to Great Wilbraham, and a direct footpath from Fulbourn to Little Wilbraham passes a gleaming windmill converted into an attractive home. One end of the great dyke is near Balsham, whose church has a 13th-century tower and inventive 14th-century choir stalls carved with grimacing animals and men, or possibly demons. Until the middle of the 19th century the church had its own band, and a few old instruments are kept in a glass case by the south door.

GAINSBOROUGH
Lincolnshire
15 miles northwest of Lincoln

Since the late 17th century, Gainsborough has been a town of warm red brick. It is a busy market town and industrial centre on the east bank of the Trent, linked to Nottinghamshire on the opposite bank by a three-arched 18th-century bridge. Danish invaders, led by King Sweyn, father of Canute, ravaged the town during a series of plundering raids in the late 10th century. Sweyn was murdered in Gainsborough by one of the townspeople in 1014.

The town's oldest building, Old Hall, is a large medieval manor house of timber, plaster, brick and stone. The original building was destroyed in 1470 and rebuilt ten years later. Richard III stayed at the house in 1484 and it was here that Henry VIII met Catherine Parr, who became his sixth wife – and his widow.

Today the river is a busy highway for the town's industries, which include flour milling, engineering and the manufacture of malt kilns, agricultural tools and road rollers. Some splendid 18th-century warehouses line the quayside.

GIBRALTAR POINT
Lincolnshire
4 miles south of Skegness

Where the North Sea coast turns inwards to form the north side of the 12 mile wide mouth of The Wash, Gibraltar Point looks out across some of the most extensive salt-marshes in Europe. Sandbanks and saltings stretching southwards into The Wash have been built up by eroded material from further north. Gibraltar Point is a lonely but peaceful spot, the southernmost tip of a 1500 acre nature reserve rich in a variety of wildlife and managed by the Lincolnshire and South Humberside Trust for Nature Conservation.

Gibraltar Point in spring resounds with the warbling songs of skylarks – they are more numerous here than anywhere in Britain – and in summer, little terns and ringed plovers nest on the shingle. In autumn, vast flocks of waders – oystercatchers, knots, dunlins and godwits – visit the reserve on passage or to spend the winter. As the tide comes in, they rise in their thousands to seek higher ground. Common seals bask on the sandbanks about a mile offshore, at Dog's Head or Outer Knock, and in summer, seal pups are often born here, ready to swim off with their mothers at high tide when they are two months old.

Sharp-spined sea buckthorn grows on the East Dunes, its bright orange berries providing autumn and winter food for migrant birds, especially large flocks of fieldfares. Small birds such as yellowhammers and whitethroats nest in the buckthorn and elder scrub, and the older dunes in summer are bright with flowers such as cowslips and lady's bedstraw, or the deep blue of tall viper's bugloss. From Mill Hill, the sand-dune that is the highest part of the reserve, you can see northwest to the Wolds, and south on a clear day

across The Wash to the Hunstanton cliffs on the Norfolk coast.

In the new salt-marsh, covered by the sea at high tide, are marsh samphire, rice grass, sea blite, sea aster, sea purslane and sea meadow-grass – all plants that can survive long periods in sea water. The older salt-marsh is covered with a lilac carpet of sea lavender in summer, and reed buntings have been known to nest among the sea couch grass.

Freshwater marshes as well as salt-marshes lie within the reserve, and there is a public hide for watching birds that visit the freshwater mere, half a mile north of the visitor centre. From the hide you may see waders and dabbling and diving ducks, as well as herons and perhaps kingfishers.

GLANDFORD
Norfolk
3 miles northwest of Holt

A village of flint and red-brick houses, Glandford has a Shell Museum containing shells from all over the world together with exquisite examples of craftsmanship in shell. The museum also includes jewels, pottery and relics of Pompeii. The display of seashells is based on the collection of Sir Alfred Jodrell of Bayfield Hall, an 18th-century house 1 mile to the south. At the beginning of this century, Sir Alfred also restored St Martin's Church and incorporated typical features of Norfolk, including a copy of the Seven Sacraments font at Walsoken, bench-ends and a rood screen. The church's carillon plays hymn tunes every three hours.

GODMANCHESTER
Cambridgeshire
Opposite and south of Huntingdon

In Roman times Godmanchester was an important settlement on the crossroads of the Via Devana and Ermine Street. It received its charter in 1213, but is now amalgamated with Huntingdon. Between them stretch the 300 acre meadow of Port Holme on one side of a 17th-century raised causeway, and West Side Common on the other. There are many old buildings with gables, dormer windows and colour washes.

GOG MAGOG HILLS
Cambridgeshire
4 miles southeast of Cambridge

Although they are only 300 ft above sea level, the Gog Magog Hills offer some fine views of the towers and spires of Cambridge. The Hills are a focus for many traditions. It is believed, for instance, that somewhere under the chalk slopes lie the bodies of Gog and

VERDANT BANKS AND DUNES *At Gibraltar Point, miles of salt-marsh have been colonised by plants and birds (overleaf).*

Magog, last of an ancient race of giants. A giant horse is buried nearby, and beneath Matlow Hill there is supposed to be a golden chariot.

Wort's Causeway, off the road to Great Abington, is crossed by the Roman Via Devana, which runs parallel with the main road and offers a wonderful 9 mile walk southeast to Horseheath. Footpaths just south of the Gog Magog Hills lead from the Roman road to Wandlebury Camp, an Iron Age fort rebuilt later by the British tribe, the Iceni.

At Whittlesford, 4 miles west of Great Abington, the road bypasses the railway station, and white railings have replaced a one-time level crossing, sealing off Duxford Chapel in a cul-de-sac beside the old Red Lion Inn. The chapel was founded soon after 1200 as a hospital. In the 14th century it became a 'free chapel' until dissolved by Edward VI. It was a tollhouse for the bridge before being converted into a barn for the inn.

Sawston Hall (not open to the public), 1 mile northeast of Whittlesford, dates from the mid-16th century and has always been in the hands of the Roman Catholic Huddleston family. Mary Tudor sheltered here when her life was threatened by Lady Jane Grey's supporters. The first Village College, founded here in 1930, provided education for children and adults on lines specially suited to a rural environment.

GOLDHANGER
Essex
4 miles east of Maldon

A rash of modern building has scarcely touched the attractive heart of the farming and fishing village of Goldhanger. A wheel-turned pump still raises water. The Chequers Inn, *c.* 1500, has a manorial courtroom which was also used for medieval marriage feasts. There are pleasant walks along the sea-wall, west and east, and Goldhanger Creek is full of small boats, oysters and wading birds.

GOWTHORPE MANOR
Norfolk
4 miles south of Norwich

Sir William Boleyn, grandfather of Anne Boleyn, acquired the Tudor manor of Gowthorpe, outside the village of Swardeston, between 1494 and 1505. It passed to Thomas Aldrych, twice Mayor of Norwich, in 1525. The west wing dates from *c.* 1530. The great chamber was shortened by 26 ft in 1669, and the oak framing by the spiral stair and the fireplace in the south room are additions, *c.* 1550. In 1669, Thomas Berney cased the oak-framed west wing with brick; and his son Thomas (1674–1720) introduced the 18th-century fireplaces in the drawing room and a bedroom, and also built a walled garden with new entrance gates. The house may be visited by appointment.

GRANTCHESTER
Cambridgeshire
2 miles southwest of Cambridge

A homesick poet immortalised the church clock in serene little Grantchester, set among meadows beside the River Cam and loved by generations of Cambridge students and dons. Travelling in Germany shortly before the First World War, Rupert Brooke mused about 'the lovely hamlet Grantchester'. His poem, *The Old Vicarage, Grantchester*, asked wistfully:

'Stands the Church clock at ten to three?
And is there honey still for tea?'

Brooke lived at The Orchard between 1909–10, then later at the Old Vicarage. There, in the garden, he wrote much of his verse. A mock-Gothic building halfway down the garden, known as Widnall's Folly, was created by Samuel Widnall, who bought the Old Vicarage in 1853 for his photographic and printing work.

The splendid chancel of the Church of St Andrew and St Mary places it above the run of Cambridgeshire village churches.

Just outside the village, on the Trumpington road, is a signpost pointing to Byron's Pool. The muddy cut, by which sat not only Byron but predecessors such as Chaucer, Spenser, Milton and Dryden, is approached by paths through the coppice.

The sumptuous Church of St Mary and St Michael, Trumpington, 2 miles east of Grantchester, contains the finely preserved brass of Sir Roger de Trumpington, dated 1289 – the second-oldest brass in England. It shows Sir Roger, legs crossed, in armour and with a shield bearing his coat of arms.

Five miles southwest of Grantchester is the village of Haslingfield, with its 14th-century Church of All Saints. It contains even earlier work and the west tower has embattled pinnacle turrets. There are remains of a three-storey pulpit and a Jacobean font cover, fragments of stained glass, and a standing figure of a man in contemporary dress, *c.* 1675, possibly by William Stanton of Holborn.

GRANTHAM
Lincolnshire
22 miles east of Nottingham

North from London, south from York, traffic has surged through Grantham for centuries. Coaching inns played a vital part in the development of the town. The Angel and Royal in the High Street is one of the oldest in Britain. It stands on the site of an even older inn where King John held court in 1213. The George, nearby, which dates from the 18th century, was described by Charles Dickens in *Nicholas Nickleby*.

One of the finest buildings in the town is the 15th-century grammar school, now King's School, which has a steep, stone-tiled roof and mullioned windows. Its classrooms produced a towering genius in Sir Isaac Newton. He carved his name on a window-ledge where it can still be seen.

It was at his parents' home in nearby Woolsthorpe that Newton formulated his theory of gravity, which gave rise to the legend of the apple falling in the orchard. A bronze statue of Newton stands in front of Grantham's Guildhall.

Near the grammar school stands the dominating feature of the town, the 14th-century Church of St Wulfram. Its massive tower and richly decorated spire climb 281 ft towards the sky. Above the south porch is a room containing a chained library, given to the church by a local rector in 1598. One of its 83 volumes is dated 1472.

In the centre of Grantham are 25 acres of open gardens and parkland surrounding Grantham House,

VINE HOUSE *Dated 1764, this small mansion with its Doric porch was probably designed by Grantham's John Langwith.*

which is now owned by the National Trust. This fine house was built in the late 14th century, but it was considerably enlarged and altered in the 16th and 18th centuries.

GREAT DUNMOW
Essex
9 miles east of Bishop's Stortford

The town of Great Dunmow lies at a junction of Roman roads and has a picturesque timbered guildhall, an old inn, called The Saracen's Head, and a pond, the 'Doctor's Pond', which was the scene of the first lifeboat experiments, carried out by Lionel Lukin in 1785.

Until recently, when the local bacon factory closed, every four years Great Dunmow was the scene of a famous 'trial' at which a flitch of bacon was presented to any married couple 'who have not had a brawl in their home nor wished to be unmarried for the last 12 months and a day'. It was an old Breton custom brought to Little Dunmow by the Fitzwalters and revived by Harrison Ainsworth, the historical novelist, in 1855. The ceremony, known as the Trial of the Dunmow Flitch, used to be conducted with mock seriousness by a bewigged amateur judge and counsel.

Set 3 miles southwest of Great Dunmow is the neatly beautiful village of Great Canfield. Dominating this village and the churchyard is the great castle mound – 50 ft high, with a dry moat 45 ft wide. It is the majestic tree-clad relic of the once-mighty castle of Aubrey de Vere, Great Chamberlain of England 800 years ago.

The village of Tilty, 3 miles northeast of Great

Dunmow, is notable for its Church of St Mary the Virgin. This church was formerly the chapel outside the gate of the neighbouring Cistercian abbey. It has a 13th-century nave and 14th-century chancel. The five-light east window has some particularly fine tracery. The chancel also contains brasses.

GREAT GLEMHAM
Suffolk
3 miles west of Saxmundham

The Church of All Saints in Great Glemham has a west tower with flushwork decoration, and a good roof with bosses. Inside is a seven-sacrament font, and fragments of medieval stained glass. All Saints was restored in the 19th century.

Little Glemham Hall lies in a park on the south side of Little Glemham, 2 miles from Great Glemham. This Elizabethan mansion was the home of the 'famous and valiant Edward Glemham', a privateer as bold and unscrupulous as Drake.

In the early 18th century, the estate passed to Dudley North, whose wife was a daughter of Elihu Yale, founder of the American university.

GREAT HOCKHAM
Norfolk
6 miles west of Attleborough

Had you paused at Great Hockham during an Easter holiday in the last century, you may well have been challenged by a fearsome character holding a huge pair of horns. Fortunately it would have been just a mock attack, averted by a 'gift' of a farthing to the horned man.

This village custom was known as 'dossing', and took place during the Easter Horn Fair. Sadly, it is no longer performed, but there is an attractive reminder on the village green – a carved and painted sign showing a horned man menacing a group of people by a row of medieval houses. And a massive set of dosser's horns hangs in the village hall.

Hockham is the 'Heathly' of Michael Home's books *God and the Rabbit* and *Spring Sowing*, published in the 1930s. They are both evocative descriptions of life in this Breckland village at the turn of the century, with *Spring Sowing* carrying a vivid impression of the Horn Fair. Even now there is lively debate among villagers as to which characters are derived from real life.

The village is compact around its triangular green, but the church is a five-minute walk away in the grounds of Hockham Hall. The tower crumbled and fell in the early 18th century (collapsed church towers tend to be a feature of East Anglian villages) and was replaced with a belfry of flint and stone. The church itself is quite old: in 1953 some 14th-century murals were discovered, and have been carefully restored.

GREAT MASSINGHAM
Norfolk
9 miles north of Swaffham

The village green of Great Massingham is immense, one of the largest in Norfolk, and has been divided by roads. Spreading out from it, the houses are mainly built from split flints, which give a colour-washed appearance in strong sunlight. To one side of the green is the Church of St Mary where, on entering through the tiny chancel door, your eyes are met by a blaze of gold – the entire front of the high altar is an inctricate woodcarving finished in gold leaf, the work of Norwich carver W. G. Cooper, in 1953. He based the central figures on Leonardo da Vinci's *Annunciation*, creating them separately in limewood and placing them upon a block of oak which forms the background.

Sadly that is the only touch of colour in this beautiful, austere church. Cromwell's destroyers of church ornaments must have had a field day here. The only ones left on the walls are two shields so aged that their blue dye has turned black, and the heads of the figures on the massive 15th-century pews have been hacked off. For some reason the destruction squads overlooked an extraordinary panel on the back of a pew. Panels on the other pews have purely formal designs, but that on the hindmost left-hand pew shows a woman wearing a horned headdress, and with a rose on her stomach. She holds a dog by the tail, and by her side is a cauldron. Who or what she represents nobody knows.

The village spreads out on both sides of the church like the wings of a butterfly. It even has a butterfly's spots – three large ponds on the green, probably once the fishponds of the abbey which created Massingham. Nothing remains of the abbey today except the name, adopted by a large farm, Abbey House, which has a few pieces of ancient stonework embedded in it.

The Church of St Lawrence at Harpley, northwest of Great Massingham, dates from between 1294 and 1332, the period when John de Gurney was rector. There is a finely carved door, and the west window, depicting angels and saints, is in the style of the Medieval Norwich School. Harpley Long Barrow, 150 ft long by 90 ft wide, is on the heath nearby.

GREAT PAXTON
Cambridge
6 miles south of Huntingdon

The Saxon Church of Holy Trinity at Great Paxton, built in about 1000, was enlarged during the Gothic period. Some medieval woodwork and fragments of stained glass remain.

Toseland Hall is an almost perfect small Tudor house about 4 miles southeast of Great Paxton. It has three fine bays with a central porch, three gables, fine mullioned windows and graceful ornamented octagonal chimney-stacks.

GREAT WARLEY
Essex
2 miles southwest of Brentwood

In the quiet village of Great Warley is an outstanding example of an Art Nouveau church, built in 1904; there is a screen in the form of trees with angels standing among the foliage. The architect was Harrison Townsend, the designer of the Whitechapel Art Gallery, London, and most of the interior fittings are by Sir William Reynolds Stevens.

NIGHT SHOT *Great Yarmouth's giant funfair comes to life after dark in a dizzy swirl of lights and music.*

GREAT YARMOUTH
Norfolk
18 miles east of Norwich

Where the River Yare flows out of Breydon Water it meets the River Bure and turns south, leaving a 3 mile long spit of land between the river and the North Sea. Great Yarmouth grew on this spit, facing inwards towards the river which formed a safe natural anchorage. As a port it flourished for more than 1000 years. Then, in the 19th century, when the Victorians discovered the delights of the seaside, Great Yarmouth extended its boundaries to take in the miles of golden sand on the seaward side of the spit, and began to cater for holidaymakers. It is now one of Britain's major seaside resorts.

The old part of Great Yarmouth is linked to the mainland by the Haven Bridge. South of the bridge the quay presents one of the finest waterfronts in England, with a mixture of buildings – Tudor, Georgian and Victorian – that were once the homes of rich merchants. Close to the bridge is the 19th-century Gothic Town Hall. Number 4 South Quay, Elizabeth House, contains a museum of domestic life in the 19th century in its fine 16th-century panelled rooms.

Behind South Quay are narrow courts and alleys called The Rows. Their alignment has remained unaltered since medieval times, and they form the basis of old Yarmouth's grid pattern of streets. There were originally 145 Rows, running east to west with three intersecting streets running north to south. The area was badly damaged during air-raids in the Second World War, but several Rows remain and some of the older buildings have been restored. In Row 117 is a

17th-century dwelling, the Old Merchants' House, which has a display of local woodwork and metal work from the 17th to 19th centuries. Numbers 6, 7 and 8 in Row 111 are typical small houses of the 17th century. The Tolhouse, in Tolhouse Street, dates from the late 13th century and is said to be the oldest civic building in Britain. Its dungeons are open to the public and there is a museum of local history.

The quay to the north of Haven Bridge runs to the northwest tower of the town walls. The walls were built in the late 13th century and protected the town on its northern, eastern and southern sides. The southeast tower has also survived, and several parts of the wall are well preserved.

Great Yarmouth's market place is one of the largest in England, and twice weekly is crammed with stalls selling a variety of merchandise. At the northeast corner is the Fishermen's Hospital, founded in 1702.

The parish church of St Nicholas dates from the 12th century, but was gutted by fire during the Second World War. It has been restored with a neo-Gothic interior, and the Norman tower and Early English west end have been preserved. At the opposite end of the market place, and beyond the town centre, is St George's Church, built in 1713. It is now used as an arts centre for exhibitions and concerts.

Yarmouth's 5 miles of sandy beach is the town's major attraction for holidaymakers, and organised entertainment of every kind can be found. There are two piers — the Wellington and the Britannia — each with a theatre. Gardens, sports and leisure centre, ornamental boating-lakes and a vast pleasure beach are among the many attractions along the length of the promenade. The Maritime Museum for East Anglia

on Marine Parade is an exhibition of shipping, ship models, life-saving apparatus and general marine equipment.

At the southern end of the town there is a monument to Lord Nelson. It was erected in 1819 on what was then a remote spot, but it is now surrounded by factories.

Officially part of Great Yarmouth, Caister, 3 miles to the north, is the site of a 15th-century moated castle which was built by Sir John Fastolf — the original of Shakespeare's Falstaff. The remains include a 98 ft high round tower with a stair turret, a gatehouse and stretches of wall. It was the home of the Paston family from 1459–1599 and some of the 'Paston letters' which give a vivid account of 15th-century domestic life were written here. In the grounds is a veteran and vintage car museum.

Great Yarmouth is nearer to Rotterdam in Holland — 114 miles — than it is to London — 135 miles — and so has become an important link in trade with Europe. The harbour entrance is guarded by two piers, one on each side of the mouth of the Yare, where the river turns sharply to enter the sea at right angles. This arrangement was suggested by Joas Johnson, a Dutch engineer in the 1560s, to speed the flow of the river and prevent silting at its mouth.

About 3 miles to the southwest is Burgh Castle, a spectacular Roman fort which was one of a chain built in the second half of the 3rd century to protect the coastline from Saxon pirate raids.

Three of the original walls still stand. The huge circular bastions were designed to support Roman ballistae — artillery machines capable of hurling stone balls and other missiles.

H

HADDENHAM
Cambridgeshire
6 miles southwest of Ely

Haddenham, the highest village in the Fen country, 120 ft above sea level, has an air of spacious dignity, enhanced by three or four good houses including the red-brick Porch House of 1657 with a central porch, and Vine House and The Limes, both of the 18th century. The Church of Holy Trinity was built in the 13th and 14th centuries and heavily restored from 1876 onwards.

About 3 miles to the west is Stretham, a village on the edge of the Fens and on the main crossroads to Ely. It is notable for its 20 ft high village cross, of *c.* 1400. The only surviving example of a scoop-wheel engine, used for Fen drainage in the early 19th century, lies just outside the village.

HADLEIGH
Suffolk
8 miles west of Ipswich

The long High Street of Hadleigh offers every kind of Suffolk domestic architecture – timber, plasterwork, with or without the decoration known as pargetting, pillars and noble doorways. Overall House was named after Bishop John Overall, one of the men who translated the magnificent Authorised Version of the Bible for James I. Church Square has a glowing 15th-century timber-framed guildhall with two overhanging storeys – a splendid monument to the wool and cloth trades that gave Hadleigh its prosperity from medieval times.

A bench-end in the church shows a wolf holding a human head by the hair, representing the legend of the recovery of St Edmund's head after his martyrdom by the Danes. Guthrum the Dane is said to be buried below the south aisle, but his supposed tomb canopy dates from long after Guthrum's death.

On Aldham Common, outside the town, is a memorial to Dr Rowland Taylor, the Protestant vicar of Hadleigh, who was burnt at the stake in 1555 during Bloody Mary's reign. Hintlesham Hall, 4 miles east, was the home of the Timperley family, who built the original Elizabethan house. It was much altered in the 18th century, and the facade dates from that period.

HADLEIGH CASTLE
Essex
4 miles west of Southend-on-Sea

In its earliest days, Hadleigh Castle was an enclosure with towers and a deep ditch around the outside, built in the 1230s and overlooking the Thames estuary. The castle was reconstructed in the 1360s by Edward III to guard the estuary against possible retaliation following his military successes in France. He also wanted to use Hadleigh Castle as a royal residence. Today its remains are classified as an ancient monument.

HADSTOCK
Essex
4 miles north of Saffron Walden

After defeating Edmund Ironside in 1016, King Canute built the large Church of St Botolph in Hadstock as a memorial to the dead of both sides. Much of St Botolph's dates from this time and it may have been Canute's minster.

The north door is Saxon and once had a piece of human skin (now in Saffron Walden Museum) nailed to it. The skin is reputed to have belonged to a thief who was flayed alive.

HAPPISBURGH
Norfolk
6 miles east of North Walsham

The tower of St Mary's Church is as important a landmark to mariners on the seas outside Happisburgh as the red-and-white striped lighthouse, half a mile to the south, in warning them of the position of treacherous sandbanks along the lonely coastline. The sea close to the beach, however, is shallow and safe for bathing. Shrapnel from German bombs dropped in 1940 can still be seen embedded in aisle pillars of the 15th-century church. The octagonal font of the same period is carved with figures of lions and satyrs.

HARLESTON
Norfolk
8 miles east of Diss

A village with a few Georgian houses and a mellow old market place, Harleston is a good centre for leisurely exploration of one of the most attractive stretches of the River Waveney – from the great 17th-century red-brick Scole Inn, 7 miles to the southwest, to Bungay, 7 miles to the northeast. In summer, the great spread of a rose nursery blazes from the green slopes just ouside Harleston. The valley is a froth of blossom in the spring, and in summer is a sparkle of cottage gardens.

The painter Sir Alfred Munnings (1878–1959), a past President of the Royal Academy, was born in the pretty hillside village of Mendham, 2 miles away over the river.

HARLOW
Essex
21 miles northeast of London

In 1947 Harlow became one of eight new towns designed to siphon off people and industry from London. But several reminders of its long history survive in the rural parishes that surround The High, its

COASTAL VIGIL *The ruins of Hadleigh Castle stand guard over the Thames estuary.*

modern centre. St Mary's Church, Latton, retains a Norman doorway and window and has a fine 15th-century triple arch. The parish church of Great Parndon is basically 15th century.

HARRINGTON
Lincolnshire
4 miles northwest of Spilsby

'Come into the garden, Maud', wrote Alfred Tennyson, apparently inspired by the secluded walled garden at Harrington Hall. The poet's father knew the Amcotts, who owned the hall, well, and Alfred spent many happy hours there.

Harrington is set deep in a pocket of woodlands. St Mary's Church, a medieval foundation but almost completely rebuilt with greenstone in 1855, is reached by a path congested with undergrowth and stands dwarfed by the surrounding trees. The church contains several memorials to past lords of the manor, including one of a cross-legged knight of about 1300, thought to have been Sir John Harrington, founder of the church. There are several monuments to the Copledykes who built the Elizabethan Harrington Hall, and to the Amcotts who followed – Vincent Amcott rebuilt the hall in 1673. A gateway leads to it from the churchyard.

The house as Amcott built it includes the original towering porch, and over the doorway is a sundial, installed in 1681, with the Amcott coat of arms above it. On one side of the tower are two rows of seven sash windows, and on the other side two rows of six, splitting the red-brick frontage into pleasing asymmetry. The house, gardens and a garden centre belong

HARRINGTON HALL *Elizabethan, Jacobean and Georgian influences unite to give the seat of the Copledykes its character.*

to the family of the late Sir John Maitland, MP for Horncastle between 1945 and 1966, and are frequently open to the public.

A mile south along the road to Hagworthingham is Stockwith Mill with its old water wheel and foaming millrace. The mill is little changed from when Tennyson wrote about it, in *The Miller's Daughter.*

HARTFORD
Cambridgeshire
Northeast district of Huntingdon

The picturesque village of Hartford has a number of charming cottages, the 17th-century manor house on the main road and the 18th-century Hartford House. In August 1964, during the construction of Longstaff Way, workmen dug up 1108 English and foreign silver coins of the 15th and 16th centuries, ultimately declared Treasure Trove. The vicarage is said to have been part of the marriage settlement of Oliver Cromwell's wife.

HARWICH
Essex
16 miles east of Colchester

A medieval atmosphere still lingers in the narrow streets and passageways of Harwich. It was once a walled town, and Edward III's fleet gathered in the natural anchorage to the north before sailing in 1340 to Sluys and victory in the first sea battle of the Hundred Years' War.

Number 21 King's Head Street was the home of Captain Christopher Jones, master of the *Mayflower*, in which the Pilgrim Fathers sailed to America in 1620. On Harwich Green can be seen what is probably the only tread-wheel crane in the world. It was built in

1667 to lift naval stores. During the 17th century the great increase in coal shipments from Newcastle to London caused demands for many coastal lights, and in 1665 two were built at Harwich. They functioned until 1818, when they were replaced by octagonal brick towers. Owing to movement of the channel, both had to be replaced in 1862 by the Dovercourt Lights which, in their turn, became redundant.

Dovercourt itself is a quiet seaside resort to the south of Harwich with long sandy beaches.

The busy continental car ferry to the Hook of Holland sails from Parkeston, 2 miles west of Harwich.

HATFIELD BROAD OAK
Essex
5 miles southeast of Bishop's Stortford

The Church of St Mary the Virgin at Hatfield Broad Oak was formerly a priory founded by Aubrey de Vere in 1135. The church consists only of the nave, but there is much 15th-century work, including the west tower and south porch. In 1708, a library was built to the east of the south chapel. The contents include a 15th-century screen, an 18th-century reredos by John Woodward, and several monuments, of which one is by J. F. Moore, another by John Flaxman.

HAUGHLEY PARK
Suffolk
3 miles northwest of Stowmarket

Although not built until 1620, the small red-brick mansion at Haughley Park is typical of an Elizabethan house with its E formation, crow-stepped gables and star-topped chimneys. Built by Sir John Sulyard, whose grandfather had been one of the first to support Mary Tudor when she stayed at Framlingham Castle in 1553, the interior was gutted by fire, in 1961, after nine months of restoration. Today it has been meticulously reconstructed. The house is set in over 250 acres of parkland, and includes a sequence of contrasted gardens and woodland.

HAWSTEAD
Suffolk
3 miles south of Bury St Edmunds

The Church of All Saints at Hawstead is Norman and later; the west tower is Perpendicular, with flushwork decoration. The nave has hammerbeams and angels, but was restored in the mid-19th century. There are attractive furnishings – benches, a 16th-century pulpit, a lectern – a large number of brasses, and monuments by Nicholas Stone, the two John Bacons and others from the 13th century onwards. The screen dates from the 15th century.

HEACHAM
Norfolk
2 miles south of Hunstanton

The village sign and a tablet in Heacham church recall Pocahontas, the Red Indian princess who married John Rolfe, of Heacham Hall, in Virginia in 1614. She was only 22 when she died, three years later; but she left a son, Tom, who returned to America and has since been claimed as the ancestor of many famous families. The hall was destroyed by fire during the Second World War.

Caley Mill, on the main King's Lynn to Hunstanton road, is a packing and dispatch centre for lavender. The lavender fields around Heacham and at Choseley Farm, $5\frac{1}{2}$ miles east, are at their best during July and early August, when the crop is picked and taken to a small distillery in a barn at Fring, 4 miles southeast. The mill and distillery, where lavender water is made, are open to the public.

HECKINGTON
Lincolnshire
5 miles east of Sleaford

Heckington's Church of St Andrew is one of the best Decorated churches in Britain, with a tall tower and spire. It was built by the abbey of nearby Bardney in 1345. Inside there is a very fine Easter sepulchre with carved figures, including a mermaid and a man playing bagpipes. Every Good Friday in the Middle Ages, the Host and the altar crucifix were placed in the sepulchre – a tomb in the recess in the chancel – and watched over day and night by celebrants until Easter morning, when the Host and crucifix were moved to the High Altar. The ritual symbolised the burial and resurrection of Christ. The loss of the chancel screen detracts from the medieval proportions, but the fine tracery work in the east window is a masterpiece.

EASTER SEPULCHRE *Mythological, biblical and lay figures decorate Heckington church's 13th-century mock tomb (above).*
LAVENDER BLUE *An August bounty of scented spikes brightens the fields near Heacham (overleaf).*

The only surviving windmill in the British Isles with eight sails was built in 1830 and stands at the southern end of the village. The replacement cap, sails and eight-armed cross were bought from a mill at Boston in 1890. Opposite, the former pea-sorting warehouse now makes an attractive setting for craft workshops and heritage displays in the Pearoom.

Further north about 1 mile is the village of Howell, whose Norman Church of St Oswald has additions in the transitional and decorated styles. Some fragments of medieval stained glass remain, and the font and bell-gable are 14th century.

HELPSTON
Cambridgeshire
6 miles northwest of Peterborough

At the crossroads on Helpston village green stands a memorial to John Clare, the 'peasant poet' who was born in Helpston in 1793. The memorial, an obelisk ornately decorated in the Gothic style, stands at the top of Woodgate, the street where Clare was born. Beside his birthplace is the Bluebell Inn, where he was once a servant.

Clare would have known the village cross, which dates from about 1300 and has a tall base with gables and battlements, and the attractive, grey-stone houses around the green. But the almshouses were built in the early 20th century.

The serene beauty of Helpston and the surrounding countryside inspired Clare who was, in his own words, 'A peasant in his daily cares, a poet in his joy'. Yet his life was one of turmoil and tragedy. He was at various times a ploughboy, herdsman, vagrant and failed farmer. He lived in constant poverty, and died in Northampton Lunatic Asylum where he had spent 23 years. Clare's body lies in the churchyard of St Botolph, the village church by the green.

To the southeast of the village is Woodcroft Castle where Clare worked as a ploughboy. The castle, now a manor house, dates from 1312, and has 15th-century additions. During the Civil War, the Royalist occupants of the castle were ruthlessly slaughtered by Cromwell's troops, and it is said that the sounds of battle and cries for mercy can still occasionally be heard resounding through the castle.

HEMINGFORD GREY
Cambridgeshire
1 mile southwest of St Ives

Graceful old houses stand by the edge of the Great Ouse at Hemingford Grey and gaze down at the houseboats, skiffs and motor-cruisers which moor there. Set among the village's brick, timber and thatched cottages is a stout-walled and moated Norman manor house, said to be the oldest inhabited home in England. The original entrance to the house was on the first floor, but the external staircase leading to it has now gone. The house is privately owned.

Nearby, on a willow-fringed bend of the river, is the 12th-century Church of St James. The upper section of its spire came down in a gale in 1741 and is locally believed to be at the bottom of the river. The parishioners did not rebuild the spire at the time, but topped the stump with eight stone balls instead. A short distance away from the church is the 17th-century

Hemingford Grey House, now a study and conference centre. In the gardens is one of Britain's biggest plane trees. It was planted in 1702, and has a girth of more than 20 ft.

A towpath leads to Huntingdon and Godmanchester water-meadows, and Hemingford Grey links with the village of Hemingford Abbots, where some attractive houses cluster around St Margaret's Church. St Margaret's was built about 1300, of brown cobbles.

HESSETT
Suffolk
5 miles east of Bury St Edmunds

The 14th-century Church of St Ethelbert at Hessett has a 15th-century west tower, nave and porch with flushwork decoration. There is a 15th-century font, a screen and benches, and a monument by Sir John Stone of c.1653. There is a good deal of stained glass preserved in the aisle windows; in one a boy holds a golf club.

Mural paintings depict the Seven Deadly Sins, St Barbara, St Christopher and Christ of the Trades. The 14th-century vestry was once an anchorite's cell and still has its own altar and squint.

HEVENINGHAM
Suffolk
5 miles southwest of Halesworth

The Hall at Heveningham is thought by some to be the grandest Georgian mansion in Suffolk. It was built in 1780 for Sir Gerard Vanneck, MP on an estate bought by his father. The estate still belongs to the Vanneck family. The exterior was designed by Sir Robert Taylor, but planning of the interior was entrusted to James Wyatt. Here is some of Wyatt's best surviving work, particularly the entrance hall with its vaulted ceiling and the dining room. The grounds, containing a lake, were laid out by 'Capability Brown' and contain an orangery by Wyatt.

HICKLING
Norfolk
3 miles east of Stalham

The village of Hickling lies to the north of the broad of the same name, which is the largest and least spoilt of Norfolk's unique waterways. The village is best approached by the Pleasure Boat Inn, whose 'staithe', a Broadland term for a quay or landing stage, is known to every regular voyager on these waters. Its Church of St Mary is mainly Decorated, though much restored, while Priory Farm retains some ruins of the 12th-century Augustinian priory.

The whole of Hickling Broad is part of a 1400 acre nature reserve maintained by the Norfolk Naturalists' Trust. Inhabited by many birds, the broad is also a home of a rare butterfly – the swallowtail, Britain's largest butterfly, with a 3 in. wingspan.

Potter Heigham, a village with shops, a supermarket and clustering sheds to provide almost anything that the holidaymaker afloat is likely to need, is just 3 miles south of Hickling. A modern road bridge has bypassed tne old single-lane hump-backed bridge, below which yachtsmen must still lower their masts and heads.

HINGHAM

Norfolk
6 miles west of Wymondham

Elegant Georgian houses and an impressive coaching inn, the White Hart, are grouped around Hingham's Market Place. In nearby Market Street are more Georgian houses, giving a dignified atmosphere to this 18th-century village – where each year fairs are still held in the street called The Fairland.

The village has strong ties with Hingham in Massachusetts, USA. In the early 17th century a rector, Robert Peck, rebelled against his superiors in the Church and emigrated to America to seek religious freedom. Some of his like-minded parishioners went with him, and together they founded Hingham, USA. A granite boulder in the Market Place was given by the citizens of America's Hingham, in exchange for an old mounting block which had stood outside a blacksmith's forge.

A local man who preceded Peck to America was Samuel Lincoln, whose direct descendant, Abraham Lincoln, became President of the USA. St Andrew's Church, where Samuel Lincoln was baptised, has a bronze bust of the President – a gift of the Americans after the First World War.

AMERICAN CONNECTIONS *The village sign at Hingham recalls local people who emigrated to the New World.*

HOLBEACH

Lincolnshire
7 miles east of Spalding

The market town of Holbeach is situated in the middle of the bulb-growing district. The Church of All Saints is of particular interest to architects, since it shows features of the transition between the Decorated and Perpendicular styles. Its austere beauty is enhanced by the total lack of structural alteration since the building was completed in 1380. Between the town and the sea wall there is a scatter of villages. One of these, Gedney, has a church with a 14th-century porch and 15th-century nave. There is a pleasant walk along the sea bank, but the sea itself is far out across a stretch of treacherous mud and marsh.

At Fleet, 2 miles east of Holbeach, is the 14th-century Church of St Mary Magdalene. It shows distinctive Fenland features, with its tower and spire detached from the main building. Apart from the chancel, rebuilt in 1862, the remainder of the church is in the Decorated style, except for Early English arcades and the Perpendicular west window.

HOLKHAM GAP

Norfolk
2 miles west of Wells

A vast, sweeping cove with a beach so flat it looks as though it has been rolled; grassy dunes of soft, golden sand; pine trees growing almost to the water's edge – this is Holkham Gap. About 100 years ago, Corsican pines were planted among the dunes to stabilise the sand, and since 1967 it has been part of a nature reserve managed by the Nature Conservancy Council.

The reserve stretches for about 10 miles along the coast, except for a narrow strip at Wells. It is mainly dunes and salt-marshes, some reclaimed for agriculture. At Holkham a driveway, called Lady Ann's Drive, leads to a point near the beach where a short walk brings the panorama of the cove into view.

Holkham Hall, nearly 1 mile southwest of Holkham, was built by Thomas Coke in 1734–62 to show how an area of dunes and salt-marshes could be reclaimed and utilised, and how the style of an Italian palace could be harmoniously introduced into an English setting. The Hall is an H-plan Palladian mansion, with four wings to a central section: the overall front is 340 ft, with a great central portico. The interior was planned to give long vistas of connecting rooms. All the main rooms have a full measure of 18th-century magnificence – ceilings, paintings, tapestries and statues. Holkham Hall was part of the inheritance of Thomas Coke's famous great-nephew 'Coke of Norfolk'.

HOLT

Norfolk
10 miles west of Cromer

Sir Thomas Gresham, who founded the Royal Exchange in London, was born in 1519 in the market town of Holt. He founded Gresham's School in 1555. Its Tudor-style building of 1858 is in the town square, although the school moved to its present building half a mile along the Cromer road, in 1900. This road runs through avenues of beech and pine, broken up by expanses of heather and bracken, to the Sheringhams.

The road to Cley next the Sea, 4 miles northwest, passes through rolling fields and woodland patches above saltings. Just over 1 mile to the west, the road to Blakeney crosses the attractive River Glaven, which runs through the gardens of 18th-century Letheringsett Hall. Baconsthorpe Castle, southeast of Holt, is a moated 15th-century ruin.

HONINGTON CAMP

Lincolnshire
5 miles north of Grantham

Hill-forts are almost unknown in Lincolnshire, but this small Iron Age fort, known as Honington Camp, must have been placed here for much the same reason that the early Roman defences at Ancaster, which preceded the civilian town of Causennae, were established. Both lay on the southern slopes of Ancaster Gap, an ancient channel eroded through the upland of Lincoln Edge. Honington's internal area of about an acre is guarded by no less than three banks with two intermediate ditches.

HORHAM

Suffolk
2 miles southwest of Stradbroke

At Horham in Suffolk is 16th-century brick Thorpe Hall, a house that has an interesting stack of four ornamental octagonal chimneys. The mullioned windows are of brick, rendered to simulate stonework. The house can be visited by appointment.

HORNCASTLE

Lincolnshire
18 miles east of Lincoln

Horncastle, a small market town, is set on the site of the Roman station at Banovallum, with traces of Roman walls and other relics remaining. Horncastle lies in the valley of the River Bain at its junction with the River Waring. The market place is pleasantly leafy, but today's markets are not on the scale of the enormous ten-day horse fairs held annually until the last century and said to be the largest of their kind in the world. There are a number of pleasant brick houses and some old inns, including The Fighting Cocks, named after a popular sport in the days of the horse fairs. St Mary's Church, near the market place, has some Civil War relics, such as pikes and scythes.

Snipe Dales, a 211 acre nature reserve, is 4½ miles east of Horncastle, adjoining a country park. To the southwest is Lincolnshire's only golf course of championship standard. It is in the town of Woodhall Spa. After the discovery of medicinal water here, a pump room was built in Victorian times.

HORNING

Norfolk
3 miles east of Hoveton

The patchwork of lakes making up the Norfolk Broads is threaded together with streams, channels and rivers, and on one of these, the River Bure, stands the village of Horning. Unlike many of the villages that have

sprung up with the popularity of the Broads, Horning is ancient. Earthworks have been found here and a ferry plied across the river for more than 1000 years.

Horning Ferry no longer exists, but the Ferry Inn is still in business. Along the river, inlets lead to attractive houses with gardens and lawns sweeping down to the water's edge. This system of waterways, crossed here and there by rustic bridges, provides mooring places for many pleasure craft and gives Horning a slightly Venetian air. The village's main street runs parallel to the river, with occasional glimpses of it between trim, thatched cottages.

The flat landscape is relieved by the soaring towers of Horning's 13th- to 14th-century Church of St Benedict, half a mile east of the village, and 14th-century St Helen's at Ranworth – 2 miles south as the crow flies, but about 8 tortuous miles by road. St Helen's has a fine 15th-century painted screen and a rare Antiphoner, bequeathed in 1478: its 285 sheep-

skin pages, beautifully written and illuminated by monks, contain daily services in medieval Latin and 19 finely painted miniatures.

From the top of Ranworth Tower there are fine views across the Broads, bejewelled in summer by myriads of dancing sails. At Ranworth is the Broadland Conservation Centre – a small area in which all types of typical vegetation and wildlife can be found. It was established by the Norfolk Naturalists' Trust in 1976.

About 3½ miles to the southeast is the ruined St Benet's Abbey, founded in the 11th century. Nobody seems to know when the last monks left – it was *not* dissolved by Henry VIII – but by 1702 only a few buildings remained. The curious outline of the gatehouse is caused by the stump of a windmill built into the ruins about 200 years ago.

About 4 miles north, in Barton Turf, is the 14th- and 15th-century Church of St Michael and All Angels, with a battlemented tower. It has 15th-century

NORFOLK BROADS *The area around Horsey has some of the most unspoilt landscape in the East Anglian waterways.*

screens with painted figures. A brass dates from c.1445, and there are monuments to local villagers from the late 18th century.

HORSEY
Norfolk
9 miles northeast of Acle

Horsey's story is of an unremitting battle for survival against the sea. Once an island in a bay – its name may mean isle of horses – the village is between 3 ft and 6 ft above sea level and surrounded by flat, wind-scoured countryside. Nevertheless, it has been occupied since Roman times – elements permitting. In

1938 the North Sea broke through the dunes, and the flood seemed to spell doom for Horsey.

The village was cut off for 4½ months and its inhabitants evacuated. Headlines over successive days in the local newspaper read like war communiqués: 'Horsey defences carried away.' Even when the flood had receded, the land was poisoned by salt, so the locals turned to the Dutch to learn to cope with their common enemy.

The area was brought slowly back to life, but if you climb the church tower you can still glimpse the menacing sea, barely a stone's throw away, beyond the dunes. Visitors are discouraged from clambering over them for fear of damage to that vital defence.

There are three quite distinctive centres to this scattered village – a pub, a windmill and the church. The 200-year-old mill, a National Trust property, is for drainage, pumping water from ditches into Horsey Mere – one of the remoter and pleasanter Norfolk Broads. These days it is powered by electricity rather than the wind.

The tiny All Saints' Church, tucked among trees, has a thatched roof and a Saxon round tower which was topped in the 15th century with an unusual octagonal belfry. From outside, the church has changed little over the centuries, and the restoration carried out by the Victorians was confined to furnishings inside. There is one outstanding Victorian relic: a stained-glass window showing the artist Catherine Ursula Rising, who was a member of a wealthy local family, painting a picture.

HOUGHTON AND WYTON
Cambridgeshire
3 miles east of Huntingdon

Houghton and Wyton have many picturesque cottages and riverside views. Houghton water mill, believed to be the oldest on the Great Ouse, is now a youth hostel. The 'Gothic' village pump on the green, an elaborate cast-iron affair, is unique.

Magdalene College Farm in Wyton was built in 1600, and an adjoining farmhouse is dated 1648. There are some wall-paintings of 1622 in the Three Jolly Butchers Inn.

HOXNE
Suffolk
3 miles northeast of Eye

Houses of timber, brick and plaster are dotted around the outskirts of Hoxne, whose attractive centre can be found down a shaded lane turning off from the main road. On the road towards Hoxne Cross, the historic Goldbrook Bridge crosses a tributary of the River Dove.

A plaque on the bridge records that there the young King Edmund was captured by the Danes in 870 after his defeat in a battle near Thetford, some 20 miles away. Edmund's capture was due, it is said, to his betrayal by a bridal party who saw the glint of his golden spurs as he hid beneath the bridge. As he was dragged away by his captors he loudly cursed all future bridal couples who should cross the bridge. For centuries the curse was taken seriously, and even today it is considered unlucky for a bride to cross Goldbrook Bridge on her wedding day.

The Danes tried to force Edmund to renounce his Christian beliefs by tying him to a tree and shooting him with arrows. A stone cross stands on the site of an ancient oak tree which, when it collapsed in 1848, was found to contain an arrowhead.

Edmund was beheaded by the Danes, and for several years his body lay buried in the chapel of a nearby Benedictine priory. Nothing remains of the priory today, but the 16th-century Hoxne Abbey Farmhouse stands on the site.

Hoxne's church, St Peter and St Paul, dates from the 14th century. A screen bearing scenes of Edmund's martyrdom was made from the fallen oak tree.

HUNSTANTON
Norfolk
14 miles northeast of King's Lynn

The largest of the west Norfolk resorts, Hunstanton is the only East Anglian seaside town which faces west. Here are great stretches of sand, and though the funfair and caravan park are an integral part of the waterfront, they do not disturb the town's essentially Victorian atmosphere. Old Hunstanton, half a mile north, is a residential village with beach huts nestling in the dunes. Holme next the Sea, a further 1½ miles northeast, has a bird observatory, and migrant birds throng the coast in autumn.

HUNTINGDON
Cambridgeshire
15 miles northeast of Cambridge

Huntingdon, formerly a county town, is more cramped than neighbouring Godmanchester, with which it is now amalgamated, but has some unspoilt corners with several fine Georgian houses.

Oliver Cromwell was born in a house close to Ermine Street, its site marked by a plaque on the Huntingdon Research Centre. He was baptised in All Saints' Church, which is partly 11th century. His father is buried here. About 1610, Oliver attended the old grammar school, a basically Norman building, where Samuel Pepys was also a pupil. It was opened as a Cromwell Museum in 1962 by the then Speaker of the House of Commons. The George Inn, once the property of Cromwell's grandfather, has an inner courtyard overlooked by a gallery where Shakespearean plays are produced occasionally.

Pay dirt: Briton unearths ancient hoard of riches

London, England —AP— A retired gardener looking for a lost hammer with a metal detector unearthed an ancient hoard of buried gold and silver that one report said could be worth $15 million.

Archeologist Judith Plouviez said the hoard found by Eric Lawes, 70, in a field near the village of Hoxne in Suffolk County "is an incredibly exciting and amazing find."

She said it was impossible to say how much the hoard, unearthed last week, was worth until experts examined it. But the London tabloid The Sun, which made the find its main front-page report on Thursday, said it could be worth 15 million.

Plouviez said it was believed to have been hidden by a rich family about 1,600 years ago during the Roman occupation of Britain, which began in A.D. 43 and lasted about 400 years.

Plouviez, who works for the Suffolk County Council, said: "It is one of the finest known from Roman Britain. It is priceless in terms of the knowledge it will give us."

It includes a solid silver model of a panther, gold chains, hundreds of gold and silver coins, spoons, ornaments, gem-studded jewelry and a gold pendant encrusted with rubies weighing more than a pound.

The hoard was unearthed on land owned by the council and will be the subject of an inquest to decide legal ownership. If, as seems likely, the hoard is ruled treasure-trove — items found buried in the ground with no known owner — it automatically becomes government property.

In such cases, the finder normally receives a large reward and the items are put on permanent exhibition.

The British national news agency Press Association said experts had told Lawes he could expect to receive more than $1.5 million.

The hoard has been sent to the British Museum in London to be cleaned and studied.

1994-1995

ICKLETON
Cambridgeshire
1 mile northwest of Great Chesterford

There are traces of a fulling-mill at Ickleton, where cloth was thickened with 'fuller's earth'. It is one of two built in the village during the Middle Ages, when the wool trade flourished there. The surviving foundations of the mill are near Frogge Hall, a 16th-century house which gets its name from the fact that frogs once infested the damp streets of the village. The oldest house in Ickleton, The Hovells, once belonged to a Cistercian monastery, and Abbey Farm stands on the site of a late-12th-century Benedictine nunnery. A fishpond and fragments of the priory wall and an archway remain.

Much of the property in the parish was in monastic hands until the Dissolution of the Monasteries by Henry VIII, and several houses take their names from their old owners: Caldrees Manor, from Calder Abbey in Cumbria; Durhams, from the Canons of Dereham in Norfolk; and Mowbrays, from the Mowbray Dukes of Norfolk who owned it before it passed to Clare College, Cambridge, in the 15th century. The poor of the parish were looked after by the Charity Commissioners at the Town Housen, a group of cottages which at one time incorporated a school. They date from the 17th century, except for one which was built about 1500.

The Romans had a military post at Great Chesterford, across the River Granta, and at Ickleton itself a Romano-British villa was excavated in 1842. The Roman Icknield Way passes close by, and it is probable that the road and the village take their names from the ancient British Iceni tribe, whose queen was Boudicca (or Boadicea).

Evidence of the Roman occupation is present in Ickleton's parish church, which has Roman tiles in the stonework of its tower and Roman columns supporting Norman arches in the nave. The church, dedicated to St Mary Magdalene, has an unusual feature in its clock bell, which is on the outside of the spire. Sadly, the interior of the church was gutted by fire, though restoration costing some £280,000 has been carried out. One happy result of the fire was the discovery of a series of 12th-century frescoes, of a type unique in England.

Medieval stone carvings in the churchyard wall represent foxes, crocodiles and other beasts now unidentifiable through years of weathering. Animals are also a feature of the church pews – weird cockerels and a two-headed dragon.

A little more than 1 mile north of Ickleton is Duxford, with two spikey-towered churches. Duxford Chapel, below Whittlesford bridge, is a 14th-century chantry which became a travellers' hospice under the Order of St John. Nearby is the RAF museum at Duxford Airfield, open daily from March to November, which has a large display of aircraft. Trapped there is a prototype Concorde, which flew in but can never fly out, because the runway was shortened to make way for a motorway immediately after its arrival.

INGATESTONE
Essex
5 miles northeast of Brentwood

The village of Ingatestone has a number of pleasant Georgian brick houses and a 16th-century inn, The Bell. The Church of St Edmund and St Mary has a splendid 15th-century red-brick tower. The south chapel was added in 1556 by the Petre family, who still live at Ingatestone Hall. There is a footpath from the church to this E-shaped Tudor house.

About $2\frac{1}{2}$ miles northeast is the little village of Margaretting, whose church has the same namesake. In addition to a famous 15th-century Jesse window, the church has good timbering in its north porch and tower and an octagonal font, all of which date from the 15th century.

IPSWICH
Suffolk
66 miles northeast of London

Ipswich, the county town of East Suffolk, is a thriving port on the River Orwell. Much of the town was built or rebuilt in the 19th century, but 12 medieval churches and several 16th-century buildings survive. Cardinal Wolsey was born here and the gate of his uncompleted college stands forlorn beneath dockland offices and warehouses. Christchurch Mansion, a Tudor country house in a spacious park, is a lively domestic museum with furniture, fine panelling, model ships, doll's houses and children's toys from the past, and an art gallery with some local scenes by Gainsborough and Constable. There is elaborate plasterwork on the Ancient House in the Butter Market. Dickens stayed at the Great White Horse when he was a reporter, and the inn provided him with the setting for Mr Pickwick's misadventure when he went into a lady's bedroom by mistake.

IRNHAM
Lincolnshire
6 miles northwest of Bourne

Four roads meet at Irnham, yet there is little through traffic to disturb the peace of this self-contained grey-stone village set among trees in a fold of hills.

The village inn, the Griffin, stands at the crossroads and is mostly Georgian. The north to south road through the village leads to Irnham Hall. The hall was built between 1510 and 1531, but a fire in 1887 destroyed much of the interior and there were some exterior alterations in the mid-18th century. It can be seen best from the churchyard of St Andrew's. The 12th-century church contains an early brass of Sir Andrew Luttrell, Lord of Irnham in 1390, and some stained glass, most of which is 19th century.

Two attractive 18th-century houses stand near the church – the Manor House and the even grander Newton House.

IRNHAM HALL *Lying next to the churchyard, the L-shaped house is surrounded by a Georgian-style landscape garden* (above).
IXWORTH THORPE *The Tudor brick of All Saints' south porch complements its thatched roof and wooden bell tower* (below).

IXWORTH
Suffolk
6 miles northeast of Bury St Edmunds

The small village of Ixworth has a house, Ixworth Abbey, incorporating the 12th- and 13th-century cloister ranges of the Augustinian priory that was founded here in 1170. There are 17th- and 18th-century additions, and much fine woodwork.

Two miles north is the Church of St Peter and St Paul at Bardwell. It contains much 15th- and 16th-century building; the south porch has flushwork decoration and arms, of about 1430. The hammer-beam roof has some of its original colour left, though most of the angels have gone. There is 15th-century stained glass, and a 17th-century monument with kneeling figures and children.

Two miles northwest is the hamlet of Ixworth Thorpe, which has a rare thatched Church of All Saints. Restored in 1972, it is a delightful example of a rustic place of worship.

KEDINGTON
Suffolk
2 miles east of Haverhill

The Church of St Peter and St Paul at Kedington dates from the 11th century and later. The Barnardiston family pew is constructed from a 15th-century screen. There are Perpendicular benches, 18th-century box-pews, and a three-decker 17th-century pulpit and screen.

Also interesting is a Saxon carved Crucifix, and several monuments to the Barnardiston family with effigies dating from the 16th to 18th centuries.

KERSEY
Suffolk
2 miles northwest of Hadleigh

Of all the times to visit Kersey, the late afternoon is best, for then the great Suffolk fields with their serpentine hedgerows are filled from horizon to horizon with the pink-gold and green light that has brought so many painters to East Anglia. Standing against the light as you approach along the Lavenham to Hadleigh road, Kersey church on its hilltop grows ever more massive. The village itself, however, is invisible until you come to a corner with an archaic wooden pump high on the right bank, turn, and then suddenly, there it is – all of Kersey, running steeply down The Street to a water-splash through a tributary of the Brett, and up again, just as steeply, to the summit of Church Hill.

Seen all of a piece like this, in a picture that fits snugly into the lens of any camera, Kersey is a peaceful, multi-coloured Toytown of a village, whose red-tiled roofs are subdued by just the right amount of weathering and lichen, and whose overhanging gables thrust forward in a quiet brilliance of red-and-yellow ochre, pink, white and café-au-lait. Only a closer look reveals how old it all is. The Corner House opposite the pump, for example, has among its ancient timbers those of a filled-in doorway that must date from the early 16th century at least, while a few yards down The Street is a group of weavers' cottages, so old that their hollowed steps and time-hardened timbers seem to grow out of the pavement. Their high lattice-paned dormer windows lean forward in faint surprise towards the White Horse Inn across the road, as near a pink-and-white birthday cake as a pub can be.

In all of The Street there is scarcely a house without character, from the timber-framed Bell pub to River House by the ford, whose inhabitants for almost 500 years have had the murmuring of the river along the walls as a background to their lives. The same walls, when the Virginia creeper dies back in winter, show a date-mark of 1490.

On the right of Church Hill, beyond the ford, are three adjoining houses – The Little Manor, Woodbine Cottage, and Aran Cottage – built before the Reformation and smothered at one end by a twisting creeper that looks nearly as old. Just downhill is the entrance to The Green, a lovely group of pastel-hued cottages.

The sheer size and magnificence of the Church of St Mary argues a prosperity and a population far greater than the village possesses now. It is a reminder of the centuries when half the men in England wore hard-wearing Kersey cloth, just as the women wore Lindsey Woolsey, made in the neighbouring village of Lindsey. Built largely in the 14th century, St Mary's is a most impressive building whose walls are decorated with a mingling of square-split flint and stone. The roof of the south porch consists of 16 intricately carved wooden panels, a masterpiece of 15th-century craftsmanship. The interior of the church suffered considerably during the Reformation, as a number of headless angels and battered carvings bear witness, though a surprising number of its earliest treasures remain. There is, for example, part of a 15th-century screen depicting kings and prophets making those curious double-jointed medieval gestures with their hands, and an engaging wooden lectern of similar date. Each generation has contributed something to the church, including our own which, in addition to preserving the bells and fabric, provided the beautifully embroidered hassocks decorated with ecclesiastical motifs.

Just before leaving the churchyard it is worth studying a sturdily independent East Anglian epitaph:

'Reader pass on nor waste thy time
On bad biography or bitter rhyme
For what I am this humble dust enclose,
And what I was is no affair of yours.'

KIMBOLTON
Cambridgeshire
7 miles northwest of St Neots

Catherine of Aragon, Henry VIII's first wife, was confined in a 13th-century fortified manor house in Kimbolton village from 1534 – the year after her marriage was annulled – until her death two years later. The original building has completely vanished under 18th-century alterations, which include a north gateway and outer gatehouse by Robert Adam. There are also reconstructions, made in early 1700s by Sir John Vanbrugh, of the Queen's room and adjacent boudoir – which have been refurnished since Catherine's time. He also added the main staircase. The building, Kimbolton Castle, is now a school, and the state rooms and extensive grounds are open to the public on Spring and Late Summer Bank Holidays and some Sunday afternoons in July and August.

Kimbolton is set among gently undulating fields stretching from Grafham Water. The River Kym winds along the northeastern fringe of the village, passing the former Baptist chapel and the section called The Rookery. There is a wide, mostly Georgian, main street, with buildings with brindled roof tiles. At the far end, the street curves around the churchyard of St Andrew's, built in 1219 with later alterations.

KERSEY *The village street dives down to this water-splash, then rises steeply to the magnificent Church of St Mary (overleaf).*

KING'S LYNN

Norfolk

39 miles west of Norwich

The Great Ouse river has brought prosperity to King's Lynn, a lively port and market town since the Middle Ages, and there are some noteworthy buildings strung along its east bank. Starting at the south end, there is the imposingly named Hampton Court, home of a 17th-century master-baker named John Hampton. Parts of this colour-washed building date back to the 1300s, and the King's Lynn Preservation Trust has converted it into flats. Behind the house's half-timbered frontage on Nelson Street, a cobbled court-yard is enclosed by lovingly restored wings dating from as early as the 14th century.

Nearby is the tall, 15th-century Hanseatic Warehouse, brick and timber framed with an overhanging upper storey which, until 1751, belonged to the Hanseatic League of north European merchants. They formed a protective trading partnership in the 14th century. The town was one of half a dozen English ports welcomed into the league because the Germans had established trading links here.

Downriver the ornate Customs House, built in 1683, has a statue of Charles II over its main doorway. In between these maritime buildings is the Saturday Market Place, the focal point of the town since the early 1100s. In the Market Place stands St Margaret's Church, built in the 13th century to replace the former St Margaret's, which was begun in 1100 by the first Bishop of Norwich. A severe storm in 1741 wrecked the nave and aisles, which were rebuilt, but the original twin towers are still there. The church contains two of the largest brasses in England, both 14th century, with extremely intricate tooling.

The remains of a Benedictine priory lie on the south side of St Margaret's, and across from the church are two adjacent buildings with a matching design of dark and pale flint squares: the Guildhall of the Holy Trinity, built in 1421, and the Victorian Town Hall. Among the trophies in the Guildhall's treasury are the King John Sword and a magnificent silver-gilt and enamel cup, called the King John Cup. Both, however, are 14th century and were made at least 100 years after the monarch died.

Between the Guildhall and the river is Thoresby College, founded about 1500 by Thomas Thoresby, a philanthropic merchant and member of the town council, as quarters for the chaplains of the Trinity Guild. It is now made over as flats for retired people, offices, a meeting room and a Youth Hostel. To the north of the college is the elegant 18th-century facade of Clifton House, hiding a much older building, former-ly the residence of a rich medieval merchant.

North along the river is the town's second Guildhall, that of St George. It dates from 1407 and is the oldest and largest Guildhall in England. In the 18th century it was turned into a theatre, and today it stages part of the annual King's Lynn Festival. To the side of the Guildhall is Tuesday Market – larger but slightly younger than Saturday Market – with the 15th-century chapel-of-ease, St Nicholas, just above it in St Ann's Street.

The monarch connected with King's Lynn is Henry VIII, who took over the manor during the Dissolution of the Monasteries in 1539. Before that, the town was called Bishop's Lynn, or just plain Lynn, as it is referred to these days by many locals.

KIRKSTEAD

Lincolnshire

7 miles southwest of Woodhall Spa

Kirkstead's Church of St Leonard was once the 13th-century south chapel of the former Cistercian abbey of Kirkstead, founded during the 12th century. It is now surrounded by the ruins of various abbey build-ings. There is an early effigy of a knight in armour, which dates from about 1250.

KIRTLING

Cambridgeshire

5 miles southeast of Newmarket

In Kirtling, a village close to the Suffolk border, is a fine tower gatehouse dating from 1530. It is built of red brick, with blue diapers and has two tall polygonal outer turrets behind and a superb semicircular oriel window squashed in between. This gatehouse is all that remains of the 15th-century mansion of Lord North, Henry VIII's Chancellor, who made great profits

CHECKERBOARD FACADE *Dark and light flint blocks make a busy pattern on the front of King's Lynn's Guildhall of 1421.*

out of monastic confiscations and was for a time the respectful jailer of Elizabeth I before she became queen. His tomb, along with many monuments to the North family, is to be seen in the village's flint-walled Church of All Saints.

Westley Waterless, some $3\frac{1}{2}$ miles west, has the Early English and Decorated Church of St Mary, which once had a round tower, but this fell down in the 19th century. There is a delicate early 14th-century brass to Sir John de Creke and his wife, with almost life-size figures, Sir John in armour.

KNAPTON

Norfolk

3 miles northeast of North Walsham

The Church of St Peter and St Paul at Knapton is mainly 14th century, notable for its massive double hammerbeam roof, added in 1503–4, and decorated with 160 carved angels and other figures. The roof is 73 ft long and about 30 ft wide.

About 1 mile northwest is the village of Trunch and the Perpendicular Church of St Botolph, which has a west tower and another of Norfolk's famous hammer-beam roofs decorated with angels. But its most renowned feature is its magnificent font canopy, of which type there are only three others in England. It stands on eight carved pillars, with much carving of foliage, and beneath the cover is a kind of fan-vault with a pendant. Above this are eight canopied niches, now without statues. A large crocket finishes off the very top. St Botolph's also has a screen with painted saints of 1502 and several carved misericords (brackets on the undersides of hinged seats in the stalls.)

L

LANGTON
Lincolnshire
9 miles east of Horncastle

The small red-brick Church of St Peter and St Paul at Langton was built in 1725. It has inward-facing pews and a three-decker pulpit, and still looks much the same as it did when Dr Johnson attended there in the 18th century, when visiting a friend who lived nearby. The roof was stripped of lead in 1792, possibly to make bullets for the Napoleonic Wars.

LAVENHAM
Suffolk
6 miles northeast of Sudbury

Gatherings of Tudor houses, sagging gracefully with age, offer in Lavenham a charming example of a Suffolk wool town as it must have looked during the prosperous times of the Middle Ages. The rich merchants have gone, as has the wool trade, but they have left their legacy in the buildings, especially the Church of St Peter and St Paul standing almost cathedral-like on a hill above the village.

The community has been so scrupulous in maintaining Lavenham's character that telegraph poles were removed in 1967 and the lines hidden underground. The market place looks much as it must have done in medieval times, with its cross which was probably originally a preaching cross. It was erected in 1501, paid for by the will of a clothier. The Angel Inn has stood for about the same length of time. The market place was laid out in the 13th century, and Water Street was so named because a river ran alongside it. The origin of Shilling Street has nothing to do with money, but comes from Schyling, one of several Flemish weavers 'imported' to teach their English counterparts how best to make their cloth. For some years after 1786, Shilling Street was lived in by Isaac Taylor, author and engraver, whose daughter Jane wrote the popular nursery rhyme *Twinkle, twinkle, little star*.

Many of the items the family used during their stay are on show in the Guildhall, one of the finest Tudor half-timbered buildings in the country. It is now a museum, with exhibits of local history and industries. A display of coopers' tools and techniques is mounted in what used to be the guild of weavers' wine cellars. Many of the weavers' cottages have craft symbols in their plasterwork, including one to St Blaise, the patron saint of clothworkers. The old Wool Hall is now a part of the Swan Hotel, where a preserved section of the bar wall is covered with the signatures of American airmen of the 487th Bomb Group, who were based at airfields nearby during the Second World War.

It was these same airmen who presented an electric blower for the organ in the Church of St Peter and St Paul, greatest of all the 'wool churches' in East Anglia and owing its magnificence chiefly to the 13th Earl of Oxford and the family of Thomas Spryng, 'the Rich Clothier'. They and other wealthy merchants endowed the church in thanksgiving for the end of the Wars of the Roses in 1485.

Brent Eleigh lies 2 miles southeast. It has a fine Decorated church, St Mary's, with a later west tower, and a 14th-century south door. Inside are a 17th-century pulpit and font cover and 18th-century box-pews. The reredos is painted, with a 13th-century rood screen; wall-paintings discovered on either side in 1961 have become a focal point for visitors. The Crucifixion may have formed part of the original reredos.

ST PETER AND ST PAUL *Surrounded by rich farms, the cathedral-like church of Lavenham is a testament to medieval prosperity.*

THE LAYERS

Essex

4–6 miles southwest of Colchester

There are three 'Layer' villages within about 2 miles of each other. Layer Breton has a great heath with a church in the middle of it, an old inn and cottages. Layer-de-la-Haye, 2 miles northeast, also has attractive houses and cottages, and fine views over the 1200 acre Abberton Reservoir, winter haunt of some 20,000 wildfowl. The church boasts a Purbeck marble tomb chest and a fine Kentish rag tower.

It is Layer Marney, 1½ miles west of Layer Breton, that is perhaps the most interesting architecturally, because of its enormous gatehouse – a folly-like building. This splendid red-brick tower gatehouse is the only completed part of a magnificent early 16th-century mansion. It is the largest of all gatehouses of its kind and is notable for its wealth of terracotta architectural decoration, largely taking the form of shells and dolphins.

LEEZ PRIORY

Essex

4 miles southwest of Braintree

A 13th-century priory at Leez, or Leighs, was rebuilt by Lord Rich in 1536. The greater part of the house was razed in 1753, leaving only outer and inner gatehouses and parts of the outer quadrangle, all richly ornamented red brick. Foundations of the priory church have been excavated.

LEIGH-ON-SEA

Essex

Western district of Southend-on-Sea

Leigh-on-Sea was an old fishing and smuggling village when Southend was a mere hamlet, and it still retains much of its old-world charm. There are cockle-boats and sheds, sailors' inns and weatherboarded cottages, fine cliff views and ships moored offshore.

The font in the church at Hockley, 6 miles to the northwest, was made from three huge blocks of Purbeck marble, nearly 900 years ago, and is a fine example of early-English craftsmanship.

LEIGHTON BROMSWOLD
Cambridgeshire
5 miles west of Alconbury

Leighton Bromswold has a medieval cruciform church, St Giles, with nave and tower rebuilt in the early 17th century. The west tower has obelisk-pinnacles and on either side of the nave are twin pulpits. The church contains 16th-century monumental effigies.

At Barham, a mile or two to the east, the Norman Church of St Giles has a nave arcade and chancel arch of the period, with a 13th-century chancel and font.

LETHERINGSETT
Norfolk
1 mile west of Holt

'Larnsett', as the village of Letheringsett is called by many older folk here, belies claims that Norfolk is a flat, dull county, being situated in the broad and beautiful Glaven valley and set among magnificent trees. The landscape is man-made: William Cobbett noted in his *Rural Rides* in 1821 that it had been 'judiciously planted with trees of various sort' by the local landowner, William Hardy, where before it had been bare. The valley looks its best on a fine winter's day, unfolding behind the branches of the bare trees, with the little river winding through brilliant green meadows or rich brown fields.

The heart of Letheringsett is curiously monumental, with a handful of huge houses or farm complexes set among the oaks, beeches and cypresses. The dominant building is the 18th-century Letheringsett Hall, seat of the Barons Cozens-Hardy (creators of the village with their forebear William Hardy) until a few years ago, but now an old people's home. The massive building, with five great columns in its portico, is adjacent to the church with its round Norman tower.

In the village, flint is a common building material, with brick used to frame doors and windows, making an attractive combination. Seashore pebbles have been used to face some of the houses, creating an unusual surface which, from a distance, resembles lizard skin. The cottages which housed estate workers are a little way from the centre. Built in handsome brick and flint, they carry the ubiquitous Cozens-Hardy crest. New houses built among them are in the same materials and manner and will have blended in with them after a decade or so.

In 1957 Basil Cozens-Hardy published an excellent history of Letheringsett, which included extracts from the diary of a formidable lady named Mary Hardy. She married in 1775 and for 37 years she made an entry every day, except when she was 'poorly'. She tells how they moved into the hall on April 4, 1781 – 'a very cold day' – and almost immediately became involved in a battle for water rights.

Her husband William was a brewer and maltster – his handsome brewery still stands sentinel at the approach to the village – and he and a neighbouring farmer, Richard Rouse, endlessly tried to divert the waters of the Glaven away from each other. Mary not only records the struggle, but also the little incidents that bring history to life: 'Old sow pigged 8 pigs' ... 'The Clerk of Snoring called and borrowed 20/- of Mr Hardy and went to the fair and lost it at cards among sharpers' ... 'The town inoculated for smallpox' (June 15, 1807).

The Church of St Andrew was thoroughly – or according to the vicar 'drastically' – restored in the 1870s, but it shelters two remarkable objects: an 18th-century barrel organ and the death mask of an obscure genius. The organ needs two people to work it, one winding the mechanism that moves the barrels, the other pumping the bellows. Skilled operators can produce rich music quite unlike the tinny clatter of street barrel organs.

Tucked away high on a shelf near the door is the other treasure, the mask of Johnson Jex, blacksmith and watchmaker. According to the epitaph on his grave in the churchyard, he passed his days as the village blacksmith but mastered 'some of the greatest difficulties of science, advancing from the forge to the crucible and from the horse-shoe to the chronometer'. The 18th-century writer Arthur Young said of him: 'It is melancholy to see such a genius employed in all the work of a common blacksmith.' But Jex seems to have led a full and happy life – and a prosperous one if his large, comfortable house, still known as Foundry House, is anything to go by. The Castle Museum in Norwich contains a watch made by him, and his lathe.

LEVERINGTON
Cambridgeshire
2 miles northwest of Wisbech

The Hall at Leverington is one of the better houses in the county, part Elizabethan and part built 1660–75. There are two chimney-breasts, mullioned windows, straight gables of the 18th century and a good staircase.

The parish has several other 17th- and 18th-century houses, including Hallcroft and Lancewood. Beechwood, half a mile south of the church, has a dovecote of 1600 or earlier. Park House and the charming yellow-brick rectory, half a mile northeast of the church, are good 18th-century houses, which may be visited by appointment.

LINCOLN
Lincolnshire
120 miles north of London

Majestic, triple-towered Lincoln Cathedral, standing on a 200 ft high limestone plateau overlooking the River Witham, is at the centre of the city, surrounded by medieval buildings. The city grew up on this site because of its strategic position. Even before the Romans built a fortified camp here, and later a town, local Britons called the site Lindun – the hill-fort by the pool. The 'pool' became an inland river port, of which part survives as Brayford Pool. The Roman town was a *colonia* – a settlement for the retired legionary soldiers – and its Roman full name of *Lindum colonia* became abbreviated to Lincoln.

LINCOLN *The medieval High Bridge is unique in England, carrying shops and houses along its west side.*

Under the Danes, Lincoln enjoyed thriving commercial links with Scandinavia – coins minted in the city and found on the far side of the North Sea are evidence of trading connections.

Lincoln's later, medieval prosperity came from wool, which was exported in huge quantities to Flanders for weaving into cloth. Since the mid-19th century, the city has developed as a major manufacturing and engineering centre.

The cathedral, the third largest in Britain, after St Paul's and York Minster, rises to 271 ft. Lincoln became the centre of a bishopric in 1072 and a cathedral was begun at once, but much of the present church dates from after an earthquake in 1185. It has been little altered since its completion about 1280. The medieval craftsmen who built it shaped a miracle in wood, glass and honey-coloured stone that seems to change colour in varying light. From the Observatory Tower at the southeast corner of the wall walk of the Norman castle there is a bird's-eye view of the west face of the cathedral. Within the castle is a unique prisoners' chapel.

Near the cathedral is the Bishop's Palace, started in the 12th century. It has fallen into ruins, but these have been restored and are open to the public.

Lincoln has well-preserved Roman remains, including the splendid Newport Arch marking the north gate of the Roman settlement. The steep cobbled streets leading to the lower town are lined by medieval houses, many of them now antique shops.

Lincoln also has several Norman domestic buildings, built c. 1170, when England's kings were encouraging the Jews to finance trade. On the roof of the Guildhall is the 14th-century Mote Bell, which is still rung to call the city fathers to council meetings. The shops on the High Bridge date from the 14th to the 16th centuries, and stand on a 12th-century bridge – the oldest in Britain still to carry buildings.

In the Usher Art Gallery are collections of Tennyson manuscripts and of paintings by Peter de Wint, one of the foremost British watercolourists of the early 19th century. There are also displays of antique watches, coins, porcelain and enamels. At the Museum of Lincolnshire Life at the Old Barracks, the daily existence of the people of the county from Tudor times is set forth.

The City and County Museum and the National Cycle Museum offer further interesting stops. The old racecourse is now used only for occasional point-to-point races. The 11 mile long Fossdyke Navigation Canal, first excavated by the Romans and linking the River Witham to the Trent, has a towpath which provides pleasant walking as far as the Pyewipe Inn; 'pyewipe' is Lincolnshire dialect for the lapwing or peewit.

LITTLE BADDOW
Essex
5 miles east of Chelmsford

Set in the north wall of Little Baddow's 14th-century church is an unadorned entrance known as a 'Devil Door'. To medieval Christians, the north side of the church was the province of Satan. It was the left hand facing the altar and Christ had said that he would 'set the sheep on His right hand and the goats on His left'. Because of this baptisms were performed in the south porch of the church. If an infant cried after being christened, it was traditionally thought to be a sign

that the Devil had been driven from its soul, and the north door, which was left open during the ceremony, allowed Satan to escape 'to his own place'.

LITTLE GIDDING
Cambridgeshire
5 miles southwest of Stilton

In 1625 Nicholas Ferrar, the son of a prosperous merchant family, turned his back on worldly things, brought his mother and many relatives to Little Gidding, and vowed to lead a life of prayer and good works. The family rebuilt the Church of St John the Evangelist, which had been used as a barn and pigsty, established a small local school, and tended to the poor and ailing. Despite their wish for seclusion, the Ferrars attracted both respectful and suspicious attention.

Charles I came to visit them – the third time, in 1646, in search of a hiding place from Cromwell's forces. Word of this last visit leaked out later, and the house and church were sacked by the Roundheads as a reprisal. The church was rebuilt in the early 18th century and added to in the 19th and 20th centuries. Outside the door of the small church is the table-tomb of Nicholas Ferrar who died in 1637, aged 45. The beliefs and practice of Ferrar's community, known as the Arminian Nunnery, inspired the last poem in T.S. Eliot's sequence 'Four Quartets' to which he gave the title 'Little Gidding'.

LITTLE WALSINGHAM
Norfolk
5 miles south of Wells-next-the-Sea

In its woodland setting, Little Walsingham village provides a splash of colour, with red-brick and timber-framed houses, whitewashed fronts and red, pantiled roofs. The High Street broadens out into a square, called Common Place, in the middle of which is a 16th-century octagonal pump-house. An iron brazier, known as The Beacon, on the stone roof of the pump-house, was once the only form of street lighting in the village. On the south side of the square is the flint-faced Shire Hall, and next to it a long building with an overhanging timber-framed upper floor.

Little Walsingham is most notable for its Shrine of Our Lady of Walsingham, one of the chief centres of pilgrimage in England from early medieval times until the Reformation. In 1601 Lady Richeldis de Faverches, the lady of the manor, had a vision in which she was commanded by the Virgin Mary to establish a *Santa Casa*, a replica of the Nazarene House of the Annunciation. The shrine she built was soon added to by Augustinian and Franciscan foundations. Henry VIII made a pilgrimage to Walsingham from East Barsham, although years later, after his quarrel with the Papacy, he had the shrine destroyed. The slipper chapel at Houghton, where pilgrims would take off their shoes before completing their journey to the shrine barefoot, is still a place of pilgrimage. Between 1931 and 1937 Anglo-Catholics established a new Italianate shrine. The grounds of the original priory, which was also destroyed by Henry VIII, contain an imposing archway remnant.

Fakenham, 4 miles southwest of Little Walsingham, is a market town with a partly 15th-century church and some Georgian buildings. A further 3 miles south-west is Raynham Hall, the home of the early 18th-century agriculturalist and politician the 2nd Viscount Townshend. He was known as 'Turnip Townshend', because he encouraged the growing of turnips and, more importantly, evolved the system of crop rotation. The hall is still the home of members of the Townshend family.

LODDON
Norfolk
6 miles northwest of Beccles

The Church of the Holy Trinity at Lodden is a 15th-century building, with large clerestory, west tower and a two-storey south porch with stair-turret. The pulpit is Jacobean. Of the monuments and brasses, the most notable is the one of a reclining Lady Williamson (*d.* 1684) sculpted in marble.

LONG MELFORD
Suffolk
3 miles north of Sudbury

The main street through Long Melford stretches 3 miles along the route of a former Roman highway. At its north end the road crosses a stream by a bridge built in 1792 to replace the ford which gave Melford part of its name. The road splays out onto an attractive village green, then carries on past the long wall and turreted gatehouse of Melford Hall towards Bury St Edmunds. On the other side of the green an uneven row of cottages crawls upwards in leisurely fashion towards Elizabethan Trinity Hospital. Beyond them the Church of the Holy Trinity presents what is probably the best display of flushwork – ornate decoration in flint – in the county.

The village is rich in tradition. For example, there is the 16th-century haunted inn, The Bull, which has an old galleried courtyard. Some years ago, there were reports of objects being thrown about and furniture being rearranged during the night. From time to time there were also inexplicable chills near the dining-room door, where a murder was committed in 1648.

When the shrine and abbey of Bury St Edmunds grew in importance during the Middle Ages, Melford Manor was the country retreat and deer park of its abbots. Around the time of the Dissolution of the Monasteries, Henry VIII granted the manor to William Cordell, a rich lawyer who built both Melford Hall and the hospital. Cordell went on to become Speaker of the House of Commons and Master of the Rolls. He entertained Elizabeth I at the hall in 1578, when she was welcomed by '200 young gentlemen in white velvet, 300 in black and 1500 serving men'.

Since 1786 the house, whose 'pepperpot' towers

LONG MELFORD *The timber-framed and galleried Bull Inn in the High Street is said to be haunted.*

stick up above the high wall, has been the home of the Parkers, a family of distinguished seafarers. Admiral Sir Hyde Parker sailed around the world with Lord Anson, and later commanded the North Sea Fleet in 1781 in the indecisive Battle of the Dogger Bank against the Dutch. His son, another Sir Hyde, is remembered as the man to whom Nelson turned his blind eye when the order was given to break off the action at the Battle of Copenhagen in 1801.

The well-kept grounds of the hall contain a charming octagonal Tudor pavilion which overlooks the village green. A large monument to Cordell, in the 15th-century Holy Trinity Church, was designed by the royal mason, Cornelius Cure, who also designed the monument to Mary, Queen of Scots in Westminster Abbey. Among other local benefactors were the Clopton family of Kentwell Hall, just visible across the parkland through a noble avenue of limes.

The Clopton chantry in the church has a frieze of painted scrolls carrying a poem by the 15th-century poet monk John Lydgate, of Bury St Edmunds. On the east wall of the beautiful Lady Chapel there is a multiplication table marked out as a memento of its days as a schoolroom from 1669 to 1880. The tower was built in 1725, replacing one destroyed by lightning. In 1903 it was encased in flushwork.

LOUTH

Lincolnshire
14 miles south of Grimsby

A Lincolnshire lad, Alfred Tennyson attended Louth Grammar School – which he loathed – from 1816 to 1820. Later the future Poet Laureate had his first book of verse, *Poems by Two Brothers,* which he wrote with his brother Charles, published in the town by the booksellers J. & J. Jackson. The shop, now called Parkers, still stands in the Market Place. They were paid £20 for their work – the payment being half in books and half in cash.

Louth was an important market centre in the days of the Domesday Survey, and remains so still; on market days the shops and stalls do a thriving trade beneath the shadow of the Victorian Gothic Market Hall. Many streets in the centre have names ending in 'gate' which, as. in other northern and east Midland towns, does not mean an opening, but is derived from the Saxon word for a street or walkway.

In May 1920 the River Lud, which winds through the centre of the town, burst its banks after heavy rainfall. Water and mud flooded the lower rooms of many of the houses, and 23 people were drowned. Nearly all of the town's bridges were destroyed and some inscribed stones in Bridge Street, Eastgate and James Street – where three houses were swept away by the torrent – record the height that the flood reached.

From whichever direction Louth is approached, the soaring hexagonal spire of the 15th-century parish church of St James is an unavoidable landmark. Reaching 295 ft high, it is said to be the tallest parish church spire in England. At the western end of the town, Thorpe Hall is an impressive 17th-century house. In Louth Park are the remains of a Cistercian abbey, founded in 1139 and dissolved in 1536.

LOWESTOFT

Suffolk
38 miles northeast of Ipswich

Wide, sandy beaches, and the inland lakes and rivers of the Broads, have made Lowestoft a major resort. Fishing was the main industry from the middle of the last century until recently. An 18th-century smoke house is still in use in Raglan Street. Lowestoft was the birthplace of Thomas Nash (1567–1601), the poet and dramatist, and of the composer Benjamin Britten (1913-76).

The main part of the port, which has a dry dock and shipyard, lies upriver and is used mainly by grain and timber ships. The outer harbour is the home of the yacht club and the Lowestoft lifeboat station which was founded in 1801, 23 years before the establishment of the Royal National Lifeboat Institution.

Cobbled steps known as The Scores lead down the cliffs to the site of the original beach village, now an industrial estate. Sparrow's Nest, named after one of the founders of the lifeboat station, is a park with a theatre and other entertainments. It includes a maritime museum, at Bowling Green Cottage. At Carlton Colville, 3 miles southwest, is the East Anglia Transport Museum. Working exhibits include trams and a narrow-gauge railway.

Oulton Broad, one of the finest stretches of inland water in the country, offers almost every type of boat for hire, coarse angling, sailing regattas and motor-boat races.

Four miles northwest of Lowestoft is Blundeston, whose Norman Church of St Mary the Virgin has a round west tower, and a 14th-century nave; the chancel was rebuilt in the 19th century. The south and north doorways are basically Norman. Inside are the remains of rood screens and benches.

LUDHAM

Norfolk
5 miles east of Hoveton

The 14th- and 15th-century Church of St Catherine at Ludham contains a decorated sedilia and a hammer-beam roof to the nave. The octagonal font is carved with figures and lions, the screen has painted figures of saints. A mural of the Crucifixion is painted on the chancel arch.

About 3 miles south is St Benet's Abbey, on the River Bure. It is an early Benedictine monastery, possibly begun in AD 816. It was certainly re-established in 955, and was endowed under King Canute to become the great, fortified abbey of St Benet-at-Holm. The few remaining ruins include the 15th-century west gatehouse, dominated by a windmill. The outer walls, once enclosing 38 acres, and the church foundations are recognisable. The barn of Horning Hall nearby was the chapel of the hospice of the abbey.

LOUTH *The 295 ft steeple of St James is thought to be one of the most perfect Perpendicular examples in the country.*

M

MADINGLEY
Cambridgeshire
4 miles northwest of Cambridge

From the uplands surrounding the American Military Cemetery at Madingley and from the byroads between the A45 and Comberton or Coton, there are many glimpses of Cambridge between long rollers of undulating farmland. Papworth Everard, in the wooded lanes further west, has an enlightened village settlement for the handicapped. Caxton, nearby, has a fine coaching inn and a pebbly 15th-century church.

At New Wimple a tree-lined avenue leads to the county's greatest mansion, Wimpole Hall, which was built by Sir Thomas Chichele in about 1640 and which was then considerably altered in the 18th century by the 1st Earl of Hardwicke. A sham castle in the park was built about the same time.

Madingley Hall, an Elizabethan mansion which today belongs to Cambridge University, was where the future Edward VII lodged when he was an undergraduate. The nearby post-mill (in which the whole body of the mill revolves on the base), removed from Ellington, Cambridgeshire to Madingley in 1936, is worth seeing.

MALDON
Essex
9 miles east of Chelmsford

Tall-masted sailing barges moored at Hythe Quay bear witness to Maldon's maritime past and present. Once they were commercial vessels on regular hauls to London and beyond. Now they give youngsters adventure holidays. The Hythe is Saxon for 'wharf', and was a port and landing-place on the River Blackwater before the Normans came. Its Maritime Centre has graphic displays and information about the barges, the port and the river. Behind The Hythe stands the Church of St Mary, its 17th-century tower topped by a tiny timber turret and spire, added in 1740. Farther along the reach, boat-building yards flourish.

Across from St Mary's, the High Street stretches up to the 13th-century Church of All Saints, which has the only triangular church tower in England. Nearby is the Moot Hall, built about 1440 by the MP for the borough, Sir Robert D'Arcy, as his town house. In 1576 it became the local council headquarters, and the Council Chamber and Old Courthouse are preserved.

A pillared balcony over the pavement was added in the 19th century, and the building is still used for some meetings. Just below it is St Peter's Tower – all that remains of a church that collapsed in the 1660s – and the brick library built onto it by a local cleric, Dr Thomas Plume, later that century. He was Archdeacon of Rochester when he died in 1704 and left his vast library and paintings to Maldon.

MALDON *The 13th-century Church of All Saints is the proud owner of the only triangular tower in England.*

Immediately below the Plume Library is Maldon Museum, which has mementos of the town's most unusual native son, Edward Bright. Born in 1721, Bright grew to weigh almost 42 stones and was the heaviest man then known to have lived in Britain (the heaviest ever was a Scot, William Campbell, 1856–78, who weighed 53½ stones). Bright died at 29 and is buried in a vault at All Saints. The Parish burial register notes that he was 'comely in his person, affable in his temper, a tender father and valuable friend'.

MANUDEN

Essex
3 miles north of Bishop's Stortford

The little River Stort and streams such as Wicken Water, which is often dry in summer, wind between some of the prettiest villages and hamlets in Essex. Walls of flint taken from the chalkland riverbeds give way to timbered and plastered houses on the arable farmlands of the boulder clay. One snug little settlement is echoed within a few miles by another.

Manuden is such a village, giving an immediate impression of whiteness – very white plaster and whitewashed brickwork. A house on the corner of Mallows Green Road combines pargetted panels of almost classical formality with white weatherboarding. But across the lane two superb barns in the farmyard of The Bury provide a contrast, with massive thatch above timber and brick. Peeping from the houses along the road and lanes are profusions of little dormer windows with tiled caps.

The Church of St Mary the Virgin has been much restored but still contains a medieval chancel screen and some interesting memorials; a 17th-century one to Sir William Waad gives a list in Latin of all the many important posts he held and claims that his father, Armigel, Clerk of the Council to Henry VIII and Edward VI, was the first Englishman to discover America. Waad's family home was Battles Hall, near to a hamlet with the undignified name of Maggots End. Battles is a corruption of Bataille, the name of the manorial family who for generations used a church transept as their chapel.

Facing the churchyard gate to The Street, a sagging house with a wavy roof and similarly undulating timbers along its overhanging upper storey was built in the 14th century, then rebuilt during the reign of Elizabeth I. Farther along, Yew Tree Inn took its name from a spreading yew tree growing in its courtyard, now replaced by a neat, conical trimmed descendant. In coaching times, the original alehouse had its own wheelwright's shop, run in conjunction with a cobbler's and a bakery.

Manuden House, a Queen Anne mansion with a 19th-century stucco coating, stands on a tight bend in The Street behind impressive iron railings, with gilded owls peering down from the gates. It possesses elegant panelling and a fine staircase. The red brick of its equally imposing Georgian neighbour, the old parsonage, is complemented by a cheerful red stable block, detached to form a private house around a cobbled yard, with a smartly repainted clock.

Manuden Hall, across a narrow, humped bridge carrying a minor road north towards Saffron Walden, is a mixture of Tudor brickwork and restoration, including Victorian windows and a slate roof, introduced after a fire started by a drunkard in 1888.

MANNINGTREE

Essex
8 miles northeast of Colchester

An attractive little port, Manningtree is famous for its swans, its maltings for fermenting barley, and its sailing barges. At neighbouring Mistley, the two great towers of the church were designed by Robert Adam and are the last remnants of an attempt by Richard Rigby, MP, Paymaster General of the Forces in 1762, to build an elegant little 18th-century spa town. There are many pleasant Victorian, Georgian and older houses, and a large stone swan admires itself in a fountain.

MARCH

Cambridgeshire
14 miles east of Peterborough

The large railway junction at March straggles beside the River Nene. The 15th-century Church of St Wendreda is dedicated to a Saxon lady who founded a small religious community here. The glory of the church is a double hammerbeam roof which has angels with outstretched wings carved in wood at the ends of the hammerbeams. Some of the angels hold medieval musical instruments, including the clarion, lute, pipe, organ and fiddle. The roof, built about 1500, has 118 angels and 18 saints and martyrs. The devil has also been included, possibly by a mischievous craftsman.

MERSEA ISLAND

Essex
Island joined to mainland by causeway across Strood Channel

The little island of Mersea is famous among small-boat sailors. West Mersea is overcrowded with houses and boats, but attractive old fishing cottages survive in the old town. The White Hart Inn stands opposite the Norman and 14th-century church; the Victory Inn overlooks the yacht anchorage. In contrast East Mersea is set amid relatively unspoilt farmland and grazing marshes.

Wealthy families of the early Roman period in southeast Britain buried the cremated remains of their dead beneath vast conical mounds of earth called tumuli. The tumulus on Mersea Island is the only one in Britain where you can actually enter the burial cavity. The cremation urn is in Colchester Museum.

MILDENHALL

Suffolk
8 miles northeast of Newmarket

The name Mildenhall will always be associated with a rich treasure of 4th-century Roman silverware. By the end of the 4th century AD, the Roman Empire in Europe was under threat from barbarian tribes battering on its borders. Troops were pulled out of Britain to defend frontiers nearer Rome, leaving the land vulnerable to attacks by Saxons, Picts and Scots. As the barbarian raids grew more frequent and more serious, Britain's villas were gradually abandoned. During these troublesome times, a wealthy family living at Mildenhall buried their silverware for safety. They never recovered it, and the hoard lay in the ground for

nearly 1600 years, until it was unearthed during ploughing in the early 1940s. Over 30 pieces were found and are now displayed in the British Museum.

In 1780 the lord of the manor, Sir Thomas Bunbury, tossed a coin with Lord Derby to decide which of their names should be given to a proposed horse race. If Lord Derby had lost, there would have been a Bunbury Day at Epsom instead of a Derby Day.

The north porch of the Church of St Mary and St Andrew is the largest in Suffolk. Over the porch is the Parvis Chamber, which was also used as a schoolroom in the Middle Ages. Arrowheads and small shot fired by Cromwell's supporters have been found embedded in the woodwork of the angel roof of the nave.

MONKS ELEIGH

Suffolk
5 miles northwest of Hadleigh

The main road – The Street – follows one bank of the meandering River Brett, while the thatched and timbered houses of Swingleton Green stand in graceful seclusion higher up on the opposite bank. The two parts of Monks Eleigh village are linked by an old footpath known as The Causeway, which incorporates a Victorian footbridge.

In Saxon times, the settlement was that of a leader called Illa and so became Illanlege – Illa's wood – and eventually Eleigh. The monks were those of Canterbury, into whose hands the property came in medieval times. During the 14th and 15th centuries, the inhabitants shared in the prosperity of neighbouring wool and cloth towns and had a guildhall on The Street. Dating from 1400, it has been a builder's workshop in modern times and is now a private house.

The imposing outline of St Peter's Church, with its buttresses and stair tower – once a familiar sight on railway posters advertising the area – crowns a rising triangular green complete with Victorian parish pump. On one side, Hall Farm shelters behind trees, on the other lies a wavering rank of variegated cottages,

MERSEA ISLAND *The marshes of the eastern island have changed little in the last century, and still feed grazing livestock.*

thatched and tiled, and at different pitches and angles, which spill down towards The Street. The house called Hobarts is a sturdy survivor of the early 15th century, and the Fenn is a 16th-century building with an elegant Georgian frontage grafted on.

On a hill southeast of the village stands Bridge Farm. Among its crops are varieties of maize developed over years of research to produce cobs coloured light and deep purple, brown and ivory. A small showroom in The Rise, by the crossroads, displays maize dolls and traditional corn dollies, the corn also being cultivated in different varieties on the farm. Visitors are welcome and may see dolls and straw decorations being made.

To the west is one of the prettiest villages in Suffolk, also on the River Brett. Chelsworth has a two-arched bridge which crosses the river, and there are attractive timber-framed thatched houses; the Grange is dated 1694 and the rectory was built in the late 18th century.

MOULTON

Lincolnshire
4 miles east of Spalding

In the village of Moulton is the impressive Church of All Saints, with a late Perpendicular tower and spire. There is fine work in the foliage capitals of the pillars in the nave, and an 18th-century font, recently restored, is embellished with figures of Adam and Eve. The village itself has a charming green.

About 2 miles to the east is Whaplode, whose Church of St Mary has four eastern bays of the original Norman church remaining, constituting the main body of the building. The three western bays are in the Transitional style, and the tower was begun in the 12th century. There are a number of monuments from the 13th century onwards, including a remarkable one of the late 16th century to the Irby family.

NARBOROUGH

Norfolk

5 miles northwest of Swaffham

Narborough is famed for its elegant Church of All Saints, which can claim Norman origins with later additions. There are some pieces of 15th-century stained glass. There are monuments dating from c.1300, to members of the Spelman family, many with effigies, and a number of magnificent brasses.

The monument to Clement Spelman (*d.* 1672), which has been mistakenly attributed to Caius Gabriel Cibber, shows him standing dressed in the costume of the period. The story is that, being a proud man, he insisted on being interred standing up so that no one would be able to walk on him. In 1865 the monument was opened, and it was found that the coffin was indeed upright.

NAVENBY

Lincolnshire

9 miles south of Lincoln

The Church of St Peter at Navenby has a fine De-corated east window that is an exceptionally good example of its kind. The Easter Sepulchre, which is on the north side of the chancel, is embellished with delicately carved figures, including those of three Roman soldiers. The westernmost of the pillars on the north side has an ancient seat at the bottom.

NAYLAND

Suffolk

6 miles north of Colchester

The centre of Nayland is a jumble of colourwashed dwellings with overhanging timbers, patches of cobble, tiles turning sometimes to near orange, and a milestone obelisk which could be mistaken for a market cross. The village stands near the mouth of the River Stour, and can trace its history back to when it was the Domesday lordship of *Eilanda* – the Old English word for 'island'. This came about because the original manor stood on a moated field, now called Court Knoll, which was once so close to the river that its moat was always full.

High Street was once divided in two along its length by a row of cottages, but is now one street with detached gabled houses on one side and a continuous stretch of buildings on the other. The hub of the village is the 15th-century Alston Court, which has a big 17th-century door and mullioned windows.

The Guildhall, in the High Street, is a survivor of 16th-century prosperity from the wool trade. It is now a private house. The bridge over the Stour was originally made of wood and was maintained by a bequest from a wealthy clothier, John Abel, who died in 1523. His symbol – the letter A and a bell on the keystone – was preserved when the bridge was rebuilt of more sturdy material in 1959.

In 1525, another Abel, William, presented a porch to the Church of St James, which dates from 1400. Its tower was damaged by an earthquake in the last century and it was replaced by the present spire in 1963. Inside, part of the Lady Altar covering was used at the coronation of Elizabeth II. On the altar is one of John Constable's rare religious paintings, showing Christ blessing the bread and wine.

NEEDHAM MARKET

Suffolk

3 miles southeast of Stowmarket

Needham Market is a graceful town that reflects the centuries-long agricultural prosperity of East Anglia. The Georgian houses in the High Street are of especial interest; so, too, is the Bull Hotel, with its carved corner post, the Friends' Meeting House and graveyard and the 17th-century grammar school.

The 15th-century Church of St John the Baptist possesses one of the most superb hammerbeam roofs in England, such a daring piece of design and carpen-try that it makes one wonder how it stays up. It has been called by one historian 'The culminating achieve-ment of the English carpenter'. It is as high as the walls upon which it rests, and if removed whole and placed on the ground it would make a substantial building of its own. It is decorated with carved angels, some with their wings outspread, others upswept, which were added in the 19th century when the church was restored. The clerestory is also incorporated into the roof. The chancel and sanctuary are spacious and the exterior of the church is unusual; it has buttresses and flint walls which seem to rise up straight from the passing street; there is no space for either a church-yard or bell tower.

NEW BUCKENHAM

Norfolk

4 miles southeast of Attleborough

The medieval pattern of streets set in rows and crossing almost at right angles has been preserved in the village of New Buckenham, though few of its buildings date from earlier than the 17th century. Georgian houses stand on the former market place, now a grass-covered green with a 17th-century market house built on nine wooden pillars. The one at the centre was the village whipping post.

The village became 'new' about 1150, when a Norman baron, William II de Albini, gave his castle at Old Buckenham to Augustinian canons and built a new one 1½ miles away. Its moated ramparts still stand, and in the centre are the remains of what is thought to be the first round keep in England. A barn near the keep was originally the castle chapel.

Until the 15th century, the castle chapel was New Buckenham's parish church. The present church, St Martin's, has roof timbers supported on stone effigies of the twelve Apostles.

THEY'RE OFF *Newmarket life revolves around horses – whether on the racecourse or exercising on the heath.*

NEWMARKET
Suffolk
13 miles east of Cambridge

The headquarters of British horse racing since the 17th century, Newmarket houses two of the turf's most revered institutions: the Jockey Club and Tattersalls. The Jockey Club, in the High Street, was founded in 1752 by a group of racehorse owners and it now governs every aspect of racing, including the licensing of jockeys, trainers and racecourses. The present building, next door to the fascinating National Horse Racing Museum, dates from 1882. However, its handsome red-brick front was added in 1933. Tattersalls – with its bowling-green turf, pristine stabling and magnificent covered sale ring, is just off the High Street in The Avenue. Horse sales – which are open to the public – have been held here since the 1880s. The station at which horses leave and arrive for the sales is a Palladian-style extravaganza.

Monarchs from James I to the present Queen Elizabeth have gone to Newmarket races. When Charles II was there in March 1683, a fire broke out which destroyed most of the town. Among the surviving buildings is Nell Gwynne's House in Palace Street, where the king's mistress is said to have stayed whenever Charles visited Newmarket.

The town, with its two racecourses, stables, horse-breeding and training establishments, is flanked by the vast expanse of Newmarket Heath. During peak periods, there may be some 2000 horses exercising on the 2500 acres here at any one time. Beside the heath is the 500 acre National Stud, which houses some of the world's finest stallions. About 20 miles of fencing have been put up to form paddocks, and thousands of trees provide shelter from the winds that can whip across the open country. The stud is open by appointment in August and September.

In Newmarket itself 'monuments' to the sport of kings include two old coaching inns in the High Street at which racegoers stay – the Rutland Arms Hotel and the White Hart Hotel opposite the Jockey Club. Just off the High Street is the traffic-free Rookery Shopping Precinct, in which a twice-weekly market is held.

The comparatively new Hall at Landwade, 3 miles northwest of Newmarket, incorporates part of the original mansion built in 1445. The treasures of this remote and quiet hamlet, which consist of Hall, church and a few cottages, are the superb tombs in the church. They commemorate the Cotton family, who first settled in Landwade in the 15th century.

NEWPORT
Essex
3 miles southwest of Saffron Walden

Lying near a motorway and bisected by the Bishop's Stortford road, Newport has always been affected by roads, as a scale of charges ('For every ass . . .½d') by the old Toll Bridge bears witness. Yet much of the village is tucked away from the main road, looped back in charming, narrow streets, with only a glimpse of traffic at their ends.

In the 13th century, Newport had a market, mills, numerous inns for travellers, and gave work to furriers, dyers, vintners and even a goldsmith. At that time, it was held by the King of the Romans, an archaic title for King John's second son. He was heartily detested by the great landowner, Roger Bigod, who seriously damaged Newport's trade by opening a rival market at Great Chesterford, 6 miles north. But like Saffron Walden, Newport began to grow the saffron crocus and entered a long period of prosperity.

Most of Newport's splendours belong to this time. The church was developed and the humbly named Monk's Barn, in the main street, was built in the 15th century. No one should miss Monk's Barn. Composed of dark red bricks, laid in herringbone pattern, it has a crumbling oak carving under one window of the Virgin in Heaven. Far from being a barn, it was the summer holiday retreat of the monks of St Martin-le-Grand in London. By The Green is a delightful group of houses. Three late medieval buildings particularly leap to the eye – Martin's Farm, with its tall pedestal of patterned Tudor chimneys, the Old Three Tuns and the Crown House, which has wonderful plasterwork and, over the door, a hood shaped like an oyster-shell and dated 1692.

To the north is the park of Shortgrove Hall, a mid-17th-century house burnt down in 1966 and, opposite, high on a hillock once occupied by a Norman castle, is the grammar school, founded in 1588, although the present buildings are mostly Victorian.

The Church of St Mary the Virgin stands on another hill in the heart of the village. Gathered round it are pleasant cottages, some Victorian, others much older; these are swaybacked, with dormer windows, and roofed with an unusual combination of thatch and tile – the thatch thrown around the shoulders of the cottages like old and friendly shawls. The church is grand, dating mostly from the 13th to the 16th centuries. Its chief treasure is an extremely rare 13th-century altar chest – a kind of travelling altar with compartments for vestments and plate. Its lid bears some of the earliest known oil paintings in the country.

Beside the road, almost opposite the grammar school, lies a very large brown boulder which holds a special place in Newport's affections. It is called the Leper Stone, and the grooves cut in its surface are said to be where alms were left for lepers; the ancient masonry in the wall beside may be part of a medieval hospice for poor travellers, or perhaps lepers.

Matters medical have frequently engaged the interest of the village. In the 1670s, Mistress Hannah Wooley, the wife of a schoolmaster, published her *Gentlewoman's Companion,* and enjoyed a considerable local reputation for her medicines. For everyday maladies she prescribed snail water, whose recipe begins 'Take a peck of snails with houses on their backs...' But for really serious illnesses, she advises that the best remedy is a dose of woodlice.

NEWPORT *Stained glass dating from the 14th century decorates the lancet windows of St Mary the Virgin.*

NORTH ELMHAM
Norfolk
5 miles north of East Dereham

At North Elmham, the ruins of an early 11th-century Saxon cathedral blend with the ruins of a manor house of 1386, lying in a moated enclosure. The Saxon remains can be distinguished by the large blocks of dark brown stone. Elmham was the See of the Bishop of the 'North Folk' from c. 600 or even earlier. Compared to other churches of the Saxon period, the cathedral was built on a grand scale: 123 ft long with an aisle-less nave and transept. There were once twin towers, but today the remains are only 10 ft high. The See was moved to Thetford in 1701, and not long after was finally settled in Norwich.

The original Church of St Mary was built in 1093 as an act of penance for simony – purchase of ecclesiastical benefices. One of the original Norman windows can be seen on the south side. Features include a rood screen with many painted saints, and 14th-century stained glass.

NORTH END
Essex
3 miles southeast of Great Dunmow

The little building in North End known as the Black Chapel is unusual for three reasons: few timber-framed church buildings survive; there are few old chapels left in Essex; and the priest's house is built into the church. Nave, chancel and the priest's dwelling are of the late 15th century, and there are some modern additions.

The attractive interior has benches and a screen of c. 1500, early 18th-century communion rails and 18th-century box-pews.

NORTH RUNCTON
Norfolk
3 miles southeast of King's Lynn

The Church of All Saints at North Runcton has the reputation for being one of the finest 18th-century churches in Norfolk. It was built in 1703–13 and is attributed to Henry Bell, designer of King's Lynn custom house. The west tower has a lantern. The nave has a slight projection north and south, while the chapel, which projects on the south side of the chancel, is a late 19th-century addition.

In the nave four Ionic columns support a dome, and there are other Ionic columns and pilasters. The panelling and reredos, designed by Henry Bell in 1684, come from St Margaret's, King's Lynn. The paintings in the reredos are Florentine.

NORWICH
Norfolk
98 miles northeast of London

East Anglia's flourishing capital, Norwich is watched over by the gleaming spire of its dignified cathedral and wrapped in the shimmering thread of the River Wensum. The name of Norwich appears on coins minted during the reign of King Athelstan, at the beginning of the 10th century AD. At the time of the

Norman Conquest the city was one of the largest in England, with a population of 5500.

The city flourished under the Normans, attracting many craftsmen and becoming a major centre for the lucrative wool trade by the end of the 14th century. Then, as now, the surrounding countryside was exceptionally fertile and, in medieval times, the Rivers Wensum and Yare provided a convenient export route to the sea. The prospering city also had its share of problems. There was a bloody riot in 1272, when the citizens fought with the cathedral monks who tried to impose tolls on the annual fair held at Tombland. In 1349 the 'Black Death' claimed an estimated 2000 people – roughly one-third of the entire population – and in 1381 Norwich was captured and its mayor was killed by rebels during the Peasant's Revolt. The insurgents were eventually defeated by an army under the warrior-bishop Henry le Despenser, who is remembered by a splendid decorated screen behind the altar which he gave to the cathedral.

Civil strife flared up in the city again in 1549. A rebel army of 20,000 yeoman farmers, protesting against the enclosure of common land, was routed by the Earl of Warwick, and the rebel leader, Robert Kett from nearby Wymondham, was hanged from the walls of Norwich Castle.

Towards the end of the 16th century the population of Norwich was increased by many settlers from the Netherlands, who did much to revive the textile industry. These and other settlers from Europe are recalled in the name of the Strangers' Hall, a large and rambling mansion in Charing Cross.

The earliest parts of the Strangers' Hall date from 1320 and, 600 years later, the house became a museum of domestic life. The rooms are decorated and furnished in many styles, from Tudor to Victorian. Exhibits range from underwear to traditional tradesmen's signs. In the coach house, a splendid Lord Mayor's carriage stands beside a car originally owned by the Hon. C. S. Rolls, one of the founders of Rolls-Royce Ltd.

The cathedral was started between 1094–96 by Herbert de Losinga, the first Bishop of Norwich. Norfolk flints formed the core of the building, but the beautiful white stone of the exterior came from Caen, in Normandy, reaching Norwich by way of Great Yarmouth and the River Wensum. On the last stage of its journey the stone was shipped along a short canal dug to link the cathedral to the river. The little canal was used for 300 years, and its course is now followed by a lane which runs from Lower Close to Pull's Ferry.

Inside the cathedral, the nave roof is a superb work

NORWICH *Greens and closes surround the clustered buildings of the cathedral and cloisters* (above).

PULL'S FERRY *Lying at the bottom of Lower Close, this was once the supply station for the local monastery* (overleaf).

of art. It was embellished between 1465 and 1510 and has bosses painted with biblical scenes telling the story of mankind from the Creation right through to the Last Judgement. The roof can be studied closely through a series of mirrors on wheels. Similar bosses, portraying everything from saints and musicians to grotesque creatures, may be seen in the cloisters, one of the largest in any English cathedral. They were rebuilt after being burned during the riot of 1272.

Set in the wall near St Luke's Chapel is a stone effigy dating from about 1100. It may represent Herbert de Losinga, Pope Gregory I or St Peter, and is possibly the oldest Christian effigy in England. St Luke's and St Saviour's chapels both contain paintings by unknown 14th-century Norwich painters that rival Italian works of the same period.

The cathedral spire was added by Bishop James Goldwell at the end of the 15th century. Its topmost point is 315 ft above the ground – the highest land in Norfolk is only 329 ft above sea-level – and only Salisbury, among British cathedrals, is taller.

Nurse Edith Cavell, executed by the Germans in 1916 for helping Allied prisoners to escape from occupied Brussels, is buried in a simple grave close to the South Door. Juliana of Norwich, a 15th-century mystic, is commemorated in the cathedral every year on May 8. Her theological treatise *XVI Revelations of Divine Love* was the first book to be written in English by a woman.

The Cathedral Close runs down to the river and has many fine buildings. The main entrances from Tombland are St Ethelbert Gate and the Erpingham Gate, opposite the cathedral's west front. This gate is carved with many figures and was the gift of Sir Thomas Erpingham in 1420. He commanded the archers at the Battle of Agincourt, and was immortalised by Shakespeare in *King Henry V*. Inside the gates, beside the cathedral, is King Edward VI School; nearby stands a statue of its most famous pupil, Lord Nelson.

THE MUSTARD SHOP *Colman's is the Norwich firm which has become synonymous with English mustard.*

Norwich Castle dates from the early part of the 12th century. The original walls were made of Caen stone, like the cathedral, but they were refaced with Bath stone in 1834–9. The huge keep – one of the largest in the country – is now a museum and houses a fascinating variety of exhibits. They include the world's finest collection of Lowestoft porcelain, weapons, musical instruments and many works by John Crome (1768–1821), John Cotman (1782–1842) and other artists of what became known as the Norwich school. From 1220 to 1887 the castle was the county gaol, and in the dungeons are the death masks of prisoners executed there.

Although the River Wensum formed a natural line of defence on three sides, the city was given the additional protection of walls 20 ft high at one end of the 14th century. There were ten fortified gateways with a series of towers between them. The remains are seen at their best on Carrow Hill, where a 50 yd section of wall climbs steeply to the Black Tower. At the foot of the hill, on either side of the river, are the remains of boom towers built to guard against attacks by water. Cargo ships and pleasure craft now moor a little higher upstream. The riverside walk from Carrow Bridge to the Cathedral Close is one of the best in Norwich. It passes Pull's Ferry, the ruined Cow Tower and the 13th-century Bishop Bridge.

The city's museums include St Peter Hungate, rebuilt between 1430 and 1460. It was saved from demolition in 1902, and now houses a collection of religious arts and crafts.

Another museum, The Bridewell, is dedicated to Norfolk life and depicts traditional local activities such as fishing, weaving, flint-knapping and brewing. The building, which dates from the 14th century, was used as a 'bridewell', or prison, from 1583 to 1828. Nearby is the unique and charming Mustard Shop. Entering the shop is like stepping back into the Victorian past. There is a small 'mustard museum' at the back of the shop and visitors are welcome.

Like the cathedral and castle, a lively open-air market has been a feature of Norwich life since Norman times. At one end of the square stands the Church of St Peter Mancroft, a fine example of Perpendicular architecture. Bells that celebrated the defeat of the Spanish Armada in 1588 still peal from its tower. Opposite is the Guildhall, built at the start of the 15th century and much restored in the 19th century. Among prized possessions preserved in the Guildhall is a Spanish admiral's sword presented to the city by Nelson after his victory off Cape St Vincent in 1797, following which he received his knighthood.

The third side of the square is flanked by the City Hall, opened by George VI in 1938. Together with the cathedral and the noble 19th-century Roman Catholic Cathedral of St John the Baptist, the Hall's 202 ft tower dominates the city skyline.

Elm Hill has perhaps more atmosphere than any other Norwich thoroughfare. Named after a great elm that once stood at its top, the cobble-paved hill runs down between timber-framed and pastel-coloured buildings housing art galleries, antique shops, picture-framers and a pottery. An unexpected feature is a brass-rubbing centre. In Magdalen Street is Gurney Court, birthplace in 1780 of Elizabeth Fry, the Quaker and prison reformer. Off Magdalen Street, Anglia Square is dominated by the concrete-and-glass headquarters of HM Stationery Office.

OLD BOLINGBROKE

Lincolnshire
3 miles west of Spilsby

The remains of a castle in which an English king was born adds atmosphere to the sleepy village of Old Bolingbroke on the southernmost edge of the Lincolnshire Wolds. Only a few fragments remain of the castle, built some 900 years ago by Ranulf, Earl of Chester, and occupied in the 14th century by the mighty landowner John of Gaunt, Duke of Lancaster. One of his friends and followers, Geoffrey Chaucer, is said to have frequently visited the castle. It was here that Gaunt's son – who was to become Henry IV – was born in 1366.

Henry's coat of arms is prominently displayed in the centre of the village, in a bed of red Lancastrian roses. Old Bolingbroke was a prosperous market town in the Middle Ages; now it is a rambling little community of narrow lanes overlooked by low, tree-clad hills.

The castle fell into ruin after being captured in the Civil War by Cromwell and his troops, who, despite being outnumbered, defeated Royalist forces in 1643 at the Battle of Winceby nearby – when Cromwell's horse was killed beneath him. For centuries, only tumbled, grassy mounds showed where the castle once stood, but recent excavations have uncovered substantial remains of the gatehouse, towers and curtain wall.

A turning past the village inn, the Black Horse, leads to the castle site. To the north, the parish church of St Peter and St Paul stands among yew trees facing a group of large houses on the other side of the road. The church is a mixture of 14th-century architecture – perhaps commissioned by John of Gaunt – and 19th-century restoration. The old work includes richly moulded windows, and a nave arcade reaching to the modern barrel roof. At the entrance to the church are two worn heads believed to represent John's parents, Edward III and Queen Philippa.

The church is flanked by 18th- and 19th-century buildings, including Bolingbroke House, with its turret-style chimneys.

ORFORD

Suffolk
9 miles east of Woodbridge

Daniel Defoe, writing in 1722, said of Orford that it was 'now decayed. The sea daily throws up more land so it is a sea port no longer'. Though the village's associations with the sea are as strong as ever, its port has been diminished by the encroachment of Orford Ness – a great gravel bank that grows by some 15 yds a year. The result, however, has not affected the beauty of Orford. It is now a quiet village of brick-and-timber buildings, which looks particularly attractive from the roof of its castle, built for Henry II c. 1165. Orford comes to life in summer, when pleasure craft come up the River Ore from the North Sea to tie up along the breezy quay.

ORFORD *On its grassy hillock, Henry II's restored keep commands a view all the way to Aldeburgh.*

From the quay, the road passes a car park where once the sea lapped. Across the way stands the Jolly Sailor, an inn with numerous secret cupboards hinting at past links with smuggling.

The road continues past a stretch of green, and a line of demure little brick cottages. Further on are sturdier terraces, and an elegant Georgian corner. Nearby is the Church of St Bartholomew, parts of which date from 1166. Benjamin Britten's operas are sometimes performed here.

Market Hill twists up to a square from which every prospect pleases. There is a house in Pump Street with a dominating black gable end with a porthole-style window. On the other side of the square is the Orford Oysterage, with a sign depicting a merman. Ralph of Coggeshall, writing in the 12th century, recorded that Orford fishermen caught a man-like creature in their nets. He was wild, naked and covered in hair. The fishermen handed him over to the governor of the newly built castle. The merman ate anything, raw or cooked, but either he could not or would not talk, even when tortured. He managed to escape back to the sea, 'and was never afterwards seen'.

When Henry II had his castle built it was revolutionary in design. It is thought to have been the first in England to abandon the traditional square or oblong shape. Instead, it had an irregular, many-sided construction, whose confusion of faces was intended to baffle attackers. The ramparts have been reduced to lurching waves of grassy ditch and hummock. But the keep has been perfectly restored and, from its roof, the view over land and sea takes in Havergate Island, a bird sanctuary where avocets now breed after being absent from Britain for well over a century. This small island in the River Alde (or Ore) estuary is owned by the Royal Society for the Protection of Birds.

VILLAGE PUMP *Like so much else in Orford, this scene evokes another century. The great years of the village were between the 12th and 18th centuries. Since then it has become a sleepy corner of East Anglia.*

ORTON
Cambridgeshire
Western district of Peterborough

The modern creation of Orton includes the two former villages of Orton Waterville and Orton Longueville. The former's name is a corruption of the feudal family name of de Waltreville. Its 13th-century church has an Elizabethan carved pulpit. Stone-built Manor Farm was erected in 1571 and retains its original mullioned windows.

To the east, Orton Longueville has the 13th- and 14th-century Church of the Holy Trinity, with a late 17th-century aisle. There are fragments of medieval glass and a 16th-century wall-painting of St Christopher, as well as a 13th-century effigy and sculpture by Sir Francis Chantrey.

The village of Castor lies just to the northwest, on the northern bank of the River Nene. It was once part of a Roman settlement. Its Church of St Kyneburgha is the only church in the country dedicated to the eldest daughter of the pagan King Penda of Mercia whose children all became Christians. Kyneburgha founded a house at Castor of which she became the Abbess. The dedication in 1124 is recorded by an inscription in stone over a door of the Norman church which contains wall-paintings dating from the 14th century.

OXBOROUGH
Norfolk
7 miles southwest of Swaffham

In 1948, the Church of St John at Oxborough suffered a great loss. Its medieval stone tower, one of only two in the country, collapsed, taking with it part of the 14th-century building.

The chantry chapel on the south side was not damaged. It contains two lavish 16th-century monuments to members of the Bedingfeld family, made in terracotta. A memorial of 1583 commemorates Sir Henry Bedingfeld, a governor of the Tower of London.

A moat surrounds the red-brick manor house of Oxburgh Hall nearby. It was built in 1482 by the Bedingfeld family, who still live there. The Bedingfelds remained staunch Roman Catholics through 300 years of persecution, and there is a hiding place for their priest near the main bedroom.

Henry VII visited the house towards the end of the 15th century, and slept in a chamber in the 80 ft gateway tower.

P

PAGLESHAM

Essex
4 miles east of Rochford

Set between the estuaries of the Roach and the Crouch, the village of Paglesham keeps its aura of salty individuality amid tree-bordered flat fields. The neighbouring hamlet of Churchend has a neat little red-brick hall, an ancient inn, some attractive cottages, mostly clapboard, and Tudor farmhouses. Across the fields, at Eastend, the Georgian Plough and Sail Inn proclaims the background of the village's inhabitants.

PAPWORTH ST AGNES

Cambridgeshire
5 miles southeast of Huntingdon

One of the most interesting houses in the county is to be found at Papworth St Agnes – part medieval, part Elizabethan, with a combination of red brick and stonework. A straight gable at one end, a great chimney with star-shaped shafts, a six-light medieval window on an upper floor, and some good stucco work give the house great character. There are also some good ceilings inside. It was built in 1585 for Sir William Mallory, thought to be a descendant of Sir Thomas Malory, who wrote *Morte d'Arthur*. Most of the south front was rebuilt in 1660.

PARSON DROVE

Cambridgeshire
6 miles west of Wisbech

For centuries, Parson Drove was a centre for the production of woad, the dye with which ancient Britons smeared their bodies. It is fermented from the woad plant, whose bright yellow flowers and blue-green leaves produced the pigment which was also used for dyeing cloth. The industry was killed by the introduction of synthetic indigo in the 1890s, and England's last mobile woad-mill operated in the village until 1914. The woad-making process can be studied in collections of old photographs in Wisbech Museum, 6 miles from the village. Recent aerial photography has also revealed that the land surrounding the village was farmed during Roman times.

When Samuel Pepys and two relatives stayed at the Swan Inn at Parson Drove, in 1663, someone stole his uncle's horse. The enraged diarist wrote of the village as 'a heathen place', an unkind description of this pleasant community in the Fens. The village lies on a long street, behind both sides of which fields and dykes stretch into the distance. There are churches at either end of the street. St John the Baptist has a 15th-century tower and arcades of seven bays, but may have lost its chancel in a flood in 1613. It is now maintained by the Redundant Churches Fund. Since the mid-1970s most of its functions have been taken over by the Victorian Emmanuel church, which stands next to the Methodist church.

PASTON

Norfolk
4 miles northeast of North Walsham

Like many of Norfolk's straggling villages, which are often more a collection of farms than centralised communities, Paston has never had a public house or inn and its church is buried in a wood. But there has been a village here for at least a thousand years and from it, in the 15th century, came a remarkable series of letters which tell us much about the turbulent days of the Wars of the Roses. Most of the Paston Letters were written by Margaret Paston, and through them we can trace her career as bride, mother and matriarch.

She went to Paston Hall in 1440 when she married (her mother-in-law asked her father-in-law to buy her a gown of 'a goodly blue or a bright sanguine') and lived there for 44 years until her death. She usually wrote to her husband John, a lawyer in London. His letters mostly dealt with major public events, but hers are more homely.

She tells how the Rector of Great Snoring has been arrested for murder and has been put in the stocks awaiting trial; she pays 4s 6d (22½p) for a cartload of herrings but cannot get any eels; her daughter Margery falls in love with the farm bailiff and is giving trouble.

The Pastons were an autocratic lot, fighting off the Dukes of Norfolk and Suffolk who coveted their lands. The letters record, too, a monumental row in church after Evensong in which villagers accused Margaret's mother-in-law of diverting a road.

The hall Margaret knew has long since gone, but another was built on its site in the last century and traces of the old one can be seen in the garden. The Church of St Margaret in which she worshipped is still there, with its thatched roof and 14th-century wall paintings, including a large St Christopher. Inside are several monuments to the Pastons, who died out in 1732, ranging from early tomb chests to more ornate and classical ones by Nicholas Stone dating from the early 1600s.

The quiet holiday village of Mundesley is just 1½ miles northwest of Paston. The waters are shallow, with sands and safe bathing, and yet between Mundesley and Trimingham, a further 2½ miles northwest, they have eroded away much of the cliffs, fields, houses and even breakwaters in the last century.

PEASENHALL

Suffolk
3 miles west of Yoxford

No hint of mystery lurks behind the friendly shops fronting The Street in peaceful Peasenhall. Yet the village was the improbable scene of one of the most celebrated unsolved murders of the century.

In 1902, Rose Harsent, a maid at Providence House – now called Stuart House – became pregnant. Gossips guessed that a local carpenter, William Gardiner, already a father of six (and a Sunday School teacher) was responsible. On the morning of June 1, Rose was found dead at the foot of the stairs in Providence House. She had savage neck wounds and burns, as if someone had tried to set fire to her body.

Gardiner, an obvious suspect, was arrested, and magistrates sitting at the Swan Inn sent him for trial to Suffolk Assizes. There was evidence about the state of the body and much circumstantial evidence besides. But the jury could not agree on a verdict and Gardiner was acquitted. After the trial, he and his wife moved to London where they opened a shop, resisting advice to go and live abroad.

The Swan, much modernised, but retaining some old timbers inside, stands on the north side of The Street. Customers here still argue about whether the carpenter was guilty or not.

The Street was originally a Roman village, built on either side of a river, and the Roman road from Saxmundham to Norwich crossed the village to the west of the church. South of The Street, a wide, shaded ditch follows the road out across the landscape.

Fine 15th-century linenfold panels, stripped out of the Swan during renovations, were rescued by the vicar and are now fitted in the parish church of St Michael. The church has an unusual welcome above the porch; a carved dragon and a woodwose – a mythical half-human woodland creature – whose origins remain a mystery.

Peasenhall's past, like its present, has centred on the land. Its only concession to industry lies behind the church, in the remnants of a factory where an ingenious corn seed drill was made. James Smyth, the village wheelwright, designed it in the early 19th century, and it proved so much more efficient than others that it is still used today by many farmers in Suffolk. One of the last of Smyth's 'Nonpareil' drills is exhibited in the Abbot's Hall museum at Stowmarket.

A footpath to the east of the village passes the jagged fragments of Sibton Abbey, founded in 1150 – the only Cistercian house in Suffolk. The abbey monks developed the wool trade in Peasenhall and their timber-framed Wool Hall, overlooking the tiny green at the eastern end of the village, has recently been restored by the Landmark Trust and converted into three flats around the central hall.

About 2 miles southwest of Peasenhall, near Bruisyard church, a successful vineyard was established in 1974, and its acres of Müller-Thurgau vines usually yield around 17,000 litres of white wine a year. Visitors are welcome from May to mid-October.

PETERBOROUGH
Cambridgeshire
73 miles north of London

The glory of Peterborough is its cathedral, one of the finest Norman buildings in the country. Today the city is a manufacturing and commercial centre, but its history goes back nearly 6000 years: excavations have revealed the site of a thatched hut dating from about 3700 BC.

The Romans built the town of Durobrivae and a 27 acre fortress (now beneath Thorpe Wood golf course), and developed local pottery into a major industry.

Modern Peterborough began with a monastery dedicated to St Peter c. 656. The Danes sacked this in 870, but 100 years later the Bishop of Winchester built another. Fire destroyed it around 1116, and the core of the present cathedral was built on the site as an abbey church between 1118 and 1258. The nave, built in 1194–7, has 11 bays and massive piers, built from the

THE STREET *Peasenhall's main thoroughfare follows an old Roman track on either side of a rivulet.*

local cream-coloured Barnack stone. The high wooden roof is decorated with 13th-century paintings. Henry VIII gave Peterborough cathedral status in 1541.

In the nave is a painting of Old Scarlett, a 16th-century gravedigger, who buried Catherine of Aragon, Henry VIII's first wife, and Mary Queen of Scots, in the cathedral.

Fronting Cathedral Square is the Great Gate, originally Norman with later additions. The chancel of the 14th-century Chapel of St Thomas of Canterbury stands left of the gate.

The impressive old Butter Cross (known as the Guildhall) dates from 1671. Next to it is Peterborough's ancient parish church of St John the Baptist. It was built in 1402–7 with stone from the nave of the Chapel of St Thomas of Canterbury.

Thorpe Hall, on the western side of Peterborough, is a dignified mid-17th-century rectangular house, built by John Webb during the Commonwealth period, for Chief Justice Oliver St John. It has two main floors, a high hipped roof with dormers, and signs that suggest Dutch influence on the later, east side. Gates with piers carrying heraldic birds frame the house perfectly.

Longthorpe Tower is a three-storey building of about 1300, once belonging to a fortified house. It was reached by a passage from a house next door and was built as protection from invaders up the River Nene. Recently, under centuries of whitewash, were discovered some of the best-surviving examples of English medieval wall-paintings.

The 16th-century Customs House is surmounted by a light which guided vessels bringing their cargo to a wharf on the River Nene.

The Town Museum is notable for its collection of carved bonework and straw marquetry made by prisoners during the Napoleonic Wars.

Adjoining the conglomeration of Peterborough to the south is Old Fletton, whose Norman Church of St Margaret incorporates Saxon carvings in two buttresses of the chancel.

PLESHEY

Essex

5 miles northwest of Chelmsford

The sight of the great mound on which Pleshey Castle once stood takes the breath away. It is first glimpsed between the pink-washed walls and thatched roofs of a row of cottages. Then, at the end of the row, gone. The only building that remains above ground is the magnificent 15th-century bridge of red brick that survives through the rather touching generosity of Queen Elizabeth's Commissioners, who in 1558 discovered that the villagers of Pleshey were keeping rabbits in the castle ruins. Since the bridge was the only means of access to the animals, it was decided not to pull it down. The church was largely restored in the mid-19th century, and contains tombs and monuments of the 15th to 17th centuries.

POLSTEAD
Suffolk
4 miles southwest of Hadleigh

Murder most foul made Polstead headline news more than 150 years ago, and it has remained famous as the scene of a crime that shocked and horrified the nation – the Red Barn Murder. It was there that 26-year-old Maria Marten, whose thatched cottage still stands in Marten's Lane, to the southeast of the village, was shot and stabbed to death by William Corder and her body buried in the Red Barn.

It was thought that Maria had eloped with Corder, by whom she had had an illegitimate child that died when it was two months old – some said by poison. But her stepmother dreamed three times that she had been murdered and buried in the barn. At her insistence, her husband went to the barn and dug at the spot indicated in the dreams and found his daughter's body buried there.

A search was then made for Corder and he was found living in Middlesex, married to a woman who had met him through a matrimonial advertisement. He was convicted of murder and hanged at Bury St Edmunds in August 1828, and an account of the trial, wrapped in Corder's own skin, is preserved, together with his skull, in Bury's Moyses Hall Museum in the Butter Market.

Apart from Maria's cottage, only one other relic of the crime remains in Polstead, the farm where Corder lived in the centre of the village, which is now called Corder's Farm. The Red Barn burned down mysteriously shortly after the murder, and Maria's tombstone in the churchyard was so chipped away by souvenir hunters that the exact location is not known. A sign marks the approximate spot.

Every road into Polstead winds among cherry orchards thick with blossom in May, and the 'Polstead Black' cherry is claimed to be unsurpassed. Clusters of thatched and colour-washed cottages border the lanes, and huddle closer together around the green at the top of Polstead Hill. At the bottom of the hill is Polstead Pond, a broad stretch of water fringed with overhanging trees, and on a rise opposite the Georgian Polstead Hall stands the Church of St Mary. It dates from the 12th century and has brick-built arches and windows. The bricks are thought to be English and the oldest-surviving examples of their kind.

In the grounds of Polstead Hall, beside the churchyard, a small oak tree grows alongside the remains of the Gospel Oak, an ancient tree which was believed to be more than 1300 years old when it collapsed in 1953. The spot may have been sacred in pagan times.

Some 2½ miles southeast is Thorington Hall, an oak-framed, plastered and gabled house within retaining walls, built c. 1600, enlarged c. 1700, and restored in 1937. The house may be viewed by appointment.

PLESHEY *This picturesque row of cottages leads to the huge moat of Geoffrey de Mandeville's castle.*

suddenly there it is: the astonishing upsurge of turf, 60 ft high and 900 ft around, on which Geoffrey de Mandeville built a castle a few years after the Norman Conquest.

He may well have reshaped a prehistoric tumulus to his purpose, adding a moat, now inhabited by ducks and moorhens, and an inner bailey that stood on another 2 acre enclosure to the south. At any rate, the castle he built was so important that it remained the home of successive Lords High Constable of England for more than 200 years. It later passed into the possession of Thomas, Duke of Gloucester – Richard II's uncle – who, in fulfilment of a vow, built a College of Canons at Pleshey. The faint outline of the building can still be seen, at the end of dry summers, near the church.

In 1397, Richard, suspecting treachery, had Thomas kidnapped and murdered. The widowed duchess, according to Shakespeare, was left to mourn among 'empty lodgings and unfurnished walls, unpeopled offices, untrodden stones'. Now, even these have

RAMSEY

Cambridgeshire
10 miles southeast of Peterborough

Ramsey is the market town for an area which is intensively productive of cabbages, leeks and celery. A Benedictine abbey founded here in 969 was dissolved in 1539. The remaining 13th-century Lady Chapel of the medieval abbey has been incorporated in the Abbey Grammar School. The ruined gatehouse, dating from c.1480, is one of the most highly decorated specimens in England. It is owned by the National Trust and can be visited. Bodsey House, 1½ miles to the north, has parts of a large 14th-century chapel and a superb 17th-century chimney-stack.

RAYLEIGH MOUNT

Essex
6 miles southwest of Southend-on-Sea

A motte and bailey was built on Rayleigh Mount by Sweyn, the son of a Norman lord who came to England in the reign of Edward the Confessor and won favour with William the Conqueror after Hastings. His grandson, Henry, strengthened it with flint and rubble, but in 1157 he was disgraced for cowardice in battle. The castle and other lands were confiscated.

For the next two centuries Rayleigh was a royal castle and buildings were added. But it was never used for military purposes.

REEDHAM

Norfolk
6 miles south of Acle

The chain ferry at Reedham provides the only crossing for vehicles over the River Yare and marshes between Norwich and the coast at Great Yarmouth. On the outskirts of the village is a taxidermy firm which does a brisk trade with theatres and film companies. Visitors can see work in progress, inspect the display of stuffed birds and animals, and also watch feathers being fashioned into ornaments and gifts. In the grounds are live peacocks, waterfowl, and other wildlife.

A few miles over the marshes, overlooked by Burgh Castle, the ruined Roman fort of Gariannonum, is Berney Arms, where there is a late-19th-century drainage windmill-pump. At 70 ft high it is the tallest marsh windmill in the county and in complete working order. It is open to the public during the summer.

REEPHAM

Norfolk
6 miles southwest of Aylsham

An air of 18th-century prosperity lingers in Reepham, then an important market town, in the centre of a barley-growing and brewing region. The old market place has mellow, red-brick houses balanced by the pink colour-washed facade of the King's Arms pub.

One of the largest houses, Brewery House, is known locally as the Dial House because of its sun-dial above the wide portico. Behind the market place there is a narrow street, Back Street, where a large timber-framed house with an overhanging upper storey stands among tiny cottages.

The east of the market place is dominated by the tall tower of St Michael's Church which, strangely, is not the parish church of Reepham but of neighbouring Whitwell. At one time three churches stood in the churchyard; Reepham's Church of St Mary is joined by its choir vestry to St Michael's, and the third church belonged to Hackford, but has been a ruin since 1543. Only a fragment of the tower wall remains.

About 2 miles south of the village is Great Witchingham, a parish with a part-13th-century church and the Norfolk Wild Life Park, which contains one of the largest collections of European mammals, including lynx, Barbary apes and wild boar. The aviaries hold a great variety of birds of prey. To the northeast of Great Witchingham lies Alderford, whose 14th-century Church of St John the Baptist has a west tower but no chancel arch. The octagonal seven-sacrament font, typical of East Anglian churches, is carved with a Crucifixion and angels. Some medieval stained glass still remains.

REVESBY

Lincolnshire
6 miles southeast of Horncastle

In summer, fallow deer can be seen grazing in the parkland close to the estate village of Revesby on the southern edge of the Lincolnshire Wolds. The deer park in the grounds of Revesby Abbey seems appropriate for a place that was the home of Sir Joseph Banks, one of England's greatest naturalists. Banks accompanied Captain James Cook on his voyage round the world between 1768–71. Sir Joseph's house stood about half a mile south of the present great house, known as the Abbey. On the main east–west road near the village, impressive iron gates open on to a long drive leading to the creepered walls of the house, built in the middle of the last century.

Surrounded by woodlands, Revesby consists of a dozen late 19th and early 20th-century cottages, almshouses and a church around a spacious green. The long, low almshouses, now empty, date from 1862. The Church of St Lawrence could almost be 14th or 15th century, but its small, fussy spire gives it away. The church was, in fact, built in 1891 by the Stanhope family. Its east window is in memory of Edward Stanhope, Secretary of State for War, who died in 1893. In the aisle is a marble bust of Joseph Banks, a lawyer, who had built an earlier church in the same place. St Lawrence's has a set of tiles from a Cistercian abbey which used to stand about half a mile south.

Revesby reservoir, 1 mile along the Horncastle road from the village, is a magnet for fishermen and migrating waterfowl.

ROCHFORD

Essex

3 miles north of Southend-on-Sea

Rochford Hall, now a golf club, is one of several places said to be the birthplace of Anne Boleyn, and one of the many houses that her overworked phantom is supposed to haunt. In this instance, she appears at Christmas as a white 'thing' that flits through the grounds.

Until 1900, the leases of Rochford tenants were renewed at a midnight 'Whispering Court' at the Hall. This originated when an earlier lord of the manor woke to hear his tenants whispering against him. He decreed that henceforward their leases would be renewed at night, and business would be conducted in whispers.

THE RODINGS

Essex

Between Chelmsford and Bishop's Stortford

Eight farming villages are strung along the valley of the River Roding, most of them picturesque with old churches, moated halls, clapboard or half-timbered cottages and set in rolling sweeps of ploughland, grassland or woodland. This is a curiously individual agricultural world of its own, with enchanting old houses and a handful of comfortable pubs.

Anthony Trollope, the Victorian novelist, loved 'the Roothings', as Essex people call them, and hunted here each winter. They are: Abbess Roding; Aythorpe Roding; Beauchamp Roding; Berners Roding, with a church in the Hall's yard; High Roding; Leaden Roding, with a picturesque Hall and outbuilding; Margaret Roding, with a fine white Georgian house facing the road behind its moat; and White Roding.

ROLLESBY

Norfolk

7 miles northwest of Great Yarmouth

The Norman church in Rollesby has a round tower which has had 14th-century upper stages added. The village is 1 mile northwest of the 200 acre Rollesby Broad which is linked to the deep Ormesby and Filby Broads. The A149 between Ormesby and Rollesby gives some of the best views found anywhere in Broadland. Navigable dykes in the group of Broads have been closed by sluices to reduce the risk of flooding. Archaeological excavations have produced evidence that around 2000 BC a community of Beaker Folk, so-called because of the metal pots which have been found in their burial barrows, lived in the area.

REVESBY *The Banks and Stanhope families designed a comfortable estate for their tenants.*

S

SAFFRON WALDEN

Essex

12 miles north of Bishop's Stortford

Although the saffron crocus is no longer grown commercially in the district around Saffron Walden, carvings of it can be seen in the town. It forms part of the coat of arms in the Town Hall portico and appears on decorations in the vast parish church of St Mary the Virgin. The bright yellow dye extracted from the golden stigma of purple crocus (*Crocus sativus*) was used to colour cloth and cakes until the end of the 18th century, when it was replaced by artificial dyes. Even so, the crocus brought prosperity to the town for some 400 years.

The crocus is also incorporated in some of the elaborate decorative plasterwork called pargetting, to be seen on a number of buildings. A particularly fine design enlivens the front of the medieval Sun Inn – now an antiques shop and bookseller's – in Church Street. It shows a legendary local hero, Tom Hicka-thrift, a carter of immense strength, overcoming the legendary Wisbech giant.

Running parallel to Church Street is Castle Street, which has the remains of the castle keep – all that is left of a fortress built by Geoffrey de Mandeville in the 12th century. In the grounds of this ruined castle, near the church, is the Town Museum, built in 1834. Among its exhibits is Prince Charles's xylophone. West of the castle gate is the medieval Church of St Mary. Although the spire was a 19th-century afterthought, it sits beautifully on the tower of the largest church in Essex – 184 ft long by 80 ft wide. Its grandeur reflects Walden's prosperity at that time.

Opposite the foot of Castle Street is the town's finest medieval building, timber-framed and built about 1500 as a malt house, but now a youth hostel. Much of its plasterwork has worn off, revealing the original window frames. In the middle of the town are the Market Square and its old Corn Exchange, built about 1850 and converted in the mid-1970s into a library and arts centre. At the west end of the town is a Saxon burial ground in which 200 skeletons were discovered. It is known as Repell Ditches.

On the outskirts of Saffron Walden are two of its prize attractions: early 17th-century Audley End, landscaped by 'Capability' Brown and added to by Adam in the 1700s, and the largest earth maze in England. The mansion and grounds are open in the afternoon from April to October, but closed on Mondays except Bank Holidays. Of unknown date and purpose, the maze is about 40 yds in diameter, but its path coils and twists for almost a mile on the Common. It was first documented in 1699.

About 4 miles to the southeast is Tiptofts Farm, a moated house of *c.* 1330 with a rare surviving aisled hall with a timber-framed extension. Nearby is Debden, a village which boasts the 13th-century Church of St Mary the Virgin and All Saints, though it was partly rebuilt in 1793 by R. Chiswell from the designs of John Carter. There are 18th- and 19th-century monuments and a Coade stone font of 1789.

ST IVES

Cambridgeshire

5 miles east of Huntingdon

Once a village called Slepe, a slippery landing place on the River Ouse, St Ives became a manor of Ramsey Abbey in 969. A priory cell of the abbey was set up *c.* 1050 and dedicated to St Ivo, a Persian Bishop whose supposed remains were miraculously found in a nearby field. The priory supplanted the village which then acquired the name of St Ives. The six-arched 15th-century bridge has a two-storey miniature chapel in its centre bay.

The best house in St Ives is the Jacobean manor house by the bridge, with fine brick chimneys. A great fire in 1680 destroyed 122 houses, and few built before that date have survived.

Oliver Cromwell had a farm nearby and his statue, in which he is depicted booted and wearing an unpuritanically rakish hat, stands in the market place.

ST NEOTS

Cambridgeshire

8 miles southwest of Huntingdon

Benedictine monks founded a priory near the River Great Ouse in the 10th century and named it after St Neot, a Saxon holy man who is said to have been a spiritual adviser to King Alfred. Neot's bones were brought to the priory – possibly stolen – from the church near Bodmin in Cornwall where they were originally buried. The priory was destroyed after the Dissolution of the Monasteries in 1539, and only the foundations remain.

The old market town, which grew up around the priory, has a large square, one side of which backs on to the river. The 15th-century Perpendicular tower of the Church of St Mary rises nobly beyond the square. The wooden vault is ornately carved with angels, birds and other animals. Beside a bridge, the 17th-century Bridge Hotel has waterside terraces and a small quay.

ST OSYTH

Essex

3 miles west of Clacton-on-Sea

The most imposing range of monastic buildings in Essex can be seen at St Osyth, a charming waterside village. The priory, which dates largely from the 12th century, was founded by St Osyth, wife of a 7th-century East Anglian king, who was beheaded by the Danes in AD 653. The buildings were extended by successive owners, notably Lord Darcy. The gatehouse is magnificent, there is an exceptional range of architecture, from the 13th to 18th centuries, and there are lovely gardens.

About 1 mile southeast is St Clare's Hall, one of the few surviving 14th-century moated farmhouses with an aisled hall. The wings were altered in the 16th century. The house may be seen by appointment.

HIGH STREET *Saffron yellow seems a fitting colour for a cottage in the one-time crocus capital of England.*

SANDRINGHAM

Norfolk
7 miles northeast of King's Lynn

There is no village of Sandringham but the 7000 acre estate and Country Park owned by the Royal Family takes in seven parishes. The house was bought for King Edward VII, when Prince of Wales, in 1862, with Duchy of Cornwall revenues accumulated while he was a minor.

The grounds and an exhibition of royal cars are open during the summer if no member of the Royal Family is in residence, and a good entry for a drive through the luxuriant woods is along the road from Castle Rising, emerging towards Dersingham.

From the large, red-brick house and its grounds the estate spreads westwards in a green apron of well-kept woodland and trim lawns. Sandringham Country Park lies east of the A149, an area of natural woodland and heath which few places can surpass in loveliness.

The best time to visit the park is in early summer, when woods and roadsides are swamped with the rich purples, blues and crimsons of rhododendrons in bloom. They pile up in great masses of colour among the pines, cedars and silver birches, almost over-powering in their splendour and compelling the eye at every turn of the road. There are footpaths through the woods, dipping into steep-banked glens where the rhododendrons cluster 20 ft above and brightly coloured jays swoop among the tree-tops.

Once the royal train would arrive at Wolverton to deliver or collect royals and their guests visiting Sandringham House. No trains run today, but the station houses a nostalgic museum of railway travel.

SHERINGHAM
Norfolk
22 miles north of Norwich

There are two parts to Sheringham. Upper Sheringham is on the hill and Lower Sheringham is the old fishing village which became a holiday resort at the end of the last century. There is a ridge of pebbles at high tide, but the ebb tide reveals extensive, clean-washed sands. Fishing boats are launched down a precipitous slipway below a concrete bridge joining east and west promenades. The lifeboat is launched by a tractor. A sail-powered lifeboat is preserved in its shed by the shore.

Upper Sheringham once depended on agriculture but is now a residential district. Sheringham Hall has splendid rhododendrons in its park, designed by Humphry Repton and his son, J. A. Repton, in 1812. The North Norfolk Railway is based at Sheringham station in the town centre. It operates a regular steam-train service between Sheringham and Weybourne along 3 miles of the old Midland and Great Northern Railway track.

Sheringham station has kept many of the features from the time the line opened in 1887, including an original signalbox which is usually open to visitors.

Just under a mile to the east are the ruins of 13th-century Beeston Priory, where the surrounding common has a fine spread of wild flowers from spring to autumn. On the inland slopes, the justifiably named Pretty Corner offers views of heath, woodland and sea. Here the land rises to a ridge running parallel to the coast and reaches a height of over 300 ft in places. The ridge is thickly wooded and wild flowers grow in profusion in spring and summer.

SHOTLEY GATE
Suffolk
At mouth of River Stour opposite Parkeston

The tip of the promontory, on the east side of the village of Shotley, was formerly occupied by HMS *Ganges*, the Royal Navy training establishment. A road westward gives glimpses of the Stour estuary and leads to the imposing Royal Hospital School at Holbrook, for sons of members of the Royal Navy and Royal Marines, active or retired. The church has a handsome double hammerbeam roof and a lovely Georgian chancel with paintings and gilding.

Erwarton is 2 miles to the west of Shotley Gate. Much of the present Hall here dates from 1858, when it was rebuilt incorporating features of Sir Philip Parker's house of 1570. The red-brick gatehouse with its rounded arch, buttresses and pinnacles belongs to a still earlier house of 1549. Anne Boleyn often visited the house, and it is said that her heart was secretly buried in the nearby church. A heart-shaped casket discovered in 1836 helps to confirm the story.

The slim, dramatic, six-storeyed tower-house at Freston, 6 miles northwest of Shotley Gate, was built of red-diapered brickwork c. 1550. It has a spiral staircase linking each floor. In its early days it was occupied by the Latimers, the early English Church Reformers. Unfortunately it is not open to the public.

TRADER MILL *A magnificent specimen, probably the last tower mill built in Lincolnshire, stands proudly at Sibsey.*

SIBSEY
Lincolnshire
5 miles northeast of Boston

Like Burgh le Marsh, Sibsey has a magnificent windmill. Beside the road west to Frithville stands Trader Mill, a well preserved tower mill with six sails and six storeys. It dates from 1877 and was probably the last one to be built in Lincolnshire. The mill was working until 1958. It has since been restored and is administered by English Heritage. It can be visited daily from April to September. A few hundred yards away, flowing under the Frithville road bridge, is a typical fenland drainage channel, running dead straight into the far distance, accompanied by a narrow road with houses and farm buildings huddled under its embankment.

The busy main road between Louth and Boston divides Sibsey, but it maintains a dignified air amid the vast emptiness of the fenland. Its houses are mostly 18th and 19th century, standing in their own grounds. In Chapel Lane there is a friendly blend of old cottages and new bungalows.

The Church of St Margaret has some Norman touches, particularly the north doorway and the nave, which has high arches.

Surrounding the village are acres of sugar beet, potatoes, cabbages and other vegetables. The immense flat landscape, networked by drains, dykes and sluices, is broken only by an occasional farmhouse.

SKEGNESS
Lincolnshire
19 miles northeast of Boston

The posters on the railway station have, for generations, described Skegness as 'bracing'. Though the east winds can deter the less hardy visitor from the town's extensive beaches, the town has many attractions for holidaymakers. The 9th Earl of Scarborough began planning Skegness as a holiday town in 1877. By 1881 its 1843 ft long pier had been built, and holidaymakers were pouring into the town. Today it has a holiday camp, swimming-pools, 34 acres of seafront gardens, two golf courses and an entertainment centre, The Embassy. The pier, however, was destroyed in the gales of January 1978.

Church Farm Museum in Church Road South contains agricultural tools that were used on small Lincolnshire farms at the turn of the century. The farmhouse is furnished in the same period.

SLEAFORD
Lincolnshire
11 miles northeast of Grantham

The ancient town of Sleaford on the western edge of the Fens takes its name from the river on which it stands. The elaborately decorated west front of the 12th-century parish church of St Denys dwarfs the other buildings in Sleaford Market Place. Its 144 ft stone spire is one of the oldest in England.

Mounds beside Castle Causeway are all that remain of the 12th-century castle where, in 1216, King John was taken with a fatal fever. He died at Newark, in Nottinghamshire. The Black Bull Inn has a carved stone dated 1689 showing bull-baiting, which was last practised in Sleaford in 1807.

SNAPE

Suffolk
3 miles south of Saxmundham

Unique among villages as an international centre of music, Snape is alive with opera, jazz, The Maltings Proms and concerts from April to October, and antique fairs, television and recording sessions are taking place throughout the year.

Centrepiece of the activities is The Maltings concert hall, home of the Aldeburgh Festival since 1967. It was burnt out after the opening night of the 1969 season – probably due to an electrical fault – but was restored and reopened by Elizabeth II a year later. The acoustics are as fine as in any concert hall in Europe.

The Maltings complex includes shops, galleries, wine and coffee bars, a centre for activity holidays, and the Suffolk Piano Workshop, which repairs old instruments and welcomes visitors. Here also is the Britten-Pears School for Advanced Musical Studies, named after the festival's founders, composer Benjamin Britten and singer Peter Pears. Britten fell in love with Snape and lived in a converted windmill north of the bridge in the 1930s and 1940s, composing his opera *Peter Grimes* there. Master classes held in the school are open to casual observers for a small admission charge.

The creeper-covered 19th-century brick maltings buildings were originally used to prepare fine Suffolk barley for brewing, the malt produced being shipped out via the River Alde. The combination of farming and shipping gave the nearby Plough and Sail pub its name. Departing seamen used to drop barley seeds into cracks in the bar and find them sprouting on their return to port.

The malting business was started by Newson Garrett in 1841. He was the father of Elizabeth Garrett Anderson, Britain's first woman to qualify as a doctor.

Salt-marshes adjoining The Maltings are the home of many species of wild birds and are the starting point for walks and river trips along the Alde to Aldeburgh and Iken. There is an old smugglers' inn, The Crown, which used to have peepholes allowing watch to be kept over river and countryside, and a windowless upstairs room for use as a hideaway.

At a crossroads stands Snape church, a flint and brick building dating from the 13th century and with a 15th-century carved font. Just east of the church, a 48 ft ship dating from around AD 625 was unearthed in 1862. A Saxon gold ring, now in the British Museum, was found on the site and all around was a cemetery of burial urns.

SNARFORD

Lincolnshire
8½ miles northeast of Lincoln

The small Church of St Lawrence at Snarford was begun in the 12th century and is worth visiting for three splendid monuments in the church which commemorate members of the St Pol family who died during the reigns of Elizabeth I and James I. The most elaborate is the earliest, to Sir Thomas who died in 1582. It is an alabaster six-poster bed, with two recumbent effigies, and children kneeling on the top. Sir George St Pol's monument (1613) has recumbent effigies, and the one to Robert, Earl of Warwick (1619), is graced with an alabaster medallion.

THE SNORINGS

Norfolk
1–3 miles northeast of Fakenham

In 1611 when the lord of the manor, Sir Ralph Shelton, sold Great Snoring to Lord Chief Justice Richardson he is reported to have said, 'I can sleep without Snoring'. Apart from being a slur on this charming little village, the remark was the forerunner of many a pun that has plagued Great Snoring and its neighbour Little Snoring over the centuries. As with so many other Norfolk villages the origin of the name is Saxon; in the Domesday Survey it is recorded as Snarringes, the home of the family and descendants of someone named Snear.

Great Snoring is a compact little place with handsome houses of flint and brick running in long terraces on either side of the narrow main street. Its large church, dedicated to St Mary the Virgin, was begun in the 13th century but mainly dates from the 15th. Two panels from that century have survived in the chancel screen. It is a handsome building, and standing beside it is an equally handsome rectory built of brick with octagonal turrets, carved chimneys and terracotta friezes above the ground and upper floors. Yet even this great house is only the remains of an earlier one, probably started about 1500 for the Sheltons. It was reduced to its present size in the 19th century and served as the rectory until 1975. Now it is a guesthouse whose owners have taken care to maintain its character both inside and out.

Little Snoring, 2 miles to the southeast, grew in size during the Second World War when a bomber airfield was established nearby. The village church, St Andrew's, stands on a knoll about half a mile away. It has a flint-built Saxon round tower which stands apart from the nave and chancel and appears to have been part of an earlier church. Round towers built of flint are common to churches of that age, because of the difficulty in shaping corners with the rough stone, but no one knows why it stands apart from the later building. The church doorway is massive and unique, with three Norman arches, each of a different design.

Inside are poignant memories of the wartime years. The Bible on its lectern was a gift by the widow of the last commandant of the airfield who was killed in an air crash in 1946, and there are also 'victory' boards which record the sorties of the RAF bombers over Germany.

SOMERLEYTON HALL

Suffolk
5 miles northwest of Long Melford

The Anglo-Italian masterpiece of Somerleyton Hall was rebuilt in 1851 by Sir Samuel Morton Peto, the railway entrepreneur, who employed John Thomas as architect. The writer George Borrow (1803–81), who lived locally, denounced the Hall in his travel book *Romany Rye* (1857) as 'pandemonium in red brick'. But Borrow held a grudge against Peto who had built a railway line across the writer's land.

In fact the Hall is a fascinating blend of architectural styles, including neo-Jacobean, Italian and Palladian. There is a daring marriage of brickwork and stone, and the hall contains tapestries, paintings and carvings by the sculptor Grinling Gibbons (1648–1721). The 12 acre garden has a magnificent yew maze.

MANOR FARM *Built in 1722 for Robert Burton, this battlemented house at Somersby is attributed to Sir John Vanbrugh.*

SOMERSBY
Lincolnshire
6 miles east of Horncastle

Little has changed in Somersby since Alfred Tennyson, who was to become Lord Tennyson and poet laureate of England, spent his boyhood here, roaming a countryside which he lovingly recalled as rich 'with plaited alleys of the trailing rose'. The church where his father preached, and the former rectory where the poet was born in 1809, are much as they were last century. Barely a dozen houses, mostly hidden away among woods and along narrow winding lanes, make up the rest of the little community.

Alfred was one of 12 children brought up by the Reverend George Tennyson at the rectory, now Somersby House. The rambling, cream-washed building is set back behind hedges of holly and yew opposite the 15th-century Church of St Margaret, but it is not open to the public.

A bust of Tennyson has a proud place in the church, where his father was buried in 1831, and a glass case contains some of the poet's possessions.

Opposite the church is a battlemented house said to have been built in the 18th century by Sir John Vanbrugh, designer of Blenheim Palace.

SOUTH BENFLEET
Essex
6 miles west of Southend-on-Sea

A narrow creek divides South Benfleet from Canvey Island, on the northern side of the Thames Estuary. On the island is a 17th-century cottage built in a style brought to England by Dutch engineers who re-claimed much of the island from the water. The Dutch Cottage Museum houses a collection of items connected with Thames shipping. Two causeways link Canvey Island with the mainland, and in summer Benfleet's streets are busy with traffic heading for the island. The beaches are concentrated along its southern shore. To the west is Bowers Marsh, the haunt of many wild birds and a favourite place for birdwatchers and wildfowlers. The sheltered waters of Benfleet Creek itself are favoured by yachtsmen.

SOUTHEND-ON-SEA
Essex
35 miles east of London

Big, brash and noisy, Southend has been a day-tripper's delight for nearly a century – since the first Thames paddle-steamers thrashed down river.

Southend-on-Sea is actually on the Thames Estuary, and when the tide goes out it leaves a vast expanse of mud stretching about a mile from the seafront in places. So Southend's $1\frac{1}{3}$ mile long pier was essential for the steamers when it was built in 1889. The trippers now arrive by road or rail, and the pier is used only by the lifeboat. Near the pier is a full-size replica of Drake's *Golden Hind*.

Away from the hustle of the seafront can be found the Southend of an earlier age. Less than 2 miles inland from the pier entrance is Prittlewell, once a village from which the town grew. The name Southend means the south end of Prittlewell.

Prittlewell Priory dates back to the 12th century. Set in acres of parkland, it now houses the South-East Essex Museum, devoted to local and natural history.

PEERLESS PIER *Southend's magnificent pier, still the longest in the world, stretches into the distance at sunset* (overleaf).

Southchurch Hall, a few minutes' walk from the seafront, is a moated, timber-framed manor house of the early 14th century and furnished in Tudor style.

To the west of the pier the Esplanade runs at the foot of the cliffs of Westcliff, and a lift climbs the steep face to the ornamental gardens. Further west is Old Leigh, a fishing village where the cockle boats can be seen unloading.

Transport of the modern age can be seen at Southend Airport, and in the appropriately named Aviation Way is the Historic Aircraft Museum.

SOUTHWOLD

Suffolk
8 miles east of Halesworth

The imposing white lighthouse which rears 100 ft above Southwold is visible from almost every part of the town. It was built in 1890 and its beam can be seen 17 miles out to sea. Even during the day the lighthouse serves as a very distinctive landmark for passing ships.

The town is a pleasant mixture of period houses and cottages, many painted in the old Suffolk colours of pink and pale blue, with roofs of black or red pantiles. Dotted among them like scatter cushions are nine greens of varying shapes and sizes. Some of these mark places where buildings were destroyed by a fire that engulfed the town in 1659.

Southwold began its long history as a Saxon fishing port, became a sizable harbour in medieval times, then declined as the seaward approaches silted up. Today it thrives as a holiday resort, but a reminder of its maritime past can be seen in Park Lane, where a ship's figurehead of a girl holding a bunch of grapes stands outside Park Lane Cottage.

There are several more figureheads in the Sailors' Reading Room at the seafront end of East Street. On Gun Hill, farther along the front, stand six cannon

thought to have been presented to the town by the Duke of Cumberland – who landed there from Flanders in October 1745 on his way to Scotland to fight Bonnie Prince Charlie.

The town is spread around the large and splendid Church of St Edmund, King and Martyr, a magnificent Perpendicular church dedicated to the king of East Anglia, who was murdered by the Danes in 870 for refusing to renounce Christianity. The church houses Southwold Jack, a realistic 15th-century mechanical figure of an armoured foot soldier, made of painted oak. Jack holds a short axe with which he strikes a bell before each service and whenever a bride arrives for her wedding. The paintwork is original, and endows him with a dark stubble of beard and blood-flecked eyes.

To the west of the church, in High Street, is a restaurant called Sutherland House that was the headquarters of the Duke of York (later James II), England's Lord High Admiral during the 17th-century wars with the Dutch. At the Battle of Sole Bay, fought off the town on May 27, 1672, the Dutch fleet took the duke's squadron by surprise and the battle raged all day. The English ships were badly battered, but as the Dutch withdrew and did not return to the attack, the honours were thought to be even. A panorama of the battle can be seen in the town museum – a pretty Dutch-style cottage facing the church. To the north of the church is Station Road, where George Orwell, author of *1984* and *Animal Farm*, lived in Montague House for a time in the 1930s.

Southwold has had its own brewery since the 16th century, and the present one – Adnams, in East Green, in the town centre – incorporates the original building. It recaptures the spirit of the past by using horse-drawn drays to deliver barrels of real ale.

SOUTHWOLD LANDMARKS *The lighthouse can be seen from all over town, while the inn name recalls the 1672 battle.*

TULIP CAPITAL *Spalding's town sign is a colourful tribute to its major produce.*

SPALDING

Lincolnshire
14 miles southwest of Boston

The River Welland flows under seven bridges through the centre of this splendid old market town. Spalding is the centre of an intensively farmed agricultural area and is the capital of 'Tulipland'. The countless tulips and daffodils provide a popular attraction for visitors who drive round the fields in April and early May to view a kaleidoscope of colour across some 10,000 acres. Tulips decorate the enormous floats in the town's popular May Flower Parade. The attractive gardens of Springfields offer a more contained, 30 acre space, to view spring flowers and roses.

The town is a happy mixture of old and new buildings. Among the oldest are the 13th-century Church of St Mary and St Nicholas, which has unusual double aisles, and the 17th-century White Hart Inn. The Gentlemen's Society, an antiquarian society founded in 1709–10, included Sir Isaac Newton and Alexander Pope among its members. Fifteenth-century Ayscoughfee Hall has a museum of local history and a fine bird collection.

SPILSBY

Lincolnshire
11 miles west of Skegness

Spilsby's fine Church of St James is famous for its monuments to the Berties and the Willoughbys, from the 14th to the 17th centuries, many with effigies. In the market place stands a statue to Sir John Franklin, the explorer, who was born in the town.

Halton Holegate, 2 miles southeast of Spilsby, has a marvellous halt for the visitor, the handsome and spacious Church of St Andrew, standing on a little hill off the Spilsby road, visible from miles away.

The doorway of the church is either 13th or 14th century. Some of the woodwork is 15th century, including several of the bench-ends which have carvings of angels, owls, monkeys, and foxes running off with geese. Other bench-end figures were carved by a local craftsman in the 19th century. The pinnacled tower was also partly rebuilt in the last century.

Set among trees on the same side of the road as the church is the Old Hall, a largely 18th-century red-brick and slate-roofed building. Its somewhat faded elegance makes it one of the village's most imposing houses.

The low-beamed Bell Inn, believed to date from 1520, stands back from the road just west of St Andrew's Rectory, a mainly 19th-century building that was frequently visited by Alfred, Lord Tennyson.

One of the village's most notable sons was Thomas Grantham, a Baptist church leader born in 1634, who was persecuted and imprisoned in the struggle for nonconformist beliefs during the reign of Charles II.

A dramatic landmark is the Boston Stump, the 272 ft high steeple of St Botolph's Church, Boston, which can be clearly seen at a distance of 15 miles from Halton Holegate, through clumps of small trees dotted around the neighbouring fields.

STAMFORD

Lincolnshire
12 miles northwest of Peterborough

Well-worn tracks of ancient Britons converged on Stamford long before the Romans built their road to the north through the town. It was the only spot for miles where the River Welland could be forded easily at all times of the year. The Normans built a castle beside the river, and in 1215 Earl Warenne assembled the barons and an army of 2000 here to march on Runnymede in order to force King John to agree to Magna Carta.

Stamford became a prosperous wool town and an important religious centre in the Middle Ages. There were four monasteries and priories, four friaries, six religious hospitals and 14 parish churches in the town. Five of these early churches remain. There are also many fine medieval, 17th- and 18th-century buildings in the local grey stone, making Stamford one of the most elegant towns in the Midlands. Six churches stand in 1 square mile. St Mary's has a magnificent 14th-century spire; All Saints' has a spire standing 152 ft; St Martin's and St John's are both fine examples of English Perpendicular architecture; and St George's was enlarged in 1449 by Sir William Bruges, first Garter King of Arms. The sixth church, St Michael's, collapsed while being restored in 1832, and the present church was built on the site four years later.

In the wall of the old grammar school is Brasenose Gate. This was part of Brasenose Hall, which was occupied by rebellious Oxford University students who established halls of learning at Nottingham and Stamford in the 13th century. By 1336 they had settled their differences with the university authorities and returned to Oxford. The 'brazen-nosed' bull from the Hall now decorates Brasenose College, Oxford.

Browne's Hospital, founded in the 15th century by a rich wool merchant of the town, is one of England's outstanding medieval almshouses. In 1552, the manor of Stamford was inherited by William Cecil. Elizabeth I's favourite adviser, who later became the first Lord

Burghley. His parents and grandparents had lived in the town. Cecil began building Burghley House, 1 mile south of the river, in 1553. It is regarded as the grandest surviving building of the Elizabethan age.

Stamford was the home of Sir Malcolm Sargent (1895–1967), the orchestral conductor. He is buried in the town cemetery.

STANSTED MOUNTFITCHET
Essex
3 miles northeast of Bishop's Stortford

Stansted is nationally famous as the hub of the fierce battle to prevent the third London Airport from being situated here in a sweep of country said to contain 540 buildings of architectural or historic interest, other than churches. The town is noisy with traffic, but side streets contain old houses of charm. Stansted Hall stands in a great park with a lake. There is a medieval church, the site of a Norman castle and a 65 ft high red-brick tower windmill built in 1787 and restored in 1966.

Mole Hall Wildlife Park at Widdington, 4 miles northeast, includes wallabies, chimpanzees and a variety of birds.

STEBBING
Essex
3 miles northeast of Great Dunmow

Rising from the grounds of Stebbing Park, on the approach to the village from Bran End, is an impressive conical earthwork known as the Great Mount. Towering 44 ft high and stretching no fewer than 225 ft across, the mound is reached by a causeway across its moat. There is thought to have been a small fortification here before the Norman invasion. It was then replaced by a more substantial defensive motte by Ranulf Peverel – one of the lords among whom the Conqueror shared out local manorial rights. Peverel married one of his king's mistresses, and their son founded the priory of Hatfield Peverel 12 miles southeast of the village.

Another moat surrounds Porters Hall, an early 17th-century farmhouse on Stebbing Green, built to an L-shaped plan with two front gables and retaining one of its original chimney-stacks. A great deal of Roman pottery and traces of a Roman building have been found close by. Porters Hall is only one of many admirably preserved buildings in the village. Most of those dating from the Middle Ages were extended or altered in the 16th, 17th or 18th centuries and, like Butlers Cottage in the High Street, many are decorated with pargetting on their facades.

Below the church, sprawling across the end of the main street beyond the war memorial, is Church Farm, an early 16th-century building now plastered over. Farther down the steep hill stands the breathtaking Priors Hall or Parsonage Farm, another of the village's former manorial seats.

At the top of the hill above the church, the frame of an old inn sign, hanging empty, and a red emblem over the door are the only reminders that the Red Lion, now a private house, was once a pub. It was built in the 16th century and extended later.

The Church of St Mary the Virgin with its shingle-tiled spire has altered little since the 14th century, when it replaced an earlier foundation. Its window tracery is a delight and the interior is enhanced by the chancel's later roofing and repairs made to the nave in 1825. The greatest revelation is the mighty rood screen filling the chancel opening, carved not in wood, as usual, but in stone.

A stroll down Mill Lane to the Stebbing Brook gives glimpses of Stebbing Park's imposing manor house between attractive cottages, including Mill Cottage, the smallest in the village. The weatherboarded water mill itself is 18th century. It still works, though powered by electricity except on occasional festive days, when the original machinery is set in motion.

STILTON
Cambridgeshire
6 miles southwest of Peterborough

At the 17th-century Bell Inn at Stilton, the famous cheeses, made in Leicestershire, were loaded on to coaches for London and the North. This village on the edge of the Fens has the reputation for a cheese that it has, in fact, never produced.

The Bell has a long range of stone-built bays and gables, with two massive chimney-stacks and an impressive coach entrance. One gable carries the date 1642 but the inn is probably earlier.

STOKE-BY-NAYLAND
Suffolk
5 miles southwest of Hadleigh

A stiff climb to the Church of St Mary the Virgin rising out of the Stour Valley is rewarded by a fine view of 'Constable Country'. Stoke-by-Nayland is regarded as the heart of the area which the painter John Constable used in his Suffolk landscapes, and the largely 15th-century church itself features in several of his paintings. Its tower of flint and mellow, peach-coloured brick rises 120 ft, looking down on a neat rectangle of village streets and providing a landmark for miles around.

Perched on a hillside to the south of the church runs a row of timbered almshouses, looking as they probably did centuries ago. A stroll from the church to School Street leads to the fine 16th-century Guildhall and the Maltings, dating mostly from the same period. Now converted into four cottages, part of the Maltings was once a medieval hall-house.

Near the lych gate in School Street is the building housing the well, down which a servant of Lord Windsor's fell to his death in 1603, and a tiny brick structure with a grating high up in one wall. This was once the village lock-up.

But the village possesses more momentous links with the past than these. Brasses and memorials inside St Mary's include a 16th-century brass of Lady Howard, an ancestor of two of Henry VIII's ill-fated wives, Catherine Howard and Anne Boleyn, who were both beheaded; and a 6 ft brass monument of a knight in full armour – Sir William Tendring, who fought most valiantly at the Battle of Agincourt and who died six years later in 1421.

The 16th-century Thorington Hall, whose tall Tudor chimneys rise southeast of the village, is a fine example of a yeoman's house, which has remained virtually unchanged by the centuries.

STOW
Lincolnshire
4 miles north of Saxilby

The village of Stow can be approached from Lincoln by two Roman roads – Ermine Street as far north as Scampton, a village of stone-walled cottages nestling below Lincoln Edge, and then Till Bridge Lane to the west.

Stow is remarkable for its 11th-century Saxon and Norman Church of St Mary which has a massive 15th-century tower. A carving of a dragon beneath the Early English font symbolises the defeated Devil. There is a fine Norman chancel in the church, which is known as the 'Mother Church of Lincoln'; it was once the cathedral of Lindsey, one of the three districts into which Lincolnshire was divided. In the north transept are the remains of a 13th-century wall-painting of St Thomas Becket.

Two miles northeast of Stow, in the village of Coates-by-Stow, is the charming little Church of St Edith. It has no aisles but has a Norman south doorway, a font, and a Perpendicular rood screen which still has its gallery, a great rarity in England. There is a monument of the Commonwealth period to Brian Cook, some fragments of medieval glass, and 15th-century pulpit and bench-ends.

STOWMARKET
Suffolk
11 miles northwest of Ipswich

Roads converge on the little country town of Stowmarket from all directions – a fact reflected in its name, for the Anglo-Saxon word *stow* means 'meeting place'. The market was added later.

Abbot's Hall, on the site of an old monastic building, is now an open-air museum of rural life. Saddle-making, barrel-making and old methods of cultivation in East Anglia are vividly re-created.

Dr Thomas Young, who was tutor to the poet John Milton, lived at Stowmarket. Dr Young is buried in the central aisle of the parish church of St Peter and St Mary, and an old portrait of him hangs in the church.

SUDBURY
Suffolk
13 miles northwest of Colchester

Weaving is still carried on in the ancient town of Sudbury, once the largest of East Anglia's woollen centres. It was a busy river port on the Stour when the great English painter Thomas Gainsborough was born here in 1727. His father's original Tudor house, with an added Georgian front, is now a museum with a lecture and exhibition centre, and an attractive garden.

The centre of the town is Market Hill. Below it lie the medieval Anchor Inn and the 15th-century Salters Hall, with its fine oriel windows. The 15th-century St Peter's Church, on Market Hill, has painted screen panels and the 'Sudbury Pall', a wonderful piece of 15th-century embroidery on velvet.

SWAFFHAM
Norfolk
14 miles southeast of King's Lynn

One story that many people have heard about Swaffham is the tale of its pedlar. He and his dog feature on the town sign just beyond the Market Place, and anyone in Swaffham can recount the adventures of

CONSTABLE COUNTRY *The little row of almshouses at Stoke-by-Nayland sprout modern antennae but seem timeless.*

John Chapman, a poor tinker who lived there in the middle of the 15th century. One night, he dreamt that if he stood on London Bridge he would meet a man who would make him rich. So John and his dog hiked to London, 100 or so miles away, stationed themselves on the bridge and waited for fortune.

After several days, a curious shopkeeper asked what they were doing there, and, on hearing John's story, recounted a recent dream of his own. He said that in his dream, a pedlar from Swaffham had found a pot of gold buried beneath a tree in his garden. John hastened back home, dug beneath the tree, and there, sure enough, he found not one but two pots of gold coins. Much of the money he gave to the parish church of St Peter and St Paul, to rebuild the north aisle. His generosity is recorded in the town's 'Black Book' – the parish records – in the church library.

The wedge-shaped Market Place, flanked by graceful 18th-century buildings, is the nucleus of Swaffham. The north end is occupied by the Assembly Rooms of 1817, once the centre of the town's social life. Nearby are the 18th-century buildings of the Sixth Form Centre, the Victorian Corn Exchange and Plowright Place, a double row of old workshops that have been converted into a pretty shopping precinct.

In the centre is the Butter Cross or Market Cross, given to the town by the Earl of Orford, nephew of the writer Horace Walpole, in 1783. Butter-sellers once displayed their wares beneath the cross – which is actually a dome held up by eight pillars. The statue on top of the cross is of Ceres, The Roman goddess of agriculture. The spire of Swaffham church, poking over the rooftops to the east of the Market Place, is crowned by a copper ball.

Three miles to the southwest, at Cockley Cley, a reconstruction of an Iceni village as it is thought to have been at the time of Queen Boudicca has been built near a 15th-century forge cottage, now a museum of local history.

At Great Cressingham, 5 miles to the southeast, are the remains of a once great house built of brick in 1545. Great Cressingham Manor has been partly re-built, but the original south front exists showing an ornate string course of terracotta forming a frieze of arches and leaves, and above it terracotta panelling decorated with such emblems as a hawk on a fist and a wreath with a monogram.

SWAFFHAM PRIOR
Cambridgeshire
5 miles west of Newmarket

Swaffham Prior gets its name from the Anglo-Saxon word 'Swaffham', meaning a 'homestead of the Swabians', an ancient tribe – and the Prior refers to the fact that it once belonged to the Prior of Ely. The village stands on one of the few hills in Cambridgeshire.

Two churches in the same churchyard stand above Swaffham Prior's curved main street which is lined by a mixture of demure cottages and Georgian houses with shady gardens. The first church, St Mary's, was built in the 12th century. It has a fine 13th-century tower on to which a Fibreglass spire was recently

added. The second church, St Cyriac's, dates from the 13th century and was built for a separate parish. The two parishes amalgamated in 1667, and both churches continued to function until St Mary's spire was struck by lightning in 1767 and the church was closed down for a time. However, it is St Mary's which is in business today, while St Cyriac's is used as a social centre.

The village of Swaffham Bulbeck, 1½ miles southwest, is named after a Norman family who founded a nunnery here. The yellow and red-brick Abbey House was built on the site in the 18th century, and the ground floor contains a small part of the nunnery crypt. In the 17th century, Swaffham Bulbeck was an inland port from which cereals were exported to the Continent. Although the waterway and quay are no longer used by commercial traffic, the port area – Commercial End, off the main road – retains much of its original character. The Dutch-style Merchant's House, the granary and the malt house are still standing, and the old stevedores' cottages are now private homes.

Just down the road from the playing-field is the 13th-century Church of St Mary, among whose treasures is a beautiful 500-year-old Italian chest – which is, in fact, a portable altar. The pew-ends are capped with the battered remains of fabulous beasts carved in the 15th century.

Much of the limestone used in Swaffham's churches comes from quarries near the neighbouring village of Reach. It claims to be the oldest settlement in the district on the basis of Stone Age flints found in the surrounding peat. It was once a Roman river port for Cambridge, and was fed by a canal from the River Cam at Upwake and the quays were in use through medieval times. Once a year the village celebrates Reach Fair, a colourful event of gaily painted swings and roundabouts held on Fair Green and opened by the Mayor and Corporation of Cambridge. A symbolic figure of the fair is 'The King of Reach', a tradition stemming from a charter given by King John granting Reach perpetual freedom, and therefore, say villagers, the right to have their own king.

At Bottisham, about 1 mile south of Swaffham Bulbeck, is the Church of the Holy Trinity. It is an impressive building of the 13th and 14th centuries, with a west tower and porch. Inside are a clerestory, a stone rood screen, and wood parclose screens. There are several interesting monuments, including two seated figures of *c.* 1740, and one with an urn and *putti* – cherub-like children – by John Bacon.

ST CYRIAC *The 1490 tower of Swaffham Prior's now-redundant church is an interesting 'round' octagonal with narrow buttresses.*

T

TATTERSHALL

Lincolnshire

8 miles southwest of Horncastle

Cromwells have been linked with Tattershall since the 14th century, and the heritage is still vividly alive in the splendours of an ancient castle, church and market cross. The magnificently restored keep of Tattershall Castle and the Church of Holy Trinity are both monuments to their builder – Ralph Cromwell, Lord High Treasurer of England under Henry VI.

The market cross on the village green serves as a reminder of the medieval times when Tattershall was a flourishing market town. Houses and shops now surround the small village green and its trees in the heart of this little community beside the River Bain where it forms part of the Horncastle Canal. Some of the buildings in and around the village, and a number of exceptionally tall trees, prevent the castle from being a major landmark. Although the keep – over 100 ft high – does not dwarf its surroundings, its battlements provide stunning views of the surrounding flatlands.

Walls some 20 ft thick form the base of the four-storey building, which is spacious enough for a large hall on each floor. It was restored by Lord Curzon of Kedleston, former Viceroy of India, between 1911–14 and subsequently handed over to the National Trust in 1925, which opens it to the public daily. The moated keep is all that is left of the castle which Ralph Cromwell built. It is one of the most splendid examples of medieval bricklaying.

Ralph Cromwell died in 1456, only a year after the castle was completed. He was buried no more than 400 yds away, in the greystone church that he also built – although, in fact, Holy Trinity was not finished until the 1480s. A gatehouse, now a museum and National Trust shop, stands between the castle and the church.

Plainly furnished and almost without ornament, the church is 186 ft long and has more than 60 windows through which light streams unimpeded. Most of its original stained glass has been broken, or taken to other churches. The interior arches have bases of up to 7 ft in height, which increase the feeling of austerity. In the north transept, among several fine brasses, a sadly mutilated one commemorates Ralph, 3rd Lord Cromwell, who gave such lustre to Tattershall.

Just south of Tattershall is the village of Coningsby. The Church of St Michael and All Angels is notable for its early 17th-century, one-handed, red-faced clock. It is 16½ ft in diameter, the largest one-handed clock in the world.

TEALBY

Lincolnshire

3 miles east of Market Rasen

Landing lights burn on not-too-distant plateaux, and black aircraft with their wheels down wobble overhead like flying dinosaurs. This is RAF country, and has been ever since the Second World War when the roar of Lancasters, Halifaxes, Wellingtons and Stirlings was the most familiar sound in the Lincolnshire landscape.

Tealby, however, set on and among the ups and downs of a hillside crowned by its church, remains aloof from most of this and concentrates on good gardening instead. Airfields apart, most of the village looks upwards and outwards to the wide, airy rim of the Wolds. From the church, the main street runs steeply down to a watersplash through the River Rase, past the Gothic school with its metal spire, the Memorial Hall, defended by a cannon and containing plaques recording Tealby's many wins in the Lincolnshire Best-Kept-Village competition, a lane called The Smooting and a good many attractive cottages of varying dates. Most of the older buildings are reddish-brown ironstone with mossy-tiled roofs, and almost all have stone-embanked gardens, richly planted and expertly maintained.

Beyond the watersplash, the river – known as the Beck – flows through some cottage gardens within the precincts of Bayons Park, where once stood a manor that was one of the most remarkable buildings in the shire. It was built in the 1830s by Alfred, Lord Tennyson's uncle – Charles Tennyson, MP – who, piqued at not being offered a peerage, capitalised on his Norman lineage by calling himself Tennyson-d'Eyncourt, and built a mock Norman castle at Bayons complete with keep, drawbridge and barbican. It was occupied by the army during the Second World War, and later fell into disrepair. It was dynamited by the Royal Engineers in 1964, and all that remains is a rocky, ivy-covered mound.

Climbing back from the river towards the church, it is worth having a look at the King's Head, a handsome stone pub with yellow shutters and a very fine Norfolk-reed thatch. The three-layer, patterned crown and the thatched cap over the door make one of the finest examples of the craft for miles around.

All Saints' Church, stoutly built in ironstone and dating in part from the mid-12th century, overlooks the entire village. The interior is rough-hewn, with a low tower arch, seemingly of greater strength than the present building requires and possibly late Norman. There are some fragments of 14th-century glass, and monuments to the Tennyson-d'Eyncourts and a number of their servants. The family must have been excellent employers, since the memorials include mention of up to 50 years' service at Bayons Manor.

On the southwestern outskirts of the village is the hamlet of Tealby Thorpe. Thorpe Mill – built in the late 18th century – is now a private residence.

TERLING

Essex

3 miles west of Witham

There is a certain magnificence about the trees, a neat uniformity of fencing and a four-square, discreet opulence about the pub, that tells any experienced wanderer in southern England that he is approaching a village whose chief means of livelihood is the working of a great estate. This is certainly the case at Terling, where the pub is called the Rayleigh Arms. Further clues are provided by milk-floats bearing the legend 'Lord Rayleigh's Dairies: A Family Business', and a number of signs indicating the whereabouts of various departments of Lord Rayleigh's Farms. These are the outer glimpses of one of the finest dairy-farms in the country. Some 2400 cattle graze in fields that are almost manicured in their perfection of fences and ditches. The originator of all this grandeur was the Hon. E. G. Strutt (1854–1930), a younger son of the 2nd Lord Rayleigh. He was made a Companion of Honour for his services to agriculture during the First World War: now he and his wife are remembered by a pair of bells in Terling's church.

Though the village is of much greater age than the farm, it would almost appear that the two were made for one another. The broad green with its clipped turf is bounded by old cottages, decently and quietly clad in primrose, ochre or white. Next to the church, which has a handsome red-brick tower of the 18th century, is a small Tudor manor with octagonal chimneys.

From the green, the road bends around into a neat pastel-coloured grouping of cottages and shops, beside which stand the discreet pillars marking the entrance of the drive to Terling Place, home of the present Lord Rayleigh. Further along, the road passes a low E-shape of red-brick estate buildings, obviously modern, yet all of a piece with this attractive village.

TETFORD

Lincolnshire
6 miles northeast of Horncastle

Tetford is the largest village in what is known as 'Tennyson Valley' – the poet was born just over a mile away at Somersby. Tetford lies below the gently billowing Lincolnshire Wolds, with their clusters of beech trees on the skyline and their roads following the contours of leisurely switchbacks, a snug little settlement of mainly red-brick houses and a church built from local greensand stone.

Memories of the past echo in the names of buildings clustered at one road junction. The National School of 1891, a well-proportioned red-brick building with a Georgian rather than Victorian air, is backed by the modernised Old School House. Both are private houses now, and across the road is another – the Old Forge. The manor house on the outskirts of the village is late Georgian and has been restored and extended.

The White Hart Inn was once the meeting place of a Gentlemen's Literary Club, attended by Lord Tennyson and before him by the much-travelled Dr Samuel Johnson, who also played skittles at the inn when staying with his friend Bennet Langton at Langton, a few miles to the southwest.

St Mary's Church dates from the 14th century, though a church at Tetford was mentioned in the Domesday Survey of 1086. In the churchyard is the stump of a medieval cross with faint traces of armorial bearings, and nearby stands a headstone of 1830 recording the death of two gypsies 'Slain by Lightening'.

Above the church porch a sun-dial sternly claims to be 'Redeeming the time because the days are evil'.

Inside the church are several memorials to the Dymoke family, the most impressive being a tablet to Captain Edward Dymoke who died in 1739. Above the tablet are arrayed a helmet, breastplate and back-plate, fitting symbols for a man who was Hereditary Grand Champion of England.

This title has existed since the time of William the Conqueror, and has been held by the Dymokes since 1377. Until 1821 the champion attended the coronation of the monarch, rode in full armour into Westminster Hall and threw down a gauntlet to challenge anyone defying the monarch's right to succeed. The Dymoke's manor house at Scrivelsby, 7 miles southwest of Tetford, no longer exists, but is marked by a Lion Gateway and a restored gatehouse where Lieutenant-Colonel John Dymoke, the present champion, lives. At the coronation of Elizabeth II his task was to bear the Standard of England.

The Roman highway from Lincoln to Burgh le Marsh skirts the northern fringe of Tetford, and crossing it the road north up Tetford Hill meets one of the loveliest stretches in the country – the Blue Stone Heath Road. It follows a track even older than that of the Romans, along the exposed ridges of the Wolds with superb vistas on either side.

TETNEY HAVEN

Lincolnshire
5 miles south of Cleethorpes

Sea-birds wheel and cry above the lonely expanse of mud-flats and salt-marsh, bright with sea asters in summer, that surrounds Tetney Haven on the North Sea coast. Silent oil tankers wait to discharge at the deep-water monobuoy, or pass upriver to Immingham, and Grimsby trawlers pass by in the estuary beyond the Haile Sand Fort – a remnant of First World War defences.

Once, the haven sheltered ships that were waiting for the tide to carry them through the narrow channel leading to the Louth Navigation, a canal extension of the River Lud by which ships of up to 30 tons could go 12 miles inland southwest to the Riverhead warehouses at Louth. They brought in coal and timber and took out wool and corn. Opened in 1770, the canal thrived until the East Coast railway arrived in 1848. It was disused by 1915, and was closed in 1924. Now it is a land drain. The old lock gates have gone and new sluice gates have been built nearer the sea. It also serves as a collector to feed the 218 acre Covenham Reservoir, Lincolnshire's largest lake.

The steep banks of the canal cutting keep the water strangely calm, disturbed only by the floats of the lone anglers strung along the canal side, fishing for pike and perch. From the bridge at Tetney Lock hamlet, $1\frac{1}{2}$ miles southwest of Tetney Haven, a path follows the canal on its southern side for the last mile or so seawards.

A nature reserve managed by the Royal Society for the Protection of Birds occupies the foreshore and saltings near Tetney Haven. Little terns nest here in summer, while later in the year many waders and flocks of Brent geese winter here. It is unwise to wander on to the saltings, for it is dangerous underfoot, with deep channels hidden by undergrowth. The reserve is open from April to August and can be visited by appointment with the Warden of Tetney Marshes Nature Reserve, c/o the Post Office, Tetney, Grimsby, South Humberside.

TATTERSHALL CASTLE *Built by an ancestor of Oliver Cromwell, the solid keep walls contain some 322,000 bricks (overleaf).*

THAXTED

Essex
6 miles southeast of Saffron Walden

At the heart of Thaxted stands the Guildhall, an ancient building of dark-silver oak framing with plaster infill. It was built about 1400 by the Cutlers' Guild as a meeting place for men of the craft, and to declare the prosperity of the Thaxted cutlery trade. It is best seen looking up the hill from the bottom of Town Street. From here, it seems protected rather than dwarfed by the slender 180 ft blade of the church spire. The cutlers' industry declined in the 16th century, possibly in part because of a shortage of trees on which they depended for fuel. At the top of the hill, opposite the church, is an imposing building, Clarence House, built of elegant red brick in 1715.

The Guildhall is at the junction of four streets. Below the Hall, in Town Street, is the Recorder's House, which probably dates from the 16th century. There, in the days of Thaxted's wealth, the Recorder, or magistrate, lived. It is now a restaurant. The other houses of Town Street belong to all kinds of periods. Few are distinguished in themselves yet, taken together, the jumble of eaves, overhangs and colour-washed walls is extraordinarily pleasant.

Also in Town Street a plaque is displayed on the house where Gustav Holst, the British composer of part-Swedish descent, lived between 1917 and 1925. He worked on several famous compositions here, including the setting of the favourite school hymn, *I vow to thee, my country*, the 'Jupiter' theme of his orchestral suite *The Planets*, which is probably his best-known work.

To the right of the Guildhall runs the appropriately cobbled Stony Lane, lined on one side by fine, overhanging medieval houses. One of them bears the legend 'Dick Turpin's Cottage', denoting where the highwayman may, or may not, have lived at some time in his career. No one seems to know for certain whether there is any truth in the legend.

At the top of the lane is the south entrance of one of the most glorious of all Essex churches. Like the Guildhall, much of its soaring mass advertises the wealth of the medieval tradesmen who dedicated their church to Our Lady, St Lawrence, patron saint of cutlers, and to St John the Baptist. The interior, some of which dates from the 14th century, is all clear light and airy spaciousness, perhaps even a little bleak, an effect accentuated by the lack of furniture in the 183 ft long building. All the same, there is much to see: the pinnacled cover that completely encloses the font; the chapel dedicated to the Blessed John Ball, priest and martyr, one of the leaders of the Peasants' Revolt in 1381; and the bright banners of six saints in the chancel. Memorials are relatively few for so large a church, but there is a charming though largely illegible one to Peter Platt, the early-19th-century builder who restored the tower.

'Where Peter lies, 'tis fit this tower should show,
But for his skill, itself had lain as low.'

A tower windmill shares the skyline with the church spire. The mill was built in 1804, and all its original machinery is intact. There is a small rural museum on the lower floors which is open to the public on weekends during the summer.

At Great Sampford, 4 miles northeast, is the Church of St Michael. Most of the church dates from the 14th century when it was rebuilt by the Knights Hospitaller, though the south chapel remains from an earlier building. It has a 14th-century font, and when the nave was redecorated in 1979 some 14th and 15th-century murals depicting the seven deadly sins were uncovered. The fine chancel has an enormous window which almost fills the wall.

THEDDLETHORPE ST HELEN

Lincolnshire
3 miles northwest of Mablethorpe

Stretching for nearly 5 miles along the seashore at Theddlethorpe St Helen the Saltfleetby-Theddlethorpe Dunes National Nature Reserve is shielded on its landward side by shoulder-high scrub of sea buckthorn, interspersed with elder, blackthorn, hawthorn, dog rose and the occasional willow. The banks of the grass-covered dunes are an important conservation area for the natterjack toad – a small toad with a yellow stripe on its back, which does not hop, but runs. Along the coast to the north, past Saltfleet Haven to Donna Nook, the sea recedes so far that, at low tide, it all but disappears across an enormous expanse of ridged sand and mud which is very rich in shells. This can be a dangerous coast, because the unwary can find themselves lost in a sandy expanse if a mist comes in off the sea. The tide floods in quickly over this flat shore. A walk along the dunes is safer and more pleasant.

The terraced promenade at Mablethorpe also gives access to miles of sandy beach for summer holidaymakers. Tree stumps that appear on the sands at very low tides are all that remain of a village and forest that was engulfed by the sea in 1289.

North of Mablethorpe, Theddlethorpe St Helen and Saltfleetby along the Lincolnshire coastline, is Tetney Haven, a lonely expanse of mud-flats and salt-marsh on the North Sea shore. A nature reserve managed by the Royal Society for the Protection of Birds occupies the foreshore and saltings near here.

THETFORD

Norfolk
12 miles north of Bury St Edmunds

When the Danes conquered East Anglia in the 9th century, they made Thetford their capital. Later, it was the See of the Bishops of East Anglia until 1091. Everywhere in the town are reminders of its past; the most prominent are the ruins of the 12th-century priory and Castle Hill, the site of Iron Age earthworks and a Norman castle mound.

The rivers Thet and Little Ouse meet in the centre of the town, and a three-way bridge spanning the junction leads to a river promenade. By Spring Walk stands a house built as a pump-room in 1818, when Thetford made an unsuccessful attempt to become a spa.

Medieval and Georgian buildings can be seen in almost every street. One of them, the 15th-century Ancient House, is Thetford's museum of local history. The Church of St Mary the Less is part Saxon, part Norman.

Thetford was the birthplace in 1737 of Thomas Paine, author of *The Rights of Man* and supporter of the American and French revolutions. A gilded bronze statue was installed in 1964 in front of the King's House in his honour.

CLUNIAC PRIORY *The crumbling walls of Thetford's monastic remains once held the Howard tombs.*

THORNEY
Cambridgeshire
7 miles northeast of Peterborough

The small island on which Thorney is built was used as a monastic settlement in the 7th century. This monastery was destroyed by the Danes in 870 and rebuilt by the Normans. Part of this abbey is now incorporated in the parish church, which was restored in the 17th century. French names and epitaphs on gravestones recall the generosity of a 17th-century Duke of Bedford who offered help to refugees from Louis XIV's religious persecution in their establishment of a community in Thorney. Two centuries later another Duke of Bedford built for his estate workers a row of 'model' houses that still stand in Wisbech Road. The yellow bricks came from the duke's brickyard at Toneham.

THORPE MARKET
Norfolk
4 miles south of Cromer

The Church of St Margaret at Thorpe Market was built in 1795 in the Gothic Revival style, and has open-work screens, porches on both sides, and at each corner of the building are turrets with little spires. The font is Perpendicular. One of the monuments is by Charles Regnart, 1796. The village green is spacious, with a 16th-century house at one end.

About 2½ miles to the southwest is Gunton, whose Adam Church of St Andrew was built by the renowned architect in 1769, and has a portico of Tuscan columns. The organ is in the west gallery, which is supported by Corinthian columns.

THURSFORD
Norfolk
5 miles northeast of Fakenham

Between the 1850s and 1930s people walked miles for the fun and spectacle of the travelling fairground, brought to them by the huge showman's steam-engine. Today the Thursford collection gives visitors all the fun of those long-ago fairs and enthusiasts still travel here from far and wide.

Steam traction engines such as *Victory* of 1920, on display at Thursford, provided haulage and supplied power for the roundabouts, ornate mechanical organs – often with mechanical figures – and electric lights.

For many people, the bright fairground lights were their first experience of electric lighting. It was the fairground also that introduced the bioscope, the earliest cinema, between 1896 and 1914. Thursford's *Edward VII*, built 1905, was used with a bioscope show.

Many steam-engines, including ploughing engines, are on display and mechanical and keyboard organs for fairs, cinemas and dance halls can be seen and heard. They include the Mighty Wurlitzer, the fourth largest cinema organ in Europe, built for the Paramount Cinema at Leeds.

TILBURY
Essex
21 miles east of London

The long landing-stage at Tilbury and the flat marshlands beyond have been a first close-up view of England for millions of travellers in the past 100 years. The largest ocean-going liners have been able to moor at the 1142 ft quay at any stage of the tide. Now that the great passenger-carrying trade has declined, Tilbury's 5 miles of docks have become London's major port for container ships. Since 1963, the

Dartford-Purfleet Tunnel has improved the town's access to the south of England.

Henry VIII built a fort at Tilbury to guard the Thames Estuary, and it was here in 1588 that Elizabeth I gathered the army that was to repel a Spanish invasion should the navy fail to defeat the Armada at sea. She told her soldiers: 'I have the body of a weak and feeble woman, but I have the heart and stomach of a king and I think foul scorn that any prince should dare to invade the borders of my realm. Rather than any dishonours shall grow by me, I will myself take up arms.' The fort itself is the finest remaining example of a 16th-century English defensive bastion.

TITTLESHALL
Norfolk
6 miles southwest of Fakenham

Tittleshall possesses a fine combined Decorated and Perpendicular church in St Mary's, whose west tower and chancel are Decorated, the nave Perpendicular, and the octagonal font Perpendicular. But the interest of Tittleshall is in its series of monuments to the Coke (Earls of Leicester) family. Nicholas Stone, the early 17th-century sculptor, carved that to Sir Edward Coke (*d.* 1634), with a recumbent effigy. Louis Roubiliac carved the busts of the 1st Earl and Countess of Leicester, *c.* 1760, and Joseph Nollekens sculpted the large marble relief showing Mrs Coke (*d.* 1800) leaning on a broken column, whilst above an angel sitting on clouds holds out his hand to her.

Wellingham lies about 2 miles northwest, and its Church of St Andrew contains a rood screen dated 1532, with good figure painting of saints, among them St Sebastian, and St George fighting the Dragon, with onlookers from a city tower.

TOLLESBURY
Essex
7 miles east of Maldon

Farmland ends and creeks and estuary marshes begin at Tollesbury, which lies close to the River Blackwater. A lane leads down to the marshes and a small boatyard on Woodrolfe Creek.

The Church of St Mary is a colourful mixture of pebble, stone, brick and tiles. The 18th-century font bears the inscription: 'Good people all I pray take care, that in ye church you do not sware. As this man did'. The font was paid for by a drunken man who swore in church and was persuaded to make the donation to avoid prosecution.

The weather-vane of the church represents a fishing boat, a reminder that Tollesbury once had a fishing fleet. At the turn of the century more than 100 sailing smacks brought in their catches of sprats for pickling.

TOLLESHUNT MAJOR, D'ARCY AND KNIGHTS
Essex
4 to 6 miles northeast of Maldon

At Tolleshunt Major is an unusual Tudor brick wall, surrounding a large courtyard and relatively small, partly 16th-century, timber and brick house. The large turreted gatehouse is the central feature of the wall and there are other turrets at each corner of the wall. Ornamental panelling from the Hall, dated 1546, is in the Victoria and Albert Museum. The house itself may be visited by appointment.

Nearby, Tolleshunt d'Arcy possesses the 15th-century Church of St Nicholas, with an embattled west tower. The ceiling in the chancel dates from the 19th century and there is a collection of brasses in the north chapel.

The Hall, which lies south of the village, is a house of *c.* 1500 with a fine moat and four-arched brick and stone bridge dated 1585. A wing, remodelled in the 17th century, has outstanding 16th-century panelling of linenfold divided by ranges of carving. In the grounds is a large 16th-century dovecote. The Hall at Tolleshunt D'Arcy can also be visited by appointment.

Tolleshunt Knights has its Devil's Wood, said to have been the fief of the Devil himself, who presided over orgies held on the banks of a bottomless pool in the wood. A house standing outside the old wood, Barnhall, still has a beam known to this day as the Devil's Beam. It bears on its blackened sides the marks of Satan's claws, left there when the arch-fiend destroyed an earlier, partially built house erected on his territory – or so the story goes.

TYDD ST MARY
Lincolnshire
3 miles south of Long Sutton

The 14th-century Church of St Mary in Tydd St Mary has a later west tower and spire. Inside, the 12th-century arcades provide evidence of the former church here. The chancel windows have fine tracery work, and there is notable carving on the fine 15th-century font. There are several good monuments, including one by J. M. Rysbrack.

VILLAGE LOCK-UP *Rowdy Tollesbury fishermen who overstepped the law could find this home for a night or two.*

WAINFLEET ALL SAINTS

Lincolnshire
5 miles southwest of Skegness

Once a port, Wainfleet All Saints is now 5 miles inland. South of the town the River Steeping winds between high banks to The Wash. William of Waynflete, a bishop of Winchester and founder of Magdalen College, Oxford, was born here c. 1395. In 1484 he left Magdalen College School, now a library, to the town.

WALBERSWICK

Suffolk
1 mile southwest of Southwold

The once-flourishing port of Walberswick has weathered gracefully into a pleasant residential community with large houses and well-tended gardens. The Church of St Andrew stands within the ruins of its larger medieval predecessor. The shore is much more sandy than most beaches on this coast, and there are gay, lopsided holiday houses among the extensive dunes planted with marram grass. Attempts have been made to bind these perpetually shifting sea defences with plastic seaweed, to avoid a repetition of the 1953 floods; but results so far have been discouraging. The village offers the best view of Southwold across the River Blyth – only 1 mile to the north yet 8 miles by car.

WALPOLE ST PETER

Norfolk
5 miles northeast of Wisbech

The Church of St Peter and St Mary at Walpole St Peter is so magnificent that it is known as 'the Cathedral of the Fens'. There has been a church on the site since at least the year 1021. The oldest part of the present building, the tower, dates from about 1300.

The altar is raised nine steps above the chancel because it is built over a passage known as the Bolt Hole. In the passage are rings to which horses used to be tethered during services.

The church has a west tower, Perpendicular windows in the aisles and clerestory, two-storey south porch with coats of arms, stone-vault and carved roof bosses, a 16th-century font with an early 17th-century cover, and a 17th-century screen across the west end. There also remains a pulpit of 1620, box-pews and fragments of stained glass.

WALSHAM LE WILLOWS

Suffolk
5 miles east of Ixworth

The picturesque village of Walsham le Willows justifies its picturesque name, but there are splendid limes and beech trees too. The village is set in the heart of parkland, and draws together roads and lanes from surrounding villages. There are weatherboarded and timber-framed cottages, and a fine confusion of eaves and roof levels.

The name of the Six Bells Inn derives from the bells of the church tower. Inside the church hangs a 'crant', a medallion used to mark the pew seats of unmarried girls who have died; until the 19th century the 'crants' were hung with wreaths by young men on the anniversary of the deaths.

WALTHAM ABBEY

Essex
7 miles southwest of Harlow

An old, small abbey, once grand, kingly and powerful, Waltham Abbey is set on the edge of Epping Forest. King Harold built a religious college here, and gave it riches. It is said that after he was slain at Hastings he was buried at Waltham – a plain slab is believed to be his tomb. Henry II built a great abbey, an offering to God to expiate the murder of Thomas Becket.

Much has gone, destroyed in the Reformation, but what remains is magnificent. The great Norman nave has been compared with Durham Cathedral. Restored in the 1860s, the abbey contains some of the finest 19th-century stained glass in the Jesse window. Dated 1861, it was designed by Sir Edward Burne-Jones who, with William Morris, Dante Gabriel Rossetti and others, formed the Pre-Raphaelite Brotherhood of artists and poets.

WANSFORD

Cambridgeshire
7 miles west of Peterborough

A fine old bridge across the River Nene at Wansford has 12 arches: the seven northern arches date from 1577, the next three were rebuilt in 1672–4. and the last two added in 1795.

East of Wansford about 1½ miles is Stibbington Hall, a country mansion built of Ketton stone, c. 1625, to an E-shaped plan. Only the exterior is available for viewing – visitors cannot go inside.

WARHAM ST MARY

Norfolk
2 miles southeast of Wells

Warham St Mary's most notable building is the Church of St Mary. Norman work includes a blocked north door, but the tower dates from the 14th century and the fittings are nearly all 18th century – for example, the fine three-decker pulpit. There is some early Renaissance German or Flemish stained glass mixed with medieval English fragments.

LINCOLN WATERSCAPE *On the outskirts of Wainfleet, the River Steeping wends its leisurely course* (overleaf).

At Warham Camp, just south of the village, an almost circular Iron Age fort lies on the lowland coastal plain, bordered on its west side by the River Stiffkey. Close to the stream there is a single defensive bank only, but the remainder of the $3\frac{1}{2}$ acre area has two banks and ditches, the banks still standing higher than a man. Excavations have shown that it was constructed late in the Iron Age and lasted at least into early Roman times.

WAXHAM HALL
Norfolk
4 miles east of Stalham

On the North Sea coast, Waxham Hall stands outside the village of Waxham, behind a long high flint wall and a 15th-century gateway. The flint and brick house, once the home of the Brograves and Wodehouses, is now a farm and is not open to the public. It is reputedly haunted by six members of the Brograve family, all of whom died violently in battle, from the Crusades to the Civil War and Ramillies. A later descendant, Sir Berney, once invited them all to dinner and drank with them until midnight.

WELLS-NEXT-THE-SEA
Norfolk
9 miles north of Fakenham

Its sprats are famous and delectable, and it does a brisk trade in whelks. Wells, no longer quite next the sea, but on an estuary, is a little port with an attractive quay, extremely narrow streets and a pleasant series of Georgian houses on the green called the Buttlands. This name probably derives from an area allocated for long-bow practice in the 16th century. Other good buildings to see are Ostrich House in Burnt Street, Marsh House in Marsh Lane, and the 16th-century St Michael's cottage in Jickling's Yard.

WENDENS AMBO
Essex
2 miles southwest of Saffron Walden

Great and Little Wenden became one parish in 1662, hence the addition of *Ambo*, Latin for 'both'. The village lies in a shady vale by a winding stream, which gives rise to the first half of its name, from the Old English verb *windan*, 'to wind'. Thatched and tiled cottages line the lane to the church.

The Church of St Mary the Virgin has a Norman tower, topped by a short lead spire known as a Hertfordshire spike, because this type of spire is common in the neighbouring county. Inside the church are wall-paintings c. 1330, depicting the life of St Margaret. The large thatched barn near the church is part of the 15th-century Wendens Hall farm.

The railway station just south of the village bears the name of Audley End, the 17th-century mansion close by. The lands of Walden Abbey, on which the mansion stands, were given by Henry VIII to Thomas Audley as a reward for his help in the Dissolution of the Monasteries. It later passed to the Howard family, and the present house was begun in 1603 by Audley's grandson, Thomas Howard, Earl of Suffolk. It still retains its Jacobean elegance.

WEST DEEPING
Lincolnshire
5 miles east of Stamford

The small village of West Deeping on the old Roman King Street is distinguished by a splendid watermill and an adjoining elegant Georgian facade. To the east, past Deeping St James, is the fenland stretch known as the Bedford Level. The church at Deeping St James was once the church of a priory founded in 1139. It is a large building offering a representation of all the architectural styles from Norman to 18th century. There is an impressive Norman arcade in the nave, and the late Norman font is adorned with a design of intersecting arches. The west tower and spire are work of the 18th century.

About 2 miles southwest of Deeping St James, across the Cambridgeshire border, is the manor house of Northborough. The gatehouse opens onto the main street. Built c. 1330, with a porch added in 1500, the house stands as a good example of a small, fortified stone-built dwelling, now carefully restored to its medieval state. Gabled with a buttress on the south side, it has a Gothic chimney and three carved doorways.

WEST SOMERTON
Norfolk
$1\frac{1}{2}$ miles west of Winterton

A quiet village at the eastern end of Martham Broad, West Somerton has a weedy reach which is good for angling. Drainage of the marshy surroundings, carried out through a maze of streams and dykes reaching the sea near Yarmouth, was once powered by windmill-pumps, most of them now shorn of their sails. In the 18th century, smugglers are said to have landed cargoes in Somerton Gap, working to instructions provided by the windmill sails, which were set at agreed angles to issue warnings of Revenue men and transmit messages.

At nearby Martham, to the south, a working agricultural museum re-creates village life in the second half of the 19th century. Craftsmen such as a blacksmith and a wheelwright work on the farm and during the summer work heavy horses in the fields.

WEST STOW
Suffolk
5 miles northwest of Bury St Edmunds

Scanty West Stow looks as if it has never been anything more than a tiny village among the inhospitable sandy heaths, known locally as Breckland. Its long and crowded past lies buried beneath 3 ft of sand, residue of a violent 14th-century sandstorm that swept over the district – a common hazard in Breckland until the Forestry Commission recently laid down trees which keep a firm hold on the soil.

An archaeologist's treasure trove is now being uncovered here. Ever since Stone Age man dug for flint, West Stow had – until that sandstorm – been a busy community. Hunters and Bronze Age farmers camped in the valley beside the River Lark, where the Romans later built pottery kilns. And between AD 400 and 650, a small Anglo-Saxon settlement was established. It was probably peopled by farmers, who came over from Denmark and Germany.

The traces of about 30 wooden buildings – now simply dark stains in the ground – have been so well preserved in the sand that it has even been possible to reconstruct some of them on their foundations. These huts were made of split tree trunks, and roofed with thatch. Pottery, bronze jewellery, spinning tools and bone combs found on the site are now on display in Ipswich Museum.

The reconstructed village – open from April to October, except on Mondays – is the main attraction in West Stow's 125 acre country park and nature trail.

The few cottages that make up West Stow today are mostly of mellow white Suffolk brick, so West Stow Hall stands out as a surprise. Its three-storey red-brick gatehouse, dating from the 1520s, has turrets and pinnacles and carries the arms of Mary Tudor, sister of Henry VIII. She became the wife of Louis XII of France, and, after his death, Duchess of Suffolk. She is buried in St Mary's Church, Bury St Edmunds.

WESTLETON
Suffolk
3 miles east of Yoxford

The little village of Westleton lies $2\frac{1}{4}$ miles back from the lost port of Dunwich. It had its beginnings when a Norseman named Vestlidhe stumbled across the site after the Romans left Britain. By the time the Normans arrived it had merged into the Saxon neighbourhood and so was entered in Domesday Book as Westlede's Tun, *Tun* meaning 'a settlement'. Since then, English history has largely passed it by. Today the whole area is a network of nature reserves among the marshes.

Throughout its history much of Westleton's activity has centred on the Green. For two centuries the parish butts were here, in the days when archery practice was compulsory. Here, also, was the village pound where stray cattle were kept. Close by were the stocks – last used in the 1870s for chastening a poacher named Bob Randall. Near the pond was the ducking-stool where many a village scold had her tongue temporarily stilled. Here, too, is the White Horse, once built of wattle and plaster with a thatched roof, but rebuilt at the turn of the century.

Close to the Green, on a rise, is St Peter's Church, which has kept its thatched roof and has stood here since 1340. In past centuries smuggling and piracy were very much a part of life, especially on the east coast, and an entry in the Westleton Churchwarden's Account for 1731–2 records the sum of one shilling and sixpence having been given to 'fifteen seamen in company, which had been taken by ye pyrates and very barbarously used'.

In medieval times Suffolk was wool country, and Westleton Heath, 6 miles southwest of Southwold, is one of the last surviving examples of east Suffolk heaths where sheep once grazed. Today the heath is a fine nature reserve and walking area.

WESTON LONGVILLE
Norfolk
9 miles northwest of Norwich

Curiously, Weston is, like Paston, famous for a very personal account of day-to-day life in a bygone age. The village, on a hill above the River Wensum, is a place of pilgrimage for admirers of Parson James Woodforde, whose *Diary of a Country Parson* is a classic. He arrived in Weston in 1776, aged 36, and kept his diary until $2\frac{1}{2}$ months before his death on New Year's Day 1803. He was an amiable, obscure man and recounts no world-shaking happenings – the only amazing ones are his meals:

Jan. 28, 1780: 'We had for dinner a Calf's Head, boiled Fowl and Tongue, a Saddle of Mutton rosted on the Side Table, and a fine Swan rosted with Currant Jelly Sauce for the first Course. The Second Course a couple of Wild Fowl called Dun Fowls, Larks, Bla-mange, Tarts etc, etc, and a good Desert of Fruit after amongst which was a Damson Cheese. I never eat a bit of a Swan before, and I think it good eating with sweet sauce. The Swan was killed 3 weeks before it was eat and yet not the least bad taste in it.' Then, by way of a change on April 15, 1778: 'My two large Piggs, by drinking some Beer grounds taken out of one of my Barrels today, got so amazingly drunk by it, that they were not able to stand and appeared like dead things almost, and so remained all night from dinner time today. I never saw Piggs so drunk in my life, I slit their ears for them without feeling.'

Dec. 31, 1780: 'This being the last day of the year, we sat up till after 12 o'clock, then drank a Happy New Year to all our Friends and went to bed. We were very merry indeed after Supper till 12. Nancy and Betsie Davie locked me in the great Parlour, and both fell on me and pulled my Wigg almost to Pieces – I paid them for it however.'

So his comfortable, tolerant life went on. He was forgotten after his death until his diaries were published in 1924.

At first sight there seems little relationship between Woodforde's village and today's. His rectory was rebuilt last century, though the pond in the grounds where he hid smuggled gin from the Excise men remains. But the Church of All Saints, with a 13th-century tower and a rare 14th-century painting of the Tree of Jesse, is still as it was. So is the great barn where he collected his tithes from local farmers, feasting them in return on roast beef, puddings, rum, wine and strong beer at a 'Frolick'. And some of the best fishing in Norfolk is still to be found at the Lenwade Bridge, where Woodforde caught a 'prodigious pike' which he inevitably served up for dinner.

WHITTLESEY
Cambridgeshire
5 miles east of Peterborough

An industrial and market town, Whittlesey has a forest of tall brickwork chimneys stretching westwards towards Peterborough. Until the 19th century, Whitt-lesey Mere was a 1900 acre lake, much broadened during floods. In winter it froze hard enough for skating, which was not only a major Fenland sport, but one of the fastest and most reliable ways of getting about. The last great drainage scheme of 1851 used a massive centrifugal pump to remove the water. This drove away many species of wildfowl, but also banished the agues and rheumatics which had plagued the fen dwellers.

The Church of St Mary has a magnificent vaulted spire. It was added in the mid-15th century to the church which had been largely rebuilt after fire damage in the 13th century. The smaller St Andrew's has graceful Perpendicular and Georgian features.

WICKEN

Cambridgeshire

2 miles southwest of Soham

Wicken, with its four village greens, stands beside Britain's oldest nature reserve – and the last stretch of natural, undrained fenland in East Anglia. Wicken Fen, just a step from the main street, is 600 soggy, peaty acres of old England. Before Roman times the Great Fens covered 2500 square miles.

The Romans raised a network of causeways and opened drainage channels through the treacherous marshes. Draining has continued since the 13th century across the whole area. It was the Dutch engineer Vermuyden who devised a workable drainage scheme in the 17th century. Employed by the 4th Earl of Bedford, Vermuyden dug the Old Bedford River and the New Bedford River, and made a large area of fenland fit for pasture. Before Wicken Fen became a reserve, it was strip-farmed for sedge and peat by local villagers; they used the sedge for thatching, kindling and animal litter, and the peat for fuel. When this work was abandoned and the surrounding water level had fallen, scrub began to choke the sedge-beds. Much of it has been cleared and the water level raised and now only Wicken is left in its original state – a treasureland of sedges, reeds and many other marsh plants, with 5000 species of insects, and a great variety of birds including warblers and breeding snipe, all jealously guarded by the National Trust, which has managed the fen since 1899. Only part of the fen is open to the public.

Wicken Fen stands out like an island above the surrounding peatland, which has shrunk as it has been drained. The water level in the reserve is kept high by a unique windpump with a scoop-wheel – carrying out

a task which is the reverse of that for which it was designed. Until the 1820s there were about 700 such pumps draining water from the fenlands. They were mostly replaced by steam pumps, but a few, like Wicken's, were used well into the 20th century. The Wicken Fen Mill, a four-sided timber building standing on a brick base and with a boat-shaped cap, was built in 1908 and has been restored on a new site to pump water back into the fen. A 2 mile nature trail wanders around the reserve, and there is a hide for bird-watching.

The village is at the other end of Lode Lane from the fen. One village green lies beside the main road, scattered about with houses. Another, Pond Green, has a duckpond and is surrounded by cottages and farm buildings. The William Thorpe Building, at the foot of Lode Lane, has displays recounting the history of the nature reserve.

St Laurence's Church stands to the east of Wicken. A chancel screen was presented to the church as a memorial to Henry, the fourth son of Oliver Cromwell, who lived at Spinney Abbey after the Restoration. Its stones were reused in building what is now a farmhouse set back from the road to Stretham, a mile to the northwest of the village. Henry is buried beside the altar with another Oliver Cromwell, one of the Lord Protector's grandsons.

Felix of Burgundy founded a monastery at Soham, 2 miles northeast of Wicken, but like many others in the region this was destroyed by the Danes. The cruciform church, begun in the 12th century but much added to, has a mighty peal of ten bells.

POND GREEN *These charming cottages line a duckpond on one of Wicken's four greens.*

WIGGENHALL ST MARY, ST GERMANS, ST PETER AND ST MARY MAGDALENE

Norfolk
4–7 miles south of King's Lynn

Three of the four villages, each named after their church's patron saint, have particularly fine woodwork in their parish church. The fittings include benches with poppy-heads and large carved figures of saints on the bench-ends, remains of painted wood screens, and early 17th-century pulpits with hour-glass stands. St Mary Magdalene dates from the 13th century in its present form and has some 15th-century stained glass.

The roofless, ruined Church of St Peter stands in its village, between St Germans and St Mary Magdalene.

WILLINGALE

Essex
4 miles northeast of Chipping Ongar

The parish churches of Willingale Doe and Willingale Spain stand in a single churchyard, though the lay-out is such that the Bell Inn separates them – hence the local joke that the two churches have only one bell between them.

Long ago, it is said, two sisters fell in love with a foreign nobleman, who returned the love of one of them and planned to marry her. But she died before her wedding day, and the grief-stricken suitor erected a church – St Andrew's of Willingale Spain – before returning heart-broken to his native land. The surviving sister, feeling that she had been slighted, ordered the construction of a much larger church – St Christopher's of Willingale Doe – right beside the first one. The tradition cannot be right, for there is a difference in age of at least 200 years between the two churches.

WIMPOLE

Cambridgeshire
6 miles north of Royston

There are two landmarks in Wimpole; the Hall, and the Church of St Andrew, which although of 14th-century origin, was almost completely rebuilt by Henry Flitcroft in 1749 and Gothicised in the late 19th century. There is a superb series of monuments, from 16th-century brasses onwards: work by Peter Scheemakers, Flaxman, Bacon the Elder, Banks and the Westmacotts may be seen on arrangement with the vicar.

WINGFIELD

Suffolk
2 miles north of Stradbroke

The charming village of Wingfield possesses an unusually ambitious church for such a small place. St Andrew's has a clerestory to the chancel as well as to the nave, and a west tower. There are monuments to members of the de la Pole family from the 14th century, and one to Sir John de Wingfield, who rebuilt the church and founded the college.

Wingfield Castle to the northwest of the village is mainly Tudor, but with a 14th-century south front with the original central gatehouse, corner turrets and door.

The College, founded in 1361, was surrendered to Henry VIII at the Dissolution.

Fressingfield lies 2 miles east. The Church of St Peter and St Paul is Decorated and Perpendicular in style, with a west tower, clerestory and vaulted two-storey south porch. Inside are good benches with carving.

WISBECH

Cambridgeshire
12 miles southwest of King's Lynn

Surrounded by bulb fields and orchards, Wisbech is a flourishing centre of a rich flower and fruit-growing area. Architecturally, it is the region's most distinguished town outside Cambridge. The Brinks, two rows of impeccable houses lining the River Nene, are among the finest examples of Georgian architecture in England. Peckover House, built on the North Brink in about 1722, is the town's most outstanding building. Presented to the National Trust in 1943 by the Peckover family, local bankers, it reflects their wealth in its rococo wood and plasterwork interior decoration. A plaque on a building on the South Brink commemorates it as the birthplace in 1838 of Octavia Hill, founder of the National Trust.

Once 4 miles from the sea, Wisbech is now 11 miles inland, as the result of land reclamation, but it is still a busy port. Ships of up to 2000 tons can navigate the River Nene.

The Rose and Crown Hotel, which dates from about 1600, has fine Tudor work and a graceful 18th-century staircase; and the Old Market and Norfolk Street contain good Georgian buildings. A Regency house at the centre of the town embodies the remains of successive castles from Norman times.

Near this house stands the Wisbech and Fenland Museum, established in 1781. It illustrates local history, and also contains the manuscript of Charles Dickens's *Great Expectations*, donated to the museum by his friend Chauncey Hare Townshend.

The parish church of St Peter and St Paul includes Norman work and a monument by Joseph Nollekens, the 18th-century sculptor.

On the northeast outskirts are two attractive marshland churches at Walsoken, which is mainly Norman, and West Walton, which has a detached 13th-century tower. At Tydd St Giles, 5 miles north, Nicholas Breakspear (d. 1159), the only Englishman to become Pope, as Adrian IV, is said to have been curate.

WITHAM ON THE HILL

Lincolnshire
4 miles southwest of Bourne

Approached from the east a steep incline leads to Witham's large village green, where the stocks survive as a relic of the village's ancient past. A tiled canopy protects the stocks, suggesting that in Witham justice was tempered with mercy. The Bywells Spring, which gushes out near the stocks, had never been known to stop flowing until the drought of 1976.

The parish is mentioned in the Domesday Book, the great land survey ordered by William the Conqueror in 1086, and Charles Kingsley in his book *Hereward the Wake* says that Hereward owned the estate. The spacious Church of St Andrew, largely 15th century, has several examples of Norman architecture – including the south aisle and the arch and doorway of the south porch. The church tower and spire were rebuilt in 1738 after the earlier ones had collapsed. Distinctive ornamental urns decorate the base of the spire.

On the opposite side of the green stands Witham Hall, an impressive mansion with bays dating from 1752. It is now a preparatory school for boys.

One of the wonders of Lincolnshire stands on farmland about 1 mile from the village but within the ecclesiastical parish. The Bowthorpe Oak, with a trunk about 40 ft in circumference, is thought to be at least 500 years old. The trunk had already been hollowed out in the 17th century, creating a room in which 39 people have stood together. On one occasion, it is said, 16 people sat down to afternoon tea inside the oak, or so the story goes.

WIVENHOE

Essex
4 miles southeast of Colchester

The village of Wivenhoe is a busy shipyard on the wooded reaches of the Colne. Its church was damaged by earthquake in 1884. The older houses include one in East Street that has fine pargetting, or decorated plasterwork.

Essex University, standing in Wivenhoe Park, is functional, with tower blocks, concrete and glass – and a lake which saves the scene.

WOLFERTON

Norfolk
6 miles northeast of King's Lynn

For about a century, Wolferton was one of Europe's glittering royal centres. Emperors and empresses, kings and queens, leading statesmen and polished courtiers passed through its little station on their way to nearby Sandringham, after the estate was bought by the Prince of Wales – the future Edward VII – in 1862. So heavy was the royal traffic through Wolferton that in 1898 the railway track from King's Lynn had to be doubled and a magnificent set of reception rooms was built at the station.

But as road transport became more popular in the 1960s, fewer people – including royals – used the line. The royal trains halted for good in 1966, so British Rail decided to demolish the unique reception rooms and build a housing estate on the site.

The rooms were saved by an act of courage and vision: Eric Walker, a senior British Rail executive, was sent to take an inventory and was overwhelmed by what he saw. He and his wife decided to buy the station and turn it into a combined house and museum, which now attracts thousands of visitors.

The rooms were filthy and neglected when the Walkers moved in, but beneath the grime everything was intact – even down to the toilet fittings. Painstaking work has created a museum of Edwardian social life and of railway history, for Mr Walker has collected and put on display much long-forgotten equipment.

Nearby is another survival from the days of glory,

the Gate House. The level-crossing keeper once lived here, and it has been lovingly restored as a private home. In the adjoining churchyard is a last surviving lamp post, exquisitely decorated with a crown on top. The nearby 'gas house' used to supply acetylene gas to all the lamps in the village and to St Peter's Church. The church is late 13th and early 14th century but has been much restored.

WOODBRIDGE

Suffolk
8 miles northeast of Ipswich

When yeoman farmer John Sayer of Woodbridge died in 1635, he left a sum of money to pay for bread to be distributed each week to the town's poor. The bread is still distributed, though the loaves his money buys now are few, and they go to the first-comer rather than the most poor. But each week a Woodbridge baker comes to the church and leaves some bread in an elegant cupboard of polished wood, purpose-built into the stone of the porch to contain it. During the Second World War, however, recipients of the bread were obliged to surrender their ration coupons.

Traditions last long in Woodbridge, which stands at the head of the Deben estuary, 9 miles from the North Sea. South of the town is Kyson Hill, a finger of land projecting into the Deben where the river makes a brief incision into Martlesham Creek and then heads for the sea. Four acres of the hill belong to the National Trust.

Down beside the river, boatbuilders and sailmakers have been at work for at least six centuries. But where their 14th-century predecessors built vessels used as warships by Edward III, they now turn out craft devoted to pleasure.

The former Boat Inn – now a private house – has stood on the Quayside since 1530, and nearby is the 17th-century Ferry House. The row of cottages at Nos 1–5 Quayside used to be the Ship Inn, built in the 16th century. The Congregationalists once held their meetings in the Ship, then in 1688 they built their own church around the corner in Quay Street. The present Quay United Reformed Church, which was formerly the Congregational Church, was built on the original site in 1805. But the most eye-catching riverside building is the weatherboarded tide mill. Built in the 18th century, it was working until 1957, when the oak shaft attached to the water wheel fractured.

In Woodbridge, it is difficult to escape reminders of the town's greatest benefactor, Thomas Seckford, a 16th-century MP and barrister, who commissioned the first systematically surveyed maps of England. He founded the Seckford Almshouses to look after 13 poor men – although the present almshouse buildings date only from Victorian times – and built the Shire Hall. This fine building, ornamented with curly gables in the Dutch manner, still looks out on the main square, called Market Hill, making a fitting memorial to its builder. An ornate Gothic pump and drinking trough in front of it were added in 1876.

Seckford was buried in 1587 in the parish church of St Mary the Virgin, connected to Market Hill by cobbled footpaths. The church also has a remarkable

TIDE MILL *The 18th-century weatherboarded mill is a prime attraction for visitors along the Woodbridge estuary (overleaf).*

three-tiered monument of Jeffrey Pitman, a local tanner and haberdasher who became High Sheriff of Suffolk and who died in 1627. In the monument, Pitman kneels piously on the top tier with his two wives and two sons kneeling facing one another in the tiers below.

As lord of the manor, Thomas Seckford lived with his family at The Abbey, just below the church. The earliest parts of the house – now a school – were built on the site of an Augustinian priory and date from 1564. However, the building has been much altered in the centuries since then.

Another Seckford family home – once connected to The Abbey by a secret tunnel – is the fine Elizabethan Seckford Hall. The hall stands 1 mile southwest of Woodbridge, on a site which was owned by the Seckfords for 520 years, and is said to be haunted by Thomas Seckford's ghost. In 1940, it was bought derelict by Sir Ralph Harwood, a former secretary to George V. He restored it and made it into a hotel, with some interesting furniture from Windsor Castle and Buckingham Palace, including the winged chair in which Edward VII died in 1910.

A mile away from Woodbridge, on the opposite bank of the Deben, is the site of the Sutton Hoo ship-burial where excavations in 1939 revealed the remains of a Saxon ship, and a vast treasure hoard. At Boulge, $2\frac{1}{2}$ miles northwest of Woodbridge, Edward FitzGerald, translator of The Rubaiyat of Omar Khayyam, is buried. On his grave is a rose bush which came from Omar Khayyam's grave in Iran.

About 3 miles northeast is Ufford. Its Church of St Mary has a 15th-century font cover which is a masterpiece of woodwork in the form of a prodigious spire rising in a mass of fine pinnacles, with a pelican at the top. Uffa, after whom the village was named, was the founder of the Sutton Hoo dynasty.

Northeast about 6 miles is Otley, site of a partly moated 16th-century timber and brick house, with a fine diapered chimney-shaft. The house has fine linen-fold panelling, a good hall screen, heavily beamed ceilings in the hall and Jacobean wall decorations. In the same parish, Otley High House is a fine contemporary timber-framed building, viewable by prior appointment.

About a mile further northwest is Helmingham, whose Tudor Hall stands within a deer park; it is moated, with functioning drawbridges, and has crenellation added by Nash in the 18th century. It was built in 1490 by the Tollemache family to whom there are many monuments in the church. The gardens are open to the public.

WOOLPIT
Suffolk
5 miles northwest of Stowmarket

A village green, complete with a roofed-over village pump, lies near the centre of Woolpit, recorded in the Domesday Book as Wolfpeta – a pit in which wolves were trapped. The wolves have gone, but the centuries-old atmosphere lingers on amid the ancient dwellings, many of late medieval and Tudor design. The 400-year-old Swan Inn is still here, although its archway and yard no longer cater for the coaches that once used it as a staging post on the way to Bury St Edmunds. Modern traffic ignores the community since a by-pass was built, and leaves the village in peace.

Many of the village houses are built of white bricks, for which the local brickyard, now closed, was famous from the 17th century. Green is another colour that figures in local history, but for a different reason. There is a legend that in the 12th century, reapers saw two children climbing out of a pit. Their bodies were green, and after learning English they spoke of coming from a mysterious land called St Martin. The boy died young, but the girl grew up to marry. The story is said to have been the basis for Herbert Read's novel The Green Child, written in 1935.

St Mary's Church stands on the north side of the village, a building of flint and stone with a 140 ft high steeple that landmarks one of the most beautiful churches in Suffolk. It dates from the 11th century, but its later additions include a fine 15th-century porch and the tower and spire which were rebuilt in 1853. The nave is 14th century, and is crowned by a magnificent hammerbeam roof with spread-winged angels decorating the beam ends. Within the nave are carved pews, a lectern said to have been given by Elizabeth I, and a pulpit designed in 1883 by George Gilbert Scott junior, son of the Victorian church architect. The 15th-century screen still has traces of medieval decorations. But many of the church's contents were destroyed in the turbulent 1640s when a puritanical Parliament ordered the general demolition or removal of altars, pictures and candlesticks. St Mary's suffered at the hands of William Dowsing, a religious fanatic selected to carry out the destruction.

Just north is Elmswell, whose Church of St John has a west tower with flint-work decoration. The chancel was restored in the late 19th century. There is a carved font, and a monument to Sir Robert Gardener, Chief Justice of Ireland, ascribed to Maximilian Colt (1619).

WORSTEAD
Norfolk
3 miles southeast of North Walsham

When Flemish weavers settled in East Anglia during the Middle Ages they introduced a technique to the wool trade which produced a cloth of fine fibres and closely twisted yarn. Worstead became the centre for the manufacture of this new material, which came to be known as worsted – after the village.

The worsted industry thrived as a cottage craft until the 19th century, when production moved to the mills that came with the Industrial Revolution. Some brick-built weavers' houses – in which 12 ft high looms were used – remain in and around the village. The last hand-loom weaver, John Cubitt, died in 1882 aged 91. The old market place is now called Church Plain – 'plain' is the Norfolk word for 'square' – and it has several large 17th-century houses.

Worstead's church, St Mary's, is a splendid memorial to the prosperous weaving days. It was built from the wealth of the 14th-century cloth-makers and has a 109 ft high tower. Inside there are copies of the designs made by Sir Joshua Reynolds for some of the windows of New College Chapel, Oxford, painted on panels in 1831. North of the village is a rise known as Meeting Hill, the remains of a 19th-century Nonconformist hamlet with a chapel and some fine cottages.

WOOLPIT *The notorious William Dowsing had 80 of St Mary's statues and paintings destroyed during the 1640s.*

WOTHORPE
Cambridge
1 mile south of Stamford

Ruins, c. 1620, are all that remain of the cruciform house at Wothorpe, originally built for Thomas Cecil, eldest son of Lord Burghley, for use as a lodge until his great house Burghley, at Stamford, was completed.

The manor house fell into ruin during the 18th century; the towers, with an octagonal top storey, are still well preserved. A gateway with a stepped gable leads to the courtyard.

WRITTLE
Essex
2 miles west of Chelmsford

Rich parklands and fragments of ancient forest abound in Writtle parish, the largest in Essex. It was once a royal manor, passing from King Harold to William the Conqueror, and later became one of King John's hunting lodges. In 1204 he granted its revenues to the Hospital of the Holy Ghost in Rome. Then, in 1391, it was sold to William of Wykeham, Bishop of Winchester and founder of the school, who used it as part of his endowment of New College, Oxford.

Drivers heading up the long slope into Chelmsford will be aware of the high brick wall climbing the hill beside them. This is part of the perimeter of Hylands Park, much of which lies within the parish. At the heart of its 400 acres of woods is an early Georgian manor.

The central green of Writtle slopes gently towards its pond, which originally supplied water for traction engines. All around the green are houses of different styles, from the Tudor-timbered splendour of Aubyns, near the church, through elegant Georgian brickwork to varieties of pargetted plaster. Some of the pargetting boasts sizable relief bosses; other examples, like a pair of 1787 cottages, have simpler, incised panels.

The Church of All Saints was built around 1230, but tiles dating from Roman times are incorporated into the structure, and an earlier church stood here at the time of the Conquest. The tower is of rough stone and rubble, with narrow red-brick buttresses and a brick parapet. Inside are medieval stone angels on the roof supports, re-coloured in recent times, and decorative shields down the centre roof beam.

WYMONDHAM *The two towers of the abbey church still compete with each other, as they have for 500 years.*

Parts of the building have been replaced or restored because of two local catastrophes. In 1802 a gale tore out one wall of the tower and left the bells swinging in the wind. Within a day the whole tower had collapsed, bells and all. The entire west end of the church had to be rebuilt, and stones from the wreckage were used in houses on the north of the green.

Then in 1974 a disastrous fire destroyed the chancel roof and the vestry and damaged much of the east end. Motifs on the wall above the west door, and embroidered ones in front of the altar, commemorate this blaze. Outside, the large wooden cross in the churchyard was fashioned from charred chancel beams.

Down the road by St John's Green is a Marconi Research Establishment. In 1899 Guglielmo Marconi, the inventor of radio, set up his first workshop in an old silk factory in Chelmsford. Soon after, he began making transmissions from Writtle, raising his aerials on the flat land by the River Wid.

WYMONDHAM
Norfolk
9 miles southwest of Norwich

Wymondham is an ancient, shapely town centred on a 17th-century market cross which has an octagonal chamber raised on arcades. The Abbey Church of St Mary and St Thomas of Canterbury has two huge towers, the result of a 14th-century dispute over the shared use of the church by townspeople and monks from the priory. The monks built for themselves the present octagonal tower, and at the same time put up a thick wall to seal off themselves and the high altar from the parishioners. In retaliation, 50 years later, the townspeople built the square west tower larger than that of the monks' tower.

Kett's Rebellion – a peasants' revolt in 1549 against encroachments on common land – began in Wymondham. The rebels, under Robert Kett, captured Norwich before the revolt was crushed; Kett was hanged in Norwich and his brother suffered the same fate in Wymondham.

YOXFORD
Suffolk
4 miles north of Saxmundham

In the 18th century, coaches travelling between London and Yarmouth turned off the Yarmouth road to call at the Three Tuns Hotel at Yoxford, a village set in a wooded hollow of the Yox Valley. Sadly the hotel burnt down in 1926 – its visitors' book is reputed to have included the signatures of Lord Nelson and Charles Dickens. A restaurant now stands on the site.

Although with the loss of the inn Yoxford has lost much of its stagecoach-days character, travellers will still find it worthwhile to make the small diversion from the London to Yarmouth road, guided by the 17th-century spire of St Peter's Church which stands out as an unmistakable landmark. Further guidance is obtainable in the village itself, given by a cast-iron signpost opposite the church, said to be one of only two such signposts in England. It dates from about 1830 and its arms, pointing to London, Yarmouth and Framlingham, are set at the height of a stagecoach driver's seat.

The High Street has a medley of styles and periods, with colour-washed cottages, Georgian balconies, Dutch gables and two 17th-century inns, mingling with the butcher's, the general store, an art gallery, the inevitable antiques shops and other tradesmen's premises. Milestone House, which takes its name from a 150-year-old milestone outside, is a particularly ornate 18th-century building with two porticoed porches topped by an elegant hooded iron balcony. The building now houses a pottery. The long High Street continues, almost without interruption, on to the next hamlet of Hemp Green.

Embracing the village are the luxuriant parklands of three large mansions, Rookery Park, Grove Park and Cockfield Hall – parklands that have given Yoxford the title 'The Garden of Suffolk'. Cockfield Hall has been the home of the Blois family since the 17th century, and their name appears on one of the village inns, the Blois Arms.

In Tudor days, Lady Catherine Grey was held in custody at the hall after imprisonment in the Tower of London. She was a sister of the tragic nine-day Queen of England, Lady Jane Grey, who was beheaded in 1554. Lady Catherine died in 1568 and was buried in Cockfield Chapel. Later, in the reign of James I, her body was taken to lie beside her husband's in Salisbury Cathedral.

Satis House, on the edge of the Cockfield grounds and now a hotel, was the home of the wealthy Mrs Clarissa Ricketts. In 1887 she lost all her money gambling at Monte Carlo and died shortly after her return to Yoxford. Mystery surrounds her funeral, which she is said to have arranged herself and which took place at nightfall. The mystery is further deepened by the rumour that she was seen leaving Darsham railway station disguised as a man after the funeral, and was later reported in Egypt.

SUFFOLK PINK *The colour of these Yoxford cottages was once obtained by mixing pig's blood or sloe juice into the plaster.*

INDEX

Page numbers in **bold** type refer to main entries in the book. Numbers in *italic* refer to illustrations

A

Abberton Reservoir, 93
Abbot's Hall Museum, 131
Abel, John, 104
Abel, William, 104
Acle, **8**
Acton, **8**
Adam, Robert, 87, 102, 120, 139
Addedomarus, 47
Addlethorpe, **8**
Adelwold, St, 10
Adnams brewery, 128
Adrian IV, Pope, 148
Affleck family, 50
Ainsworth, Harrison, 71
Albini, William de, 40
Albini, William II de, 104
Alcock, John, Bishop of Ely, 38
Alde, River, 8, 111, 124
Aldeburgh, **8**, 124
Alderford, 118
Aldewood, Forest of, 56
Aldrych, Thomas, 70
Alford, **8**, 9
Alfred the Great, 24, 120
Alvingham, **8–10**
Amcott, Vincent, 76
Amcott family, 76
Ancaster, **10**, 82
Ancholme valley, 34
Anderson, Elizabeth Garrett, 124
Anne of Denmark, 63
Anson, Lord, 99
Arlington, Isabella, 60
Arlington, Lord, 60
Arminian Nunnery, 96
Ashdon, **10**, *10–11*
Ashurst, Robert, 40
Athelstan, King, 106
Attleborough, **10–11**
Audley, Thomas, 144
Audley End, **11**, *12–13*, 120, 144
Aylmerton, **11**
Aylsham, **11**
Ayscoughfee Hall, 129

B

Babingley, River, 40
Babraham, **14**
Bacon, Francis, 38
Bacon, John, 77, 133
Bacon the Elder, 148
Baconsthorpe Castle, 82
Bacton, **14**, *15*
Bacton Wood, **14**
Badingham Manor, 42
Bain, River, 53–6, *54–5*, 82, 134
Ball, Blessed John, 138
Balsham, 66
Balsham, Hugh de, Bishop of Ely, 34
Banks, 148
Banks, Joseph, 118
Banks, Sir Joseph, 118
Bardfield Saling, 14
The Bardfields, **14**
Bardolph, Lord, 52
Barham, 94
Barnack, **14–15**
Barnardiston family, 87
Barsham, 15–16
Bartlow Hills, 10
Barton Turf, 83
Basildon, **15**
Battles Hall, 102
Bawburgh, **15**
Bayfield Hall, 67
Bayon's Park, 134

Beacon Hill, 49
Beaufort, Lady Margaret, 38
Beaumont, G. F., 46
Beaumont, Henry de, 62
Beccles, **15–16**
Becket, St Thomas, 131, 141
Bedford, Dukes of, 139
Bedford, 4th Earl of, 146
Bedford Level, 144
Bedingfeld, Sir Henry, 113
Bedingfeld family, 56, 113
Bedingfield, 50
Beeston, **16**
Beeston Priory, 123
Bek, Gilbert de, 23
Bell, Henry, 106
Belton, **16**, *16*
Berney, Thomas, 70
Berney Arms, 118
Bertie family, 129
Bigod, Roger, 105
Bigod family, 26, 57
Bildeston, **16–17**
Binbrook, **17**
Binham Priory, **17**
Biscathorpe House, 56
Black Death, 107
Blackmore, **17**
Blackwater, River, 24, 50, 100, 140
Blaise, St, 92
Blakeney, **17–20**, *18–19*
Blaxhall, **20**
Blickling Hall, **20**
Blois family, 155
Blue Stone Heath Road, 135
Blundeston, 99
Blyborough, **20**
Blyth, River, 141
Blythburgh, **20**, *21*
Bodley, G. F., 66
Bodsey House, 118
Boleyn, Anne, 20, 119, 123, 130
Boleyn, Sir William, 70
Boleyn family, 20, 41
Bolingbroke, Old, 111
Bonner, Bishop of London, 58
Boothby Pagnell, **20**
Borrow, George, 58, 124
Boston, **22–3**
Boston Stump, 22, *22*, 129
Bottisham, 133
Boulge, 152
Bourne, **23**, *23*
Bourne Mill, Colchester, 47
Bowers Marsh, 125
Bowthorpe Oak, 149
Boxford, **23**
Boxted, **23–4**
'The Boy's Grave', 50
Bradwell-on-Sea, **24**
Braintree, **24**
Bramfield, **24**
Brampton, **24**
Bran Ditch, 31
Brancaster, **24–5**
Brandon, **25**
Brant Boughton, 66
Brant Valley, 66
Breakspear, Nicholas, 148
Brecklands, 56, 71, 144
Brent Ditch, 31
Brent Eleigh, 92
Brentwood, **25**
Bressingham, **25**, *25*
Brett, River, 87, 133
Breydon Water, 72
Bright, Edward, 102
Brightlingsea, **26**
British Rail, 149
Britten, Benjamin, 8, 99, 111, 124
BRM racing cars, 23
Broadland Conservation Centre, 83
Broads, 82–3, *82–3*, 84, 99, 119
Brograve, Sir Berney, 144
Brograve family, 144
Brooke, Rupert, 70
Broomholm Priory, 14
Brown, Lancelot 'Capability', 11, 33, 80, 120
Brownlow family, 16
Bruges, Sir William, 129
Buckden, **26**
Bunbury, Sir Thomas, 103
Bungay, **26**
Bure, River, 8, 11, 72, 82, 99
Bures, **26**

Bures, Sir Robert de, 8
Burgh, Elizabeth de, 42–3
Burgh Castle, 73, 118
Burgh le Marsh, **26**, 135
Burghley House, 14, **28**, 130, 154
Burn, River, 29
Burne-Jones, Sir Edward, 141
Burnham Market, 29
Burnham Norton, 29
Burnham-on-Crouch, **28–9**
Burnham Overy, 29
Burnham Thorpe, *28–9*, 29
The Burnhams, 29
Burwell, 29–31, *30*, *31*
Bury St Edmunds, **31–3**, 97, 117, 152
Bushnell, John, 14
Butley Priory, **33**
Byrons's Pool, 70
Bywells Spring, 148

C

Caistor, **34**, 73
Caius, Dr John, 35
Calceby, **34**
Caley Mill, 77
Calthorp, Sir William, 29
Cam, River, 11, 34, 38, 63, 70, 133
Cambridge, 14, **34–8**, *35–7*, 100, 133
Campbell, William, 102
Can, River, 42
Canterbury, 25, 103
Cant's nurseries, 47
Canute, King, 31, 67, 74, 99
Canvey Island, 125
Car Dyke, 63
Carlton Colville, 99
Carter, John, 120
Castle Acre, **38**, *39*
Castle Hedingham, **40**, *40*
Castle Rising, **40**
Castlemaine, Barbara, 60
Castor, 113
Catherine of Aragon, 26, 87, 116
Caton, Richard Bewley, 17
Causennae, 10, 82
Cavell, Nurse Edith, 110
Cavendish, **40–1**, *41*
Cavendish, Thomas, 40
Cawston, **41**
Caxton, **41**, 100
Cecil, Thomas, 154
Cecil, Sir William (Lord Burghley), 23, 28, 129–30, 154
Cedd, St, 24
Chantrey, Sir Francis, 113
Chapman, John, 133
Charles, Prince of Wales, 120
Charles, I, King, 48, 56, 96
Charles, II, King, 60, 66, 90, 105, 129
Chaucer, Geoffrey, 14, 70, 111
Chelmer and Blackwater Navigation, 42
Chelmsford, **41–2**, 154
Chelsworth, 103
Chester, Ranulf, Earl of, 111
Chichele, Sir Thomas, 100
Chigwell, **42**
Chippenham, **42**
Chipping Ongar, **42**
Chiswell, R., 120
Christchurch Mansion, 85
Church Farm Museum, 123
Churchend, 114
Churchill, Randolph, 57
Cibber, Caius Gabriel, 104
Cinque Ports, 26
Clacton-on-Sea, **42**
Clare, **42–3**, *43*
Clare, Earls of , 42
Clare, John, 80
Clavering, **43**
Cley next the Sea, 20, **43–6**, *44–5*, 82
Clopton family, 99
Coates-by-Stow, 131
Cobbett, William, 94
Cock Hill, 26
Cockfield Hall, 155

Cockley Cley, 133
Coddenham, **46**
Coggeshall, **46–7**, *46*
Coke, Sir Arthur, 24
Coke, Sir Edward, 24, 140
Coke, Lady Elizabeth, 24
Coke, Mrs, 140
Coke, Thomas, 81
Coke family, 140
Colchester, **47**
Cole, Old King, 47
Collingwood, Admiral, 17
Colman, Jeremiah, 15
Colman's, *110*
Colne, River, 26, 40, 47, 149
Colsterworth, **47–8**
Colt, Maximilian, 152
Coningsby, 134
Constable, John, 34, 47, 50, 57–8, 85, 104, 130
Constable, Maria, 58
Constantine, Emperor, 47
Cook, Brian, 131
Cook, Captain James, 118
Cooper, W. G., 72
Copford Green, **48**
Copledyke family, 76
Cordell, William, 97, 99
Corder, William, 33, 117
Cotman, John, 110
Cotton, John, 22
Cotton family, 105
Courtauld family, 24
Covehithe, **48**
Covenham Reservoir, 135
Cowper, William, 58
Cozens-Hardy, Barons, 94
Cozens-Hardy, Basil, 94
Crabbe, Rev. George, 8
Cranwell, **48**
The Creakes, **48**
Creke, Sir John de, 91
Cressing, **48–9**
Crome, John, 110
Cromer, **49**, *49*
Cromer Ridge, 62
Cromwell, Henry, 147
Cromwell, Oliver, 20, 24, 38, 50, 58, 61, 62, 66, 72, 76, 84, 96, 103, 111, 120, 147
Cromwell, Ralph, 134
Cromwell, Sir Richard, 24
Crouch, River, 28, 114
Crowland, **49**
Crozier, Eric, 8
Cubitt, John, 152
Cumberland, Duke of, 128
Cure, Cornelius, 99
Curzon, Lord, 134
Cutlers' Guild, 138

D

Dalham, **50**
Danbury, **50**, *51*
Darcy, Lord, 120
D'Arcy, Sir Robert, 100
Darsham, 155
Dartford-Purfleet Tunnel, 140
de la Pole family, 148
de Vere family, 40
Debden, 120
Deben, River, 50, 149, 152
Debenham, **50**
Dedham, **50–2**
Deeping St James, 144
Defoe, Daniel, 111
Deleval, Sir John, 53
Dennington, **52**
Denton, **52**
Denver, 56
Department of the Environment, 38
Derby, Lord, 103
Devil's Dyke, **31**, 52
Devil's Punchbowl, 58
Devil's Wood, 140
Devonshire, Dukes of, 40
Dickens, Charles, 70, 85, 148, 155
Diss, **52–3**, 61
Doddington, **53**, *53*
Dogdyke, **53**
Domesday Book, 34, 38, 124, 135, 148–9, 152

Donington on Bain, **53–6**, *54–5*
Donna Nook, 138
Dove, River, 84
Dovercourt, 77
Downham Market, **56**
Dowsing, William, 20, 24, 152
Drago, 47
Drake, Sir Francis, 50, 125
Dumpling Green, 58
Dunwich, **56**, 56, 145
Dutch Cottage Museum, 125
Duxford, 85
Dymoke, Captain Edward, 135
Dymoke, Lt-Colonel John, 135
Dymoke family, 135

E

Earl Soham, **57**
Earsham, 26
East Anglia Transport Museum, 99
East Bergholt, **57–8**, *57*
East Dereham, **58**
East Harling, **58**
East Wretham Heath, **58**
Eastend, 114
Easton, **58**, *58*
Edmund, King, 26, 31, 74, 84, 128
Edward I, King, 50
Edward II, King, 40
Edward III, King, 40, 58, 74, 76, 111, 149
Edward VI, King, 70, 102
Edward VII, King, 100, 121, 149, 152
Edward the Confessor, 43, 59, 118
Eliot, T. S., 96
Elizabeth I, Queen, 91, 97, 129, 140, 152
Elizabeth II, Queen, 104, 105, 124, 135
Elmswell, 152
Elsing, 58
Ely, 14, 29, 38, 50, **59**, 59
English Heritage, 123
Epping Forest, 141
Erasmus, 35
Ermine Street, 10, 47, 48, 67, 84, 131
Erpingham, Sir Thomas, 110
Erwarton, 123
Essex Archaeological Society, 47
Essex University, 149
Ethelbald, King, 49
Etheldreda, St, 59
Etheridge, William, 35
Eustace, Count of Boulogne, 42
Euston Hall, **60–1**, *60–1*
Exeter, 6th Marquis of, 28
Exeter family, 28
Eye, **61**

F

Fakenham, 96–7
Fane, Sir Francis, 66
Fane family, 66
Fastolf, Sir John, 20, 73
Faverches, Lady Richeldis de, 97
Felbrigg, **62**
Felbrigg, Simon de, 62
Felix of Burgundy, St, 56, 147
Felixstowe, **62**
Fens, 53, 56, 63, 74, 81, 123, 130, 144, 145, 146–7
Ferrar, Nicholas, 96
Filby Broad, 119
Finchingfield, **62**
Fitz-wimarc, Robert, 43
FitzGerald, Edward, 152
Fitzroy, Henry, 60
Fitzwalter family, 71
Fitzwilliam, Viscount, 34
Flatford, 58
Flaxman, John, 77, 148
Fleam Dyke, 31, 52, 66
Fleet, 81

Fletcher, John, 35
Flitcroft, Henry, 148
Folkingham, **62–3**, *63*
Fordham, 56
Forestry Commission, 14, 56, 144
Fossdyke Navigational Canal, **63**, 96
Fowl Mere, 58
Framlingham, **63–6**, *64–5*, 77, 155
Franklin, Sir John, 129
Freiston Shore, 23
Fressingfield, 148
Freston, 123
Fring, 77
Frinton-on-Sea, **66**
Fry, Elizabeth, 110
Fulbeck, **66**
Fulbourn, **66**
Fydell, William, 22

G

Gainsborough, **67**
Gainsborough, Thomas, 85, 131
Gardener, Sir Robert, 152
Gardiner, William, 114–15
Garrett, Newson, 124
Gatwood, 41
Gedney, 81
Gentleman's Society, 129
Geoffrey of Monmouth, 47
George V, King, 152
George VI, King, 110
Gershom-Parkington, Frederic, 31
Gibbons, Grinling, 28, 35, 61, 124
Gibraltar Point, **67**, *68–9*
Glandford, **67**
Glanville, Ranulf de, 33
Glaven, River, 43, 82, 94
Glemham, Edward, 71
Gloucester, Thomas, Duke of, 117
Godmanchester, **67**, 80, 84
Gog Magog Hills, **67–70**
Goldhanger, **70**
Goldwell, James, Bishop of Norwich, 110
Gonville, Edmund, 35
Good, Jabez, 26
Gosfield Hall, 24
Gowthorpe Manor, **70**
Grafham Water, 26, 87
Grafton, Dukes of, 60
Granta, River, 85
Grantchester, **70**
Grantham, **70–1**, *71*
Grantham, Thomas, 129
Grantham, Museum, 10
Great Bardfield, 14
Great Canfield, 71
Great Cressingham, 133
Great Dunmow, **71**
Great Eau, 34
Great Glemham, **71**
Great Hockham, **71**
Great Massingham, **71–2**
Great Mount, 130
Great Ouse, 84, 90, 120
Great Paxton, **72**
Great Sampford, 138
Great Snoring, 124
Great Stoughton, 26
Great Warley, **72**
Great Wilbraham, 66
Great Witchingham, 118
Great Yarmouth, **72–3**, *72–3*, 107, 144, 155
Green, Thomas, 8
Greenstead, 42
Gregory I, Pope, 110
Gresham, Sir Thomas, 81
Grey, Lady Catherine, 155
Grey, Lady Jane, 14, 26, 70, 155
Grime's Graves, 25
Grouse, Dr, 16–17
Grove Park, 155
Gunby Hall, 26, 27
Gunton, 139
Gurney, John de, 72
Guthlac, St, 49
Guthrum the Dane, 74
Gwynne, Nell, 105

H

Haddenham, **74**
Hadleigh, **74**
Hadleigh Castle, **74**, *75*
Hadstock, **74**
Haile Sand Fort, 135
Hakluyt, Richard, 50
Halton Holegate, 129
Hamilton, Duke of, 58
Hampton, John, 90
Happisburgh, **74**
Hardwicke, 1st Earl of, 100
Hardy, Mary, 94
Hardy, William, 94
Harlaxton, 52
Harleston, **74**
Harling family, 58
Harlow, **74–6**
Harold II, King, 141, 154
Harpley, 72
Harpswell, 20
Harrington, Sir John, 76
Harrington Hall, **76**, 76
Harsent, Rose, 114–15
Harsnett, Samuel, Archbishop of York, 42
Hartford, **76**
Harvey, Captain Eliab, 42
Harwich, 62, **76–7**
Harwood, Sir Ralph, 152
Haslingfield, 70
Hastings, Sir Hugh, 58
Hatfield Broad Oak, **77**
Hatfield Peverel, 130
Haughley Park, **77**
Havergate Island, 8, 111
Hawstead, **77**
Heacham, **77**, *78–9*
Heckington, **77–80**, 77
Helena, St, 47
Helmingham, 152
Helpston, **80**
Hemingford Grey, **80**
Hemp Green, 155
Henry II, King, 111, 141
Henry IV, King, 111
Henry V, King, 46, 52
Henry VI, King, 35, 134
Henry VII, King, 113
Henry VIII, King, 20, 38, 66, 67, 83, 85, 90, 97, 102, 116, 140, 144, 145, 148
Hereward the Wake, 23, 49, 59
Herrold, Margaret, 46
Hessett, **80**
Heveningham, **80**
Hickathrift, Tom, 120
Hickling, **80**
Hill, Octavia, 148
Hills and Holes National Nature Reserve, 14
Hinchingbrooke House, 24
Hingham, **81**, *81*
Hintlesham Hall, 74
Historic Aircraft Museum, Southend, 128
Hitcham, Sir Robert, 63
Hobart, Sir Henry, 20
Hobson, Thomas, 34
Hockley, 94
Holbeach, **81**
Holkham Gap, **81**
Holkham Hall, 81
Holly Trees Museum, Colchester, 47
Holme next the Sea, 84
Holst, Gustav, 138
Holt, **81–2**
Honington Camp, **82**
Honywood, Mary, 47
Horham, **82**
Horncastle, **82**
Horncastle Canal, 134
Horning, **82–3**
Horning Hall, 99
Horsey, *82–3*, **83–4**
Houghton, **84**, 97
Howard, Catherine, 130
Howard, Cecilie, 11
Howard, Lady, 130
Howard, Richard, 11
Howard family, 25, 40, 66, 144
Howell, 80
Hoxne, 31, 84

Huddleston family, 14, 70
Hunstanton, 67, **84**
Huntingdon, 67, 80, **84**
Hyams, Elizabeth, 23
Hylands Park, 154

I

Ickleton, **85**
Icknield Way, 26, 52, 85
Ickworth, *32–3*, 33
Ingatestone, **85**
Ingoldmells, 8
Ipswich, **85**, 145
Irby family, 103
Irnham, **85**, *86*
Isabella, Queen, 40
Isleham, 42
Ivo, St, 120
Ixworth, **86**
Ixworth Thorpe, *86*, 86

J

James I, King, 11, 63, 74, 105
James II, King, 128
James, M. R., 56
Jarvis family, 53
Jex, Johnson, 94
Jodrell, Sir Alfred, 67
John, King, 31, 40, 70, 90, 123, 129, 133, 154
John the Evangelist, St, 43
John of Gaunt, 111
Johnson, Joas, 73
Johnson, John, 42
Johnson, Dr Samuel, 62, 92, 135
Jones, Captain Christopher, 76
Juliana of Norwich, 110

K

Kedington, **87**
Kempe, C. E., 16, 34
Kempe, William, 62
Kennett, River, 50
Kent, William, 60
Kentford, 50
Kentwell Hall, 99
Kersey, **87**, *88–9*
Kessingland, 48
Ketsby, 34
Kett, Robert, 107, 154
Kett's Rebellion, 154
Kimbolton, 26, **87**
King's Lynn, **90**, *90–1*, 106, 149
Kingsley, Charles, 15, 149
Kirkstead, **90**
Kirtling, **90–1**
Knapton, **91**
Knights Hospitaller, 31, 40, 48, 138
Knights Templar, 48
Kym, River, 87
Kyneburgha, St, 113
Kyson Hill, 149

L

Laindon, 15
Landmark Trust, 115
Landwade, 105
Langton, **92**, 135
Langton, Archbishop, 26
Langton, Bennet, 135
Lark, River, 144
Latimer family, 123
Lavenham, **92**, *92–3*
Layer Breton, 93
Layer Marney, 93
Layer-de-la-Haye, 93
The Layers, **93**
Le Despenser, Henry, 107

Leez Priory, **93**
Leicester, Countess of, 140
Leicester, 1st Earl of, 140
Leigh-on-Sea, **93–4**
Leighton Bromswold, **94**
Lenwade Bridge, 145
Leonardo da Vinci, 72
Letcham, 16
Letheringsett, 82, **94**
Letheringsett Hall, 82
Leverington, **94**
Lexden Tumulus, 47
Lincoln, 22, 63, **94–6**, *95*, 135
Lincoln, Abraham, 81
Lincoln, Samuel, 81
Lincolnshire and South
    Humberside Trust for Nature
    Conservation, 67
Lindsey, 87, 131
Little Baddow, **96**
Little Bardfield, 14
Little Gidding, **96**
Little Glemham Hall, 71
Little Maplestead, 40
Little Ouse, 60, 138
Little Snoring, 124
Little Walsingham, **96–7**
Little Wilbraham, 66
Loddon, **97**
Long Melford, **97–9**, *97*
Longthorpe Tower, 116
Lord Rayleigh's Dairies, 135
Losinga, Herbert de, Bishop of
    Norwich, 107, 110
Louis XII, King of France, 145
Louis XIV, King of France, 139
Louth, 10, *98*, **99**
Louth Navigation, 10, 135
Lovell family, 58
Lowestoft, **99**
Lud, River, 99, 135
Ludham, **99**
Lukin, Lionel, 71
Luttrell, Sir Andrew, 85
Lutyens, Sir Edwin, 46
Lydgate, John, 99
Lyminge, Robert, 20

M

Mablethorpe, 138
Macaulay, Lord, 38
Mace, Jem, 16
Maddison, Sir Edmund, 34
Madingley, **100**
Madingley Hall, 100
Maitland, Sir John, 76
Maldon, **100–2**, *100–1*
Mallory, Sir William, 114
Mallory, Sir Thomas, 114
Mandeville, Geoffrey de, 31,
    117, 120
Manningtree, **102**
Manuden, **102**
March, **102**
Marconi, Guglielmo, 154
Margaret, Queen of Edward I,
    50
Margaret of Anjou, 35
Margaret of Antioch, St, 52
Margaretting, 85
Marlowe, Christopher, 35
Marten, Maria, 33, 117
Martham, 144
Martham Broad, 144
Martlesham Creek, 149
Mary, Queen of Scots, 99, 116
Mary Tudor, Duchess of Suffolk,
    145
Mary Tudor, Queen, 14, 66, 70,
    77
Matlow Hill, 70
Meeting Hill, 152
Melford Hall, 97
Melford Manor, 97–9
Mendham, 74
Mendlesham, 14
Mersea Island, **102**, *103*
Mildenhall, **102–3**
Mildmay, Sir Walter, 38
Mills, Thomas, 63
Milton, John, 38, 70, 131
Ministry of Defence, 58
Minsmere Nature Reserve, 56
Mistley, 102

Mole Hall Wildlife Park, 130
Monks Eleigh, **103**
Moore, J. F., 77
Morris, William, 141
Moulton, 50, **103**
Mundesley, 114
Munnings, Sir Alfred, 52, 74

N

Napoleon I, Emperor, 42
Napoleonic Wars, 25, 92, 116
Nar, River, 38
Narborough, **104**
Nash, John, 152
Nash, Thomas, 99
National Cycle Museum, 96
National Horse Racing Museum,
    105
National Nature Reserves, 66
National Stud, 105
National Trust: Belton House, 16
    Blakeney Point, 20
    Blickling Hall, 20
    Bourne Mill, Colchester, 47
    Burnham Overy, 29
    Bury St Edmunds, 31
    Dunwich, 56
    Grantham House, 71
    Gunby Hall, 26
    Horsey Mill, 84
    Ickworth, 33
    Kyson Hill, 149
    Paycocke's, Coggeshall, 46–7
    Peckover House, Wisbech,
        148
    Ramsey, 118
    Tattershall, 134
    Wicken Fen, 146
    Woolsthorpe Manor, 47–8
National Union of Agricultural
    and Allied Workers, 17
Nature Conservancy Council,
    81
Navenby, **104**
Nayland, **104**
Needham Market, **104**
Nelson, Edmund, 29
Nelson, Lord, 15, 20, 29, 42, 73,
    99, 110, 155
Nene, River, 63, 102, 113, 116,
    141, 148
Neot, St, 120
Nether Hall, 41
Nettleton Hill, 34
Nevile, Thomas, 38
New Bedford River, 146
New Buckenham, **104**
Newmarket, **105**, *105*
Newport, **105–6**, *106*
Newton, Sir Isaac, 38, 47–8, 70,
    129
Noel-Buxton, Lord, 46
Nollekens, Joseph, 140, 148
Norfolk, Dukes of, 25, 85, 114
Norfolk, Earls of, 57
Norfolk, Roger Bigod, Earl of, 63
Norfolk, Thomas Howard, 3rd
    Duke of, 66
Norfolk Broads, 82–3, *82–3*, 84,
    99, 119
Norfolk Naturalists' Nature
    Reserve, 58
Norfolk Naturalists' Trust, 46, 80,
    83
Norfolk Rural Life Museum, 58
Norfolk Wild Life Park, 118
North Dudley, 71
North, Lord, 90–1
North Cockerington, 8
North Creake, 48
North Elmham, **106**
North End, **106**
North Norfolk Railway, 123
North Runcton, **106**
Northampton, Henry Howard,
    Earl of, 40
Northborough, 144

O

Old Bedford River, 146
Old Bolingbroke, **111**
Old Fletton, 116
Old Leigh, 128
Old Scarlett, 116
Omar Khayyam, 152
Ongar Castle, 42
Ore, River, 8, 111
Orford, 8, **111**, *111*, *112–13*
Orford, Earl of, 42, 133
Ormesby Broad, 119
Ormsby Hall, 34
Orton, **113**
Orwell, George, 128
Orwell, River, 85
Osbournby, 63
Osyth, St, 120
Otley, 152
Otter Trust, 26
Oulton Broad, 99
Ouse *see* Great Ouse; Little
    Ouse
Overall, Bishop John, 74
Overstrand, 49
Owen, Nicholas, 14
Oxborough, **113**
Oxburgh Hall, 56, 113
Oxford, 13th Earl of, 92
Oxford, 17th Earl of, 40

P

Paglesham, **114**
Paine, James, 62
Paine, Thomas, 138
Palmer, William, 8
Papworth Everard, 100
Papworth St Agnes, **114**
Parker, Admiral Sir Hyde, 99
Parker, Sir Philip, 123
Parker family, 99
Parr, Catherine, 67
Parson Drove, **114**
Pasco, Richard de, 17
Paston, **114**
Paston, John, 114
Paston, Margaret, 114
Paston, Margery, 114
Paston family, 73
Patrick, Simon, Bishop of Ely, 50
Paycocke, John, 46
Paycocke, Thomas, 46
Paycocke family, 47
Paycocke's, Coggeshall, 46–7
Pears, Peter, 8, 124
Peasenhall, **114–15**, *115*
Peck, Robert, 81
Peckover House, Wisbech, 148
Peddars' Way, 26, 38, *39*
Pembroke, Earl of, 34
Penda, King of Mercia, 113
Penn, William, 42
Pepys, Samuel, 24, 38, 84, 114
Peter, St, 110
Peterborough, 14, **115–16**, 145
Peto, Sir Samuel Morton, 124
Petre family, 85
Peverel, Ranulf, 130
Philip II, King of Spain, 66
Philippa, Queen, 111
Pilgrim Fathers, 22, 76
Piper, John, 14
Pitman, Jeffrey, 152
Platt, Peter, 138
Pleshey, **116–17**, *116–17*
Plume, Dr Thomas, 100
Pocahontas, 81
Poley, Sir John, 24
Poley family, 23
Polstead, 33, **117**
Pope, Alexander, 129
Potter Heigham, 80
Pre-Raphaelite Brotherhood,
    141
Prittlewell, 125
Puritans, 22, 48

R

Rabett family, 24
Ralph of Coggeshall, 111
Ramsey, **118**
Randall, Bob, 145
Ranworth, 82–3
Rase, River, 134
Rayleigh, 2nd Lord, 135
Rayleigh Mount, **118**
Raynham Hall, 97
Read, Herbert, 152
Red Barn Murder, 117
Red Hill, 56
Redgrave, 25
Redundant Churches Fund, 114
Reedham, **118**
Reepham, **118**
Regnart, Charles, 139
Rendlesham Forest, 56
Repell Ditches, 120
Repton, Humphry, 11, 123
Repton, J. A., 123
Revesby, **118**, *119*
Reynolds, Sir Joshua, 152
Rhodes, Cecil, 50
Richard II, King, 40
Richard III, King, 67
Richard the Lionheart, King, 33
Richardson, Lord Chief Justice,
    124
Richmond, Earl of, 24
Ricketts, Clarissa, 155
Rigby, Richard, 102
Ring Mere, 58
Rising, Catherine Ursula, 84
Roach, River, 114
Rochford Hall, **119**
Roding, River, 119
The Rodings, **119**
Rolfe, John, 77
Rollesby, **119**
Rolls, C. S., 107
Romans, King of the, 105
Rookery Park, 155
Rossetti, Dante Gabriel, 141
Rotherham, Edward, 17
Rothwell, 34
Roubiliac, Louis, 140
Rouse, Richard, 94
Royal Air Force, 134
Royal Society for the Protection
    of Birds, 111, 135, 138
Rubens, Peter Paul, 35
Ruggles-Brise family, 62
Ryder, Lady, 41
Rysbrack, J. M., 140

S

Saffron Walden, 105, **120**, *121*
St Benet's Abbey, 83, 99
St Clare's Hall, 120
St Ives, **120**
St John, Oliver, 116
St Neots, **120**
St Osyth, **120**
St Pol, Sir George, 124
St Pol, Sir Thomas, 124
St Pol family, 124
Sall, 41
Saltfleetby-Theddlethorpe
    Dunes National Nature
    Reserve, 138
Sandringham, **121**, 149
Sandwich, 1st Earl of, 24
Santon Downham, 25
Sargent, Sir Malcolm, 130
Satis House, 155
Sawston Hall, 14, 70
Saxtead Green, 57
Sayer, John, 149
Scarborough, 9th Earl of, 123
Scheemakers, Peter, 148
Scole, 52–3
Scolt Head Island, 24–5
Scott, Captain, 38
Scott, George Gilbert junior,
    152
Scott, Sir Gilbert, 8
Scrivelsby, 135

Seckford, Thomas, 149, 152
Seckford Hall, 152
Shakespeare, William, 20, 84, 110, 117
Shell Museum, Glandford, 67
Shelton, Sir Ralph, 124
Sheringham, **123**
Sherman family, 52
Shotley Gate, **123**
Shrieking Pits, 11
Sibsey, *122*, **123**
Sibton Abbey, 115
Sidestrand, 49
Sidney, Lady Frances, 38
Skegness, **123**
Sleaford, **123**
Smyth, James, 115
Smythson, Robert, 53
Snape, **124**
Snarford, **124**
Snipe Dales, 82
The Snorings, **124**
Soham, 147
Somerleyton Hall, **124**
Somersby, **125**, *125*, 135
Somerton, William de, 17
Somerton Gap, 144
South Benfleet, **125**
South Creake, 48
South-East Essex Museum, 125
South Ormsby, 34
Southchurch Hall, 128
Southend-on-Sea, 93, **125–8**, *126–7*
Southwold, 20, 56, **128**, *128*, 141
Spains Hall, 62
Spalding, **129**, *129*
Spelman, Clement, 104
Spelman family, 104
Spilsby, **129**
Spinney Abbey, 147
Spryng, Thomas, 92
Stamford, **129–30**
Stane Street, 47
Stanhope, Edward, 118
Stanhope family, 118
Stansted Mountfitchet, **130**
Stanton, William, 70
Staverton Forest, 33
Stebbing, **130**
Steeping, River, 141, *142–3*
Stephen, King, 31, 47
Sterne, Laurence, 26
Stevens, Sir William Reynolds, 72
Stibbington Hall, 141
Stiffkey, River, 144
Stilton, **130**
Stockwith Mill, 76
Stoke-by-Clare, 43
Stoke-by-Nayland, **130**, *131*
Stone, Sir John, 80
Stone, Nicholas, 77, 114, 140
Stort, River, 43, 102
Stour, River, 26, 40, 50, 52, 57, 104, 123, 130, 131
Stour Gardens, 57
Stow, **131**
Stowmarket, 61, 115, **131**
Stratford St Mary, 52
Stretham, 74
Strutt, E. G., 135
Stuteville, Sir Martin, 50
Stuteville family, 50
Suckling, Sir John, 15
Sudbury, **131**
Sue Ryder Foundation, 41
Suffolk, Dukes of, 114
Suffolk, Michael de la Pole, Earl of, 33
Suffolk, Thomas Howard, 1st Earl of, 11, 144
Sulyard, Sir John, 77
Sussex, Earl of, 38
Sutton Hoo, 152
Swaffham, **131–3**
Swaffham Bulbeck, 133
Swaffham Prior, *132*, **133**
Sweyn, King, 67, 118

Tattershall, **134**, *136–7*
Taylor, Isaac, 92
Taylor, Jane, 92
Taylor, Sir Robert, 80
Taylor, Dr Rowland, 74
Taylor, Thomas, 53
Tealby, **134**
Tendring, Sir William, 130
Tennyson, Alfred, Lord, 38, 76, 96, 99, 125, 129, 134, 135
Tennyson, Charles, 99, 134
Tennyson, Rev. George, 125
Tennyson-d'Eyncourt family, 134
Terling, **134–5**
Tetford, 135
Tetney Haven, **135**, 138
Thames Estuary, 74, 125, 139–40
Thaxted, **138**
Theddlethorpe St Helen, **138**
Thet, River, 138
Thetford, 84, 106, **138**, *139*
Thetford Forest, 25
Thomas, John, 124
Thoresby, Thomas, 90
Thorington Hall, 117, 130
Thorney, **139**
Thorold, Mrs Cecil, 20
Thorpe, William, 147
Thorpe Hall, 82, 116
Thorpe Market, **139**
Thorpeness, 8
Thursford, **139**
Tilbury, **139–40**
Tilty, 71
Timperley family, 74
Tiptofts Farm, 120
Tittleshall, **140**
Tollemache family, 152
Tollesbury, **140**, *140*
Tolleshunt d'Arcy, **140**
Tolleshunt Knights, **140**
Tolleshunt Major, **140**
Tolpuddle Martyrs, 42
Torksey, 63
Toseland Hall, 72
Townsend, Harrison, 72
Townshend, Chauncey Hare, 148
Townshend, 2nd Viscount, 97
Trader Mill, *122*, **123**
Trent, River, 63, 67, 96
Trollope, Anthony, 119
Trumpington, Sir Roger de, 70
Trunch, 91
Tunstall, 8
Tunstall Forest, 56
Turner, J. M. W., 34, 42
Turpin, Dick, 138
Tydd St Giles, 148
Tydd St Mary, **140**
Tyler, Wat, 40

Uffa, 152
Ufford, 152
Ulceby, 8
Upwake, 133
Usher Art Gallery, Lincoln, 96

Valence, Lady Mary de, 34
Vanbrugh, Sir John, 87, 125
Vanneck, Sir Gerard, 80
Vere, Aubrey de, 71, 77
Vermuyden, Sir Cornelius, 56, 146
Via Devana, 67, 70
Viking Way, 53–6

Waad, Sir William, 102
Wainfleet All Saints, **141**, *142–3*
Walberswick, 56, **141**
Walden Abbey, 144
Walker, Eric, 149
Walpole, Horace, 133
Walpole, St Peter, **141**
Walsham le Willows, **141**
Walsingham, 96–7
Walsoken, 67, 148
Walstan, St, 15
Waltham Abbey, **141**
Walton-on-the-Naze, **66**
Waltreville family, 113
Wandlebury Camp, 70
Wansford, **141**
Warenne, Earl, 129
Warenne, William de, 25, 38
Warham Camp, 144
Warham St Mary, **141–4**
Waring, River, 82
Warwick, John, Earl of, 107
Warwick, Robert, Earl of, 124
The Wash, 26, 67, 141
Waveney, River, 15, 26, 74
Waxham Hall, **144**
Waynflete, William of, 141
Webb, John, 116
Webbe, Thomas, 52
Weeting Castle, 25
Welby, William, 52
Welby family, 52
Welland, River, 49, 129
Wellingham, 140
Wells-next-the-Sea, 81, **144**
Wendens Ambo, **144**
Wendreda, St, 102
Wenhaston, 20
Wensum, River, 106, 107, 110, 145
Wensum Forest, 14
West Deeping, **144**
West Somerton, **144**
West Stow, **144–5**
West Tofts, 58
West Walton, 148
Westleton, **145**
Westleton Heath, 145
Westley Waterless, 91
Westmacott, Sir Richard, 148
Weston Longville, **145**
Wetheringsett, 50
Wethersfield, 62
Weybourne, 123
Whaplode, 103
Whittlesey, **145**
Whittlesey Mere, 145
Whittlesford, 70
Wicken, **146–7**, *146–7*
Wicken Fen, 146–7
Wicken Water, 102
Wid, River, 154
Widdington, 130
Widnall, Samuel, 70
Wiggenhall St Germans, **148**
Wiggenhall St Mary, **148**
Wiggenhall St Mary Magdalene, **148**
Wiggenhall St Peter, **148**
William the Conqueror, King, 23, 24, 25, 38, 43, 59, 118, 130, 148–9, 154
William of Norwich, 16
Williamson, Lady, 97
Willingale, **148**
Willingale Doe, 148
Willingale Spain, 148
Willoughby family, 129
Willy Lott's Cottage, 58
Wimpole, **148**
Wimpole Hall, 100, 148
Windsor, Duke of, 16
Windsor, Lord, 130
Wingfield, **148**
Wingfield, Sir John de, 148
Wint, Peter de, 96
Wisbech, 114, **148**
Wisbech and Fenland Museum, 148
Witham, River, 22, 23, 47, 53, 63, 94, 96
Witham on the Hill, **148–9**
Withburga, St, 58
Witton Wood, 14

Wivenhoe, **149**
Wodehouse, 46
Wodehouse family, 144
Wolds, 34, 53–6, 67, 111, 118, 134, 135
Wolferton, **149**
Wolseley, Sir Garnet, 49
Wolsey, Cardinal, 85
Wood, Sir Henry Evelyn, 48–9
Woodbridge, 56, **149–52**, *150–1*
Woodcraft Castle, 80
Woodforde, Parson James, 145
Woodhall Spa, 82
Woodrolfe Creek, 140
Woodville, Elizabeth, 35
Woodward, John, 77
Wooley, Hannah, 106
Woolpit, **152**, *153*
Woolsthorpe Manor, 47–8, 70
Worlingham Hall, 16
Worstead, **152**
Worth, Frederick, 23
Wort's Causeway, 70
Wothorpe, **154**
Wren, Sir Christopher, 16, 26, 35, 38, 60
Writtle, **154**
Wyatt, James, 16, 80
Wyatville, Sir Jeffry, 16
Wykeham, William of, Bishop of Winchester, 154
Wymondham, **154**, *154*
Wyton, **84**

Yale, Eliahu, 71
Yare, River, 72, 73, 107, 118
Yarmouth, 72–3, *72–3*, 107, 144, 155
Yaxley, 61
Young, Arthur, 94
Young, Dr Thomas, 131
Yox Valley, 155
Yoxford, **155**, *155*

ACKNOWLEDGMENTS

The illustrations in this book were commissioned by Reader's Digest from the following photographers except those in italics.

9 Tim Woodcock; **10–11** Patrick Thurston; **12–13** Neil Holmes; **15** Michael Freeman; **16** Jon Wyand; **18–19** Michael Freeman; **21** Jon Wyand; **22** Tim Woodcock; **23** Tim Woodcock; **25** *The Harry Smith Collection;* **28–29** Trevor Wood; **30** Neil Holmes; **31** Neil Holmes; **32–33** Neil Holmes; **35** Trevor Wood; **36–37** Penny Tweedie; **39** Trevor Wood; **40** Patrick Thurston; **41** Neil Holmes; **43** Mike Taylor; **44–45** Neil Holmes; **46** Neil Holmes; **49** Penny Tweedie; **51** Neil Holmes; **53** Jon Wyand; **54–55** Tim Woodcock; **56** Neil Holmes; **57** Neil Holmes; **58** Neil Holmes; **59** *Neville Fox-Davies;* **60–61** Neil Holmes; **63** Tim Woodcock; **64–65** *Michael Holford;* **68–69** Patrick Thurston; **71** Jon Wyand; **72–73** Neil Holmes; **75** Neil Holmes; **76** Tim Woodcock; **77** Tim Woodcock; **78–79** Penny Tweedie; **81** David Gallant; **82–83** *Tim Woodcock;* **86 (top)** Tim Woodcock; **86 (bottom)** Neil Holmes; **88–89** Patrick Thurston; **90–91** *Neville Fox-Davies;* **92–93** Neil Holmes; **95** Philip Llewellin; **97** Neil Holmes; **98** Malcolm Aird; **100–101** Neil Holmes; **103** Neil Holmes; **105** David Gallant; **106** Neil Holmes; **107** Trevor Wood; **108–109** Trevor Wood; **111** Patrick Thurston; **112–113** Patrick Thurston; **115** David Gallant; **116–117** Neil Holmes; **119** Tim Woodcock; **121** Neil Holmes; **122** Tim Woodcock; **125** Tim Woodcock; **126–127** *Richard Jemmett;* **128** David Gallant; **129** Tim Woodcock; **131** Neil Holmes; **132** Neil Holmes; **136–137** Tim Woodcock; **139** Neil Holmes; **140** Neil Holmes; **141–142** Tim Woodcock; **146–147** Rich Newton; **150–151** Martyn Chillmald; **153** Trevor Wood; **154** David Gallant; **155** Jon Wyand.

The publishers express their thanks to local authorities, Tourist Boards and Tourist Information Centres throughout East Anglia and Lincolnshire for their help in checking material, and to Hilary Bird who compiled the index.